Organizing Creativity

Organizing Creativity

Context, Process and Practice

STEPHAN M. SCHAEFER

OXFORD
UNIVERSITY PRESS

OXFORD
UNIVERSITY PRESS

Great Clarendon Street, Oxford, OX2 6DP,
United Kingdom

Oxford University Press is a department of the University of Oxford.
It furthers the University's objective of excellence in research, scholarship,
and education by publishing worldwide. Oxford is a registered trade mark of
Oxford University Press in the UK and in certain other countries

Published in the United States of America by Oxford University Press
198 Madison Avenue, New York, NY 10016, United States of America

British Library Cataloguing in Publication Data
Data available

Library of Congress Control Number: 2023941276

ISBN 978–0–19–889350–9
ISBN 978–0–19–886414–1 (pbk.)

DOI: 10.1093/oso/9780198893509.001.0001

Printed and bound by
CPI Group (UK) Ltd, Croydon, CR0 4YY

For Ebba

Preface

Emma sighs loudly. She has been tinkering with this hardware component all day. She tried the new software, but it did not work. She even changed some of the wiring on the component. Still nothing. She goes online to search for some white papers published by engineers at CalTech who work on similar issues. *Interesting*, she thinks, *but not really anything that will help me*. She is deep in thought when one of her colleagues knocks loudly on the door. Time for lunch. She and her colleagues drive to the little coffee place downtown and start talking about their latest smart home gadgets. Terry, one of her colleagues, has found some amazing pieces of hardware and ordered them from China. Sam, another colleague, quizzes Terry on the details, and a long conversation ensues. Emma, still somewhat absent-minded, listens occasionally while poking at her potatoes. Back in the office, she decides to leave early as there is no use sticking around. She gets on her bike and cycles home.

That night she goes to bed early. During her morning shower the next day, she suddenly thinks about the wiring of the hardware component. *What did Terry say about his smart home applications? Could that be a way of rewiring elements?* Suddenly she feels a burst of energy. *Yes!* She hastily gets out of the shower and runs to the computer. *This could work.* Excitedly, she fires off a short text to Terry on the internal messaging system. *Does he have time for a chat?* He does, and suggests meeting Emma at the office to talk about her idea. Once she arrives in the office, she goes over to his desk and they have a coffee. Terry listens sceptically. Did she consider the different layouts of the two components? It seems to be incompatible. *Oh, no*; she realizes her error, and her heart sinks.

Three weeks later, Emma is busy working on another project when a message from Terry pings on her screen. It is an article that someone shared on Facebook this morning. She reads it attentively. *Yes, there may be a way, but it would require speaking to the people at the software division.* Emma opens her email program and writes to Amy in software who uploaded the document. Does she have some time? She does, so they share some thoughts over coffee. Emma's solution makes more and more sense.

She decides to present it at the morning meeting. Sally, her line manager, listens attentively. Emma explains that she needs more time and new components. Sally, who had encouraged all of the energy going into this project, generally welcomes new ideas. Now, she looks at Emma and says, 'Top management has cut off the funding for new components, and I have spent the budget for the year. They also proposed new and more concrete key performance indicators. We need to report how projects will generate return on investments. Can you give me some numbers?' Emma is taken aback. She has no answer for Sally, who tells her to come back once she can make things more concrete. In the meantime, she must focus on her current projects.

Emma feels a sense of disappointment and anger. How can she know how much money her idea will bring in? In addition, what about the large creativity strategy that top management announced last week? Are they not supposed to come up with something new and creative? Emma sighs. *Here goes another idea*, she thinks as she closes her folders.

Creativity is Everywhere

This episode from Emma's life is fictive. Yet it is inspired by my extensive fieldwork in organizations in which I observed and interviewed employees, creatives, and managers. It illustrates some of the struggles and experiences of being creative in an organization: facing a difficult problem that does not seem to be solvable, trying to learn more from different sources, talking to colleagues to receive some advice, realizing that an idea may not work, seeing suddenly how that idea may work after all just to be disappointed again, experiencing the exhilaration of finally finding a solution, discussing with superiors about developing the idea, and dealing with the different expectations of what this idea could and should effect in an organization. This episode—or at least parts of it—may also resonate with each individual's experiences, either working for an organization, for a university project, or even as a distinguished member of a local rock band.

To describe these struggles and experiences, the noun *creativity* or the adjective *creative* is typically used. In today's world, the word 'creativity' appears everywhere, especially in organizations. For instance, commuters may read advertisements for 'creative products' on trains and subways, social media profiles tout creative skills for professionals, consultants praise new methods for creativity, and top management develops strategies for increasing creativity in business meetings. It is very hard to avoid creativity these days. Everyone talks about it, but does anyone really know what creativity is? How are people creative and whom do we consider to be creative? What is good or valuable creativity? Can creativity be influenced or even managed? What role do others play in creativity? Is creativity always good? Obviously, the concept of creativity raises many questions when reflected on, and there are certainly plenty of answers. The aim of this book is to provide deeper and systematic engagement with answers to these questions and how they may be relevant when working for or engaging with organizations.

Ultimately, creativity is about *ideas*—how people get them, and how they evaluate them. Of course, everyone has creative ideas. A child paints creative pictures, a teenager writes creative poems, a student writes creative essays, and so on. To focus on creativity, it is therefore necessary to choose a context. In this book, the context is organization. Not necessarily a specific organization, such as Google or the Red Cross, but the general act of organizing and the resultant organization.

Organization, like creativity, is everywhere and a crucial part of human life. Consider breakfast in the morning. The milk (or milk substitute) that is drunk or added to a cup of coffee has been collected from farms, treated in a creamery, packaged, and shipped to the store from which it was bought. In this process, multiple types of organizations were involved in a finely tuned interdependence, including dairy farms, milking equipment suppliers, various packaging and logistics companies that transport the milk, the store which sells the milk, refrigerating companies, and so on. If avocado toast is also consumed with that milk, the number of organizations involved—in picking, sorting, storing, shipping, and selling avocados—may triple.

However, organizations not only make sure to satisfy their customers' existing needs; they may also create new needs or aspire to run their operations more efficiently, from substitutes for milk to better transport solutions. New ideas from and for organizations thus may make people's lives easier and more efficient. People are, however, not only customers exposed to new ideas from organizations; most are also employees or even owners of an organization. Some may also often wonder how they can improve work processes, products, and services or simply make work more productive. This implies the desire to generate new ideas for their respective organizations because ideas are their lifeblood. For that reason, the question of how ideas are generated, evaluated, and developed is an important issue for any organization.

Why Another Book on Creativity?

Books on creativity abound. Browse the bookshelves in a local bookshop or type 'creativity' in an online bookshop or search engine, and it becomes clear that a lifetime would not be sufficient to read all of these books. So why did I choose to pen yet another book on creativity?

First, much writing on creativity has not been supported by systematic scientific evidence. There is a tendency in many books on creativity to simplify the subject. Many authors tout their insights as a silver bullet for becoming more creative, which means they suggest oversimplified solutions to complex problems. Yet, considering the complex nature of creativity, readers should be suspicious about such generalizations. For example, this book demonstrates that brainstorming, while certainly not ineffective, may not necessarily be the most effective way to be creative. In some contexts, discussing the problem framework first and then brainstorming ideas may be much more effective (Harvey and Kou, 2013). This book also demystifies conceptions that the top-rated engineer of a company is definitively the brain behind all the good ideas. Creativity is not the prerogative of some lone genius, but in almost all cases a collective and relational effort (Håkonsen Coldevin et al., 2019). Moreover, the process of organizing is equally complex and deserves more than cursory treatment when related to creativity (Fortwengel et al., 2017). Lastly, people should reflect more seriously on how creativity is always considered a positive outcome. Since not many books reflect critically on this concept, an entire chapter of this book is devoted to a critical discussion of how creativity has become instrumental to unrestrained and unsustainable economic growth.

Second, there is a desire to explain and control creativity. Explanation seeks to predict causes and effects and to generate generalizable laws concerning creativity. However, past researchers have not come to unanimous conclusions about creativity, and a more modest attitude could be in order. Therefore, rather than explaining creativity, researchers should strive to understand it. Understanding is not primarily interested in using knowledge to predict and control creativity, but in finding insights into how individuals interpret and make sense of creativity and their and other people's actions. The different experiences and interpretations of individuals and social collectives make creativity rather unpredictable and messy. Yet, though creativity may not lend itself easily to explanation, it is certainly possible to learn something useful about how creativity *may* work from previous research.

Third, many books on creativity adopt a single perspective and, in some cases, propose simple answers to the complex problem of creativity. However, it is necessary to ask reflective questions about creativity and avoid premature conclusions. The philosopher Socrates was famous for asking inquisitive questions and exposing simple answers as potentially premature. Socrates' questions made people so nervous that they eventually sentenced him to death. Many questions certainly make people feel uncomfortable about their ignorance, but that is not a reason not to ask them. Simply accepting common wisdom without critical reflection leads to what the social critic and philosopher Herbert Marcuse has called 'one-dimensionality' (Marcuse, 1964). For example, it is fundamentally different to believe that creativity is the prerogative of only exceptional individuals or to believe that everyone can be creative. Both are extreme positions, yet both contain a kernel of truth. However, if either of them dominates, there arises a one-dimensional view of creativity. It is much harder to be reflective, open-minded, and critical on the multiple dimensions and meanings of concepts such as creativity (and many other things in life for that matter). Acknowledging multidimensionality is highly important for current and future decision makers, both in organizations and society. If people do not question the buzzwords and simple solutions, they cannot learn to stop and think for themselves, and will not experience any transformative changes. Hence the first, almost automatic questions that should appear in their heads are always 'What does this mean?' and 'How can we know that?'

These three aspects have prompted the decision to write a book on organizational creativity that does not try to simplify creativity or serve up recipes on how to be creative. Instead, this is a text that presents research, concepts, and arguments that should prompt thinking and inspiration on how to make sense of and use the elusive phenomena known as creativity. In addition, the book includes an entire chapter that critically reflects on the concept of organizational creativity as such. One of the puzzling aspects of the field of organizational creativity is that very few scholars have questioned the concept more fundamentally. Organizational creativity tends to be regarded as inherently benign, which means that we tend to accept creativity as fundamentally positive and do not consider further its purpose and outcomes. For a critical mind, this calls for further scrutiny.

Acknowledgements

Writing a book is a sizeable creative project and creativity is—despite the persistent myth about the lone creative genius—a collective effort. Without all the people who have contributed in one way or another to the development of the book over the last two years, and the generous funding from the Jan Wallander and Tom Hedelius Foundation, it would surely not have seen the light of day.

George Payne from Oxford University Press discussed with me and convinced me that a book on creativity may be needed and relayed the idea to commissioning editor Nicola Hartley, who helped me develop my initial proposals and drafts until eventually Jenny King took over at later stages of the project.

Friends and colleagues have read drafts and discussed ideas throughout the writing process. I am especially indebted to Olof Hallonsten for taking the time to read the entire manuscript from front to back, and giving helpful and badly needed feedback. Mats Alvesson, Nichola Lowe, Wendy Smith, and Jörg Sydow have read selected parts and provided valuable comments. I am also grateful for Sam Franklin´s insights into the history of creativity, which provided a useful canvas for sorting out and developing initial ideas. Moreover, during the writing process I had the privilege of spending extended periods at Copenhagen Business School (CBS) and at Freie Universität (FU) Berlin, the latter funded by a Hedelius Scholarship from the Jan Wallander and Tom Hedelius Foundation. At both places I had countless intriguing discussions and conversations with people that sparked and challenged my fledgling ideas. Thank you Christian de Cock and Morten Knudsen for hosting me at CBS, and Jörg Sydow at FU.

The impetus for writing this book was mostly a result of teaching a course on creativity as part of the master's programme 'Managing People, Knowledge and Change' at the School of Economics and Management at Lund University. Students enrolled in the course read drafts of the text and discussed ideas and concepts during lectures and seminars, while some even chose to write their master's thesis based on selected concepts we had talked about. The students' curiosity and eagerness to learn, their evocative examples to make sense of concepts, their demands for clarifications, and their scepticism and constructive critique have been invaluable, and many of their ideas, explanations, and examples have been woven into the text.

I am also grateful for all the insights about the creative process that numerous practitioners shared with me. Most are mentioned in the text with their real names, but for those who chose to remain anonymous, you know who you are. Thanks for taking the time to talk to me and share your wisdom.

While I was working on the book, my beloved father passed away. From him I learned the values of passion and loving what you are doing (even if it is hard sometimes) and nurturing the curiosity to understand and explore the physical and symbolic world. It is to his memory I dedicate this book. In those difficult times my extended family lent invaluable support to each other and eased the difficulties of coping with our incredible loss.

The most important support I could have ever imagined has come from Sofie and Ebba, who patiently put up with periods of absent-mindedness and frustration and who made life joyful and bright when it was sorely needed. From the bottom of my heart: thank you!

Malmö, 30 May 2023

Contents

List of Tables, Figures, and Spotlights

Tables

Figures

Spotlights on Practice and Research

1

Introduction

This book is about how individuals and groups *influence and are influenced by* creative processes in an organizational context. Rather than asking how it is possible to produce more creativity or suggesting a specific creativity model, the book aims to provide a detailed and systematic analysis of organizing creativity based on three overarching analytical dimensions: context, process, and practice. This chapter sets the scene for the analysis by locating creativity in its historical context, and suggests a sensitizing conception of organizational creativity. History offers many lessons about current experiences as well as individual and collective behaviours. As such, it provides pointers about what may or may not have worked in the past. The history of creativity enables the assessment and classification of different interpretations, objectives, and implications that studies of creativity have generated in the past and that have an enduring influence today. The brief historical narrative of creativity in the first part of this chapter transitions to a *sensitizing concept* of organizational creativity that will inform the further discussions in the book. The chapter concludes with an outline of the book's contents.

A Short History of Creativity

Tracing the roots of the word and concept *creativity* has filled whole books (Weiner, 2012). A good point to start a historical account is the middle of the eighteenth century during the Enlightenment. Enlightenment thinkers emphasized individuals' ability to reason and the primacy of their senses in gathering knowledge about reality. Individuals were supposed to be rational and not imaginative. Towards the end of the eighteenth century, an opposition to the dominance of Enlightenment and rational thinking emerged: Romanticism. In contrast to the ideal of reason that was advocated during the Enlightenment, Romanticism emphasized irrationality, mystery, and emotions. The Romantics believed in individual self-expression, spontaneity, and emotional practices. Creative outcomes emerged through the connection with an inner self and the articulation of one's imagination without deliberately considering its link to an external reality. The source of creative outcomes was mysterious, however, because it was based on the spontaneous outpouring from an inner self. Since some individuals generated more creative outcomes than others, the notion of the *creative genius* emerged. The idea of the genius was nothing new. Before the eighteenth century, genius was associated with a supernatural being with an almost demonic power. Creative genius thus referred to individuals who seemingly possessed inexplicable, supernatural creative powers.

From the mid-nineteenth century, humankind experienced an explosive rate of new technological inventions and economic progress. Factories sprang up everywhere, and gigantic trade shows took place in London, Paris, and Philadelphia, showcasing the latest scientific inventions. Inventors, such as Benjamin Franklin, Graham Bell, Louis Daguerre,

Organizing Creativity. Stephan M. Schaefer, Oxford University Press. © Stephan M. Schaefer (2023).
DOI: 10.1093/oso/9780198893509.003.0001

and Thomas Edison, were central to these developments. One could think that these inventors strongly believed in reason and not supernatural powers yet the mystery of creative genius was still a belief central to the process of discovery, even in the rational natural sciences. Consider the words by the German physician and physicist Hermann Ludwig Ferdinand von Helmholtz:

> We venerate in him [the artist] a genius, a spark of divine creative energy, transcending the limits of our rational and self-conscious thought. And yet the artist is a man [sic] as we are, in him [sic] the same intellectual forces are at work as in ourselves.
>
> (cited in Weiner, 2012: 90).

It seemed that rational scientific thought had to be supported by a somewhat inexplicable force that created something new and unique. Most scientists thus acknowledged mysterious forces for their creative process. The personal narratives from August Kekulé, a pioneer of modern chemistry and the discoverer of the hexagonal structure of the benzene molecule, is a vivid example. He recounted the decisive episode that led to his discovery as follows:

> I turned my chair to the fire and dozed. Again, the atoms were gamboling before my eyes. This time the smaller groups kept modestly in the background. My mental eye, rendered more acute by the repeated visions of the kind, could now distinguish larger structures of manifold conformation; long rows sometimes more closely fitted together all twining and twisting in snake-like motion. But look! What was that? One of the snakes had seized hold of its own tail, and the form whirled mockingly before my eyes. As if by a flash of lightning I awoke; and this time also I spent the rest of the night in working out the consequences of the hypothesis.
>
> (Japp, 1898: 100).

Kekulé's account illustrates the shift between a trance-like state in which he sees snakes dancing and his sudden flash of insight into how this could lead him to a scientific discovery. His experiences illustrate how the creative process involved unaccountable inspiration, subconscious processes, and a subsequent rational development of an emergent idea.

However, scientists also sought to understand the process of imagination more systematically. The philosopher Whitehead (1925: 136) famously remarked that 'the greatest invention of the nineteenth century was the invention of the method of invention'. One method which is still in wide use today was first articulated by Helmholtz and later translated and further developed by the political scientist Graham Wallas. The model described a series of stages in the creative process: *preparation*, *incubation*, *illumination*, and *verification* (Wallas, 1926). The incubation stage was associated with the unconscious and inexplicable part of the creative process during which sudden flashes of insight occur that the individual cannot explain—much like Kekulé's dream. The expansion of the Romantic notion of imagination to the natural sciences thus retained the idea of creative genius and the inexplicable mysterious forces for being creative.

Instrumental and Humanist Research Camps

The general acceptance of an inexplicable element in the creative process changed dramatically in 1950, which was a pivotal moment for creativity research. In that year, J. P. Guilford, the president of the American Psychological Association, held his annual address to discuss a previously ignored topic for psychology: creativity. Guilford complained that creativity had been neglected as a research topic in psychology despite its importance for individuals and society. He called the neglect of creativity 'appalling' and admitted that though some scholars had been interested in creativity, few had contributed to an 'understanding or control of creativity very much' (Guilford, 1950: 445). Guilford urged psychologists to explore creativity systematically and scientifically, and they heeded his advice.

From the 1950s onwards, creativity became an inherent part of the discipline of psychology and a topic of systematic and intense research efforts. Between 1950 and 1965, more research studies were published on the subject than in the previous 200 years, and between January 1965 and June 1966, more were published than in the previous five years. One of the major sites for research into creativity in the US was the Institute for Personality Assessment and Research (IPAR), which published one of the most comprehensive studies on creativity. The researchers at IPAR strove to demystify creativity and had hopes 'to discover what kinds of individual possess in high degree the powers of constructive imagination and original thought' (Barron, 1958: 151). Clearly, there seemed to be an urge to demystify creativity through concerted research efforts. The increased interest in creativity, however, was not only based on Guilford's powers of persuasion and scientific curiosity, but also linked to broader issues.

Scholars have identified two main camps that influenced the systematic study of creativity: 'instrumentalists' and 'humanists' (Bycroft, 2014; see also Franklin, 2023). The instrumentalists studied creativity mainly as a reaction to the global challenges after the Second World War. A new world order had emerged in which communist and capitalist systems competed for economic, scientific, and military supremacy. Both systems needed new technology for their military, economic, political, and industrial systems. Controlling and systematically organizing the production of new ideas was therefore important and constituted a major background against which the systematic study and demystification of creativity emerged. There was a clear need to understand how creative ideas were produced and how exceptionally creative people could be identified. Thus, the instrumentalist stream of psychological research challenged assumptions that creativity was an inexplicable trait of creative geniuses. Researchers were interested in predicting and explaining creative personalities, which would enable them to control and unleash creative potential. Explaining and uncovering creative potential would help advance military and industrial progress. Not surprisingly, the main efforts then focused on the establishment of creativity tests to detect individuals' creative potential and connection to creative processes. Moreover, government institutions and large-scale organizations established large science laboratories in which teams of scientists were systematically organized.

Another reason for an increased interest in creativity—at least in the western hemisphere—was the ascendancy of democratic and humanistic values. The humanistic strand of psychological research assumed that creativity should not only serve the narrow interest of problem solving and instrumentalist aims. Rather, creativity was an essential need for each human being. For example, the psychologist Abraham Maslow, known for his pyramid of needs, studied the ways in which extraordinary people developed a special attitude towards life—one in which self-actualization and curiosity about life and nature was predominant. Creativity was not seen as something to be harnessed for specific purposes, but as a defence against the increasing dominance of an alienating world and fears of the polarized world order. Creativity was a psychological safety mechanism to retain one's well-being and break out of the perceived dullness of life and monotonous work. For humanist psychologists, all ideas were equally valuable if they satisfied the inner needs of the individual. Maslow therefore declared self-actualization—by which he meant the possibility for an individual to develop their authentic self—as a universal need for individuals and the highest goal to strive for (Maslow, 1950).

William Whyte, the famous author of *The Organization Man*, even went so far as to claim that 'the messiness of intuition, the aimless thoughts, the unpractical questions—all these things that are so often the companion to discovery are anathema to the world of the administrator' (Whyte, 1956: 52). Whyte highlighted one of the central contradictions of organizing creativity, namely that controlling creativity may have a negative impact on the individual. In the spirit of a humanist approach he therefore urged that creativity should remain an individual pursuit.

In both camps, instrumentalist and humanist, researchers worked hard to explain creativity and published study after study. Yet after decades of feverish work, observers still bemoaned the lack of a clear definition of the concept. The subject matter of creativity turned out to be much more complex than expected. Curiously, rather than establishing clarity through strict definitions, procedures, and systematic studies, creativity had become even harder to grasp and demarcate from other concepts. Looking back on a decade of psychological creativity, the organizers of a popular annual research conference on creativity expressed a blend of optimism and resignation: '[l]ike creative effort itself, research on creativity must be able to live with imperfections, inevitable incompleteness, a poignant sense of unrealized intention, a need finally to recognize that in many ways it has fallen short' (Taylor and Barron, 1963: 372). Indeed, the busy activity of creativity research that characterized the post-Second World War years abated at the end of the 1960s.

It was another address from the president of the American Psychological Association, by then Quinn McNemar, in 1964 which highlighted the problems of creativity research since its inception in 1950. McNemar remarked that 'anyone who peeks over the fence into this field [of creativity research] is apt to be astonished at the visible chaos', and he continued his scathing attack by stating that 'so little is known about the creative process that measuring instruments are seemingly chosen on a trial-and-error basis' (McNemar, 1964: 876). Indeed, researchers had encountered tricky definitional issues and argued over distinctions from other concepts, such as intelligence (which McNemar favoured) or perseverance. This meant that researchers were not sure whether they were studying creativity or another related phenomenon.

These arguments had two consequences. One was that psychological research on creativity broadened its scope, which meant that researchers tried to elaborate their measurement techniques or broadened the study of creative traits to creative processes. These efforts led to what scholars in creativity have called the 'second golden age of creativity' (Plucker and Renzulli, 1999). The second consequence was that the field of creativity research became receptive to influences from other disciplines. Simultaneously during the 1970s and 1980s, many scientific disciplines questioned their methods and philosophical foundations—the developments usually referred to as 'turns'. One highly influential change in perspective within several fields was the 'cultural turn', which shifted perspectives towards the meaning and interpretation of phenomena rather than their explanation and prediction. While the cultural turn mainly affected the social sciences, it did have an effect on creativity research and began a 'new science of creativity' (Sawyer, 2011).

Basically, researchers started to acknowledge that to understand the complexity of creativity, it is necessary to account for more than just the individual. In other words, they began to see creativity not as something with an unchanging essence that must be discovered with tests or more refined methods, but as a process in which people's interpretations, meanings, and actions are decisive for what counts as creative. Hence one of the key insights in creativity research was that rather than focusing on the cognitive processes of individuals, creativity may be dependent on a variety of cultural and linguistic systems in which it is embedded. Accordingly, creativity researchers contemplated the influence of the broader cultural context. Two key figures in creativity research must be identified here. One is Mihaly Csikszentmihalyi, who proposed the theory that creativity is dependent on its acceptance by dominant actors within a particular field (Csikszentmihalyi, 1990). Similarly, Teresa Amabile argued that creativity is context-dependent. She claimed that rather than an individual trait or outcome, creativity is essentially a social achievement in which context and individual interact. Amabile also introduced the concept of creativity to organization and management studies, which had taken little notice of this concept up to that time (Amabile, 1988). Slowly, other researchers began to take interest in different aspects of creativity—for example, how geographical spaces influence creativity (Florida, 2012) or how creativity was understood in different historical periods (Weiner, 2012).

The Spread of Creativity Techniques

Others were not much bothered by the science of creativity; they were more concerned with what someone could do to become more creative. Rather than systematically studying creativity, these individuals and groups were interested in *how to be* creative. This interest had already emerged during the 1930s, when the fledgling advertising industry sought more refined techniques to improve its trade. Advertising required new ideas and imagination to come up with quirky ideas, appealing images, and catchy slogans. After the Second World War, advertising became even more central to distinguishing between products—not by function, but by appealing to the aesthetic sensibilities of consumers. Ad men or creative directors were key figures. Similarly, investment in research and development (R&D) was growing as industries sought to succeed in increasingly competitive markets. Techniques that were used in advertising came to be more frequently adopted by R&D departments for problem solving and creative product development.

Advertising and R&D were all about the application of creative practices either to create awareness of new products or to generate and develop new ideas. So, while researchers struggled with definitions and insights into the nature of creativity, consultants started to spread the idea of using creativity techniques. Techniques of creativity proposed that the creative process could be broken down into predefined steps, which could then be executed by groups or individuals. It was another effort to demystify creativity—not through scientific explanation, but by reducing it to manageable chunks of action.

One of the most influential consultants was, not surprisingly, a former advertising executive who had co-founded the agency BBDO: Alex Osborn. Osborn had invented a simple method for producing creativity: brainstorming. The main idea was that an individual enters a relaxed mood and starts writing down every idea that comes into their head. In this way, groups as well as individuals can come up with ideas that may have some creative potential to be developed further (Osborn allegedly brainstormed 600 ideas for his book *Your Creative Power*). Osborn, of course, was not the only one who advised organizations and individuals how to become more creative. Another more recent representative of the practitioners camp is Edward de Bono, who has been hugely influential with creativity techniques such as the six thinking hats technique or lateral thinking (de Bono, 2014), which will be discussed in more detail in Chapter 3.

The shift from the mass production of products based on labour and capital to knowledge-intensive and creative industries in which branding, services, and symbolism are central has put creativity advice in even higher demand. Self-help books on creativity for all kinds of purposes abound, and more and more consultancies provide advice on how to become more creative. The sheer mass of publications and consultancies which all tout different advice or simplify scientific studies has made creativity a widely used buzzword. The number of creativity initiatives makes organizational members tired of hearing about creativity, especially if there are no substantial organizational changes. The critically minded innovation consultant Alf Rehn once recounted multiple episodes from his experience where members of organizations experienced creativity more and more as empty talk devoid of meaning (Rehn, 2019).

While techniques of creativity are important, it seems that practice has lost its connection to research and vice versa, which means that research findings do not inform creativity practices and researchers seldom engage in an active dialogue with practitioners concerning their techniques (Kieser et al., 2015). This book discusses certain creativity practices, ensuring that they are informed by systematic and rigorous scientific research, and to provide a deeper insight into research designs on creativity, the focus now turns to different research philosophies and knowledge interests.

Research Philosophies and Knowledge Interests

The short history of creativity suggests that different research philosophies influenced the study of creativity. A research philosophy is a set of assumptions about the nature of reality (ontology), how valid knowledge is obtained (epistemology), and how and what values influence research (axiology). Generally, it is possible to distinguish between objectivist and subjectivist research philosophies, and since Chapter 2 will go deeper into objectivist and subjectivist research on organizational creativity, this section only sketches the main ideas.

An objectivist research philosophy seeks to emulate the methods and assumptions of the natural sciences and assumes that the world exists as an objective, external reality that is independent of an observer. The underlying assumption is that reality is ordered and structured, which means that it is assumed that creativity follows ordered and discrete patterns. It is those patterns and factors that an objectivist creativity researcher wants to explain. Knowledge that is valid in an objectivist approach should then be based on measurable, observable, and quantifiable data. For example, patent applications or formalized ideas are in many cases taken as measurable indicators of creative outcomes (Oldham and Cummings, 1996).

The goal of objectivist research is to be able to generalize findings and propose new theories or add to existing ones. Objectivism mainly uses quantitative research methods, which collect standardized data sets expressed in numbers. To analyse quantitative data, researchers use statistical methods. The main methods based on an objectivist approach to creativity are, for example, psychometric tests, surveys, and experiments. Overall, an objectivist research philosophy has dominated creativity research, presumably driven by the desire to propose objective criteria and general explanations for creativity (Rickards and De Cock, 2012).

Although in the minority, some creativity scholars have based their work on a subjectivist research philosophy. Their main assumption is that reality is socially constructed. Conceptions of social constructionism abound, and assume different degrees and scopes. The general notion, however, is similar throughout. In particular, rather than believing that the world exists independently of individuals, those individuals are seen to shape their understanding of the world through talking with each other, agreeing on an interpretation of reality, and acting based on these interpretations. Hence researchers of this mindset do not assume an objective, essential reality, but explore people's interpretations of their reality and processes of how these interpretations may have been legitimized—that is, how they have become the dominant form of interpretation. Thus, one of the ambitions of a subjectivist researcher is to understand the context of a phenomenon to explore what dominant interpretations are, how they were legitimized, and how they influence individual and collective actions. People do not live in a world with one single interpretation; there are different interpretations that may be used to make sense of a phenomenon such as creativity. Of course, multiple interpretations make reality much more chaotic, which in turn makes it difficult to propose generalizations related to organizing creativity. The upshot is that rather than seeking simple explanations and causal connections, conceptions of creativity should account for its dependency on subjective and collective interpretations.

Preferred research methods for a subjectivist researcher are qualitative, which means that they are based on non-standardized data sets which express meaning, experiences, and emotions through text and images. For example, a subjectivist researcher who would like to understand creative processes in a specific organizational context would inquire about how individuals discuss their idea of creativity, which stories are shared about creative individuals or groups, and what managers do and think when they want their subordinates to be creative. The analysis of qualitative data is non-standardized and involves the identification of recurrent patterns and themes, such as interpretations of creativity that many people use or frequent experiences and practices of managers.

Objectivist and subjectivist research philosophies imply different *motives for generating knowledge*. The sociologist Jürgen Habermas called these 'knowledge interests', which refers to the reasons and objectives behind generating knowledge by asking what purpose it serves (Habermas, 1968). The first knowledge interest that Habermas discussed is technical. A *technical knowledge interest* involves finding cause-and-effect relationships which can be used to dominate and control the environment. For example, trying to identify causes of creative behaviour means that this knowledge can be used to control the creative process and produce the desired outcomes. A *practical knowledge interest* focuses on how people make sense of and understand their environment. The goal is to create a mutual understanding of people's motivation, meaning, and goals. For example, evaluating how engineers and managers make sense of creativity may lead to an improved understanding of each other's interests and problems. Lastly, a *critical knowledge interest* aims to question assumptions and generate reflections about dominant knowledge and ideologies. For example, someone may reflect on what ideologies drive current forms of organizational creativity and how this may come to serve some people's interests while suppressing others. Table 1.1 summarizes the purpose, focus, orientation, and projected outcomes of the three knowledge interests with a view to organizational creativity.

This book focuses on the less dominant approach to studying organizational creativity— a subjective research philosophy and a practical and critical knowledge interest. This means that the arguments and framing of the book are based on a constructionist ontology. It is not the aspiration of the book to come up with generalizable laws or recommendations for how to control and predict creativity. Rather, the knowledge interest is mainly practical and somewhat critical in the sense that it strives to create an appreciation for different perspectives on organizing creativity. While the book advocates a practical and critical knowledge interest and leans heavily on a subjective research philosophy it does not aspire to proclaim these as the truth. Rather, by drawing attention to practice, process, and context, the book aims to foster a broader and more reflective perspective on organizational creativity

Table 1.1 The three knowledge interests

Knowledge interest in organizational creativity	Purpose	Focus	Orientation	Projected outcomes
Technical	Predict and control creative outcomes	Identify and manipulate variables that influence organizational creativity	Calculation of the most efficient and effective organization for organizational creativity	Provide the most rational form of producing creative outcomes
Practical	Improve understanding about organizational creativity	Interpret meanings and symbols	Appreciation of different perspectives and interpretations	Remove misunderstandings concerning organizational creativity
Critical	Realize more just, fair, and rational outcomes and processes of organizational creativity	Expose dominant forms of knowledge and practice	Transformation of suppressing forms of organizational creativity	Remove unnecessary forms of domination and suppression and create more just conditions

and organizing processes. This means that it would not be fitting to provide a definitive definition of organizational creativity here; instead, it would be better to suggest a framing which sensitizes readers to certain aspects of organizational creativity. It is to such a framing that the conversation now turns.

A Sensitizing Concept

A reflection on the history of creativity illustrates that discovering the true nature of creativity may have been misguided and, admittedly, in vain. The difficulties of discovering the true nature of creativity are reflected in the efforts and failures of psychologists to suggest a comprehensive definition of what creativity is and what distinguishes creative individuals. After decades of study, one finding is certain: creativity is complex, elusive, and multidimensional. This finding is, however, seldom reflected in studies on organizational creativity, presumably because it makes the study of creativity more cumbersome and challenges the dominance of the natural science ideal of creativity research.

In a recent overview of creativity studies and leadership, Hughes et al. (2018) showed that many definitions of creativity do not account for individuals' engagement in the actual process of being creative. They argued that because most definitions and conceptions of creativity are outcome-based, they consider only successful creative outcomes. The objective of these studies was, of course, to learn from successful ideas by extrapolating factors that have been influential in creating successful outcomes, which are the hallmark of technical knowledge interests. However, if only outcomes are considered, all other aspects of the creative process, that may not have led to a successful outcome but are nonetheless part of organizational creativity, are neglected. This is important knowledge, however, as the nature of the creative process also includes failures, dead ends, attempts, interactions, ambiguity, and complexity. Not engaging closely with the process and context of creativity thus means that individuals have only a very partial perspective on organizational creativity (Schüßler et al., 2021).

To capture multiple aspects of the creative process, a conclusive definition of creativity is neither feasible nor desirable, as it would limit a broader understanding of the complexity and multidimensionality of creativity. However, it is also not productive to have an 'anything goes' approach to what creativity is, because if every activity, product, or other entity is potentially creative, it becomes futile to study it. In other words, if a concept starts to mean everything, it begins to mean nothing.

The sociologist Herbert Blumer proposed a way out of this predicament. He argued that sociological definitions should neither be definitive nor completely open, but *sensitizing* (Blumer, 1954). Sensitizing means that the description of a concept, such as creativity, should offer signposts to guide the understanding of a situation but not define it conclusively. Sensitizing concepts start from how actors experience creativity from *within their contexts and actions* rather than defining creativity *from an external point of view*. So if people refrain from defining a situation clearly and instead attend closely to the experience of actors, it is more likely that they will gain a deeper insight into a variety of dimensions and influences. In addition, sensitizing concepts clarify a person's assumptions about a concept such as creativity. It is human nature never to be free of preconceived notions or

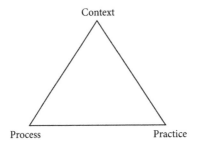

Figure 1.1   Context, process, and practice

biases. People are not blank slates, and for that reason a sensitizing concept is useful in making assumptions and values about a phenomenon explicit without letting its conception determine what people see.

In this book, the conception of *organizational creativity* sensitizes the reader to situations which are characterized by *individuals and groups of individuals, who generate, develop and evaluate potentially transformative ideas continuously within an organizational context over time.* This sensitizing concept integrates the three key dimensions—context, process, and practice—and associated assumptions which frame the presentation and discussions in this book. All three dimensions are mutually dependent and inextricably linked to each other, as illustrated in Figure 1.1. The triangle of context, process, and practice will inform the analysis of each chapter in the book by discussing each aspect in depth related to the generation, development, and evaluation of ideas, efforts to organize creativity, and the suggestion of an alternative conception of organizational creativity.

In this book's conception of organizational creativity, context refers to meaningfully enabling and constraining factors of process and practices. Process describes creativity's temporal dimension, referring to its unfolding over time. Practices are the concrete activities of individuals and collectives involved in organizational creativity. The triangle of context, process, and practice should be seen as scaffolding, and the content of each chapter will provide material for building a more comprehensive and deeper understanding of organizing creativity (see Watson, 1994 for a similar approach). The following sections discuss each dimension in more detail regarding the sensitizing concept suggested above.

Contexts: 'Transformative Ideas Within an Organizational Context'

First, context refers to the constraining and enabling factors that influence the meanings and practices in a specific situation (Johns, 2006). As discussed earlier, this book is based on a subjectivist perspective and, more specifically, the notion that contexts are socially constructed (Berger and Luckmann, 1966). Here, the focus is on a sociological interpretation, and the term *social constructionism* will be used (see Egholm, 2014 for the distinction between constructionism and constructivism). Social constructionism has been controversially debated over the last decades.

The debate can be explained using the example of a stone. A stone is a real thing in my hand, so how could it be a construct? While some sceptical philosophers would even question the ontological reality of the stone, a less radical perspective would point out that while the stone may be real, one's interpretation of the stone is imbued with socially constructed meaning. Consider the possibility that everyone agreed that all stones symbolize a stone god that should be worshipped. Suddenly, the stone on the ground would acquire a completely different meaning—as a symbol for a god. An object like a stone can therefore be evaluated based on how its meaning is socially constructed.

The assumption that creativity is socially constructed draws attention to some important aspects. First, a context influences how people interpret, and act in, a situation. For example, if stones were declared a symbol for a deity, people would interpret situations involving a stone differently, i.e. investing godly powers in a stone or using the stone in religious ceremonies. Hence, interpretations of the meaning of a context influence how people think and act with regard to practices like generating, developing, and evaluating ideas. Second, if a context is not unchanging but constructed, it can be transformed (Hacking, 1999). Hence people potentially hold powers to change the meanings of objects, situations, and organizational processes. While contexts influence people's interpretation and practices their practices could also potentially change the meaning of the context (Giddens, 1984). For that reason, an individual's conception of organizational creativity sensitizes them to potentially transformative ideas, which are influenced by the context but carry the potential to change the meaning of a context at the same time. This relates back to what this book is fundamentally about with regard to creative processes—how individuals and groups exert *influence* over but are at the same time *influenced by* an organizational context. Third, the constructed nature of meaning allows people to explore how to influence the meaning and interpretation of a context (Smircich and Morgan, 1982). Such an analysis provides an understanding of how to make organizational values and meaning systems more conducive to creativity.

This book focuses specifically on organizational contexts. However, a problem is that, much like creativity, an organization is difficult to define. For that reason, different metaphors are drawn upon to discuss specific conceptions of organization. Chapter 2 expands on the concept of metaphor and describes how different metaphors can be used to make sense of organizations. In general, the metaphors of culture and flux and transformation inform the arguments of the book, which will be discussed in more detail in the next chapter. Yet in the spirit of providing a holistic, multidimensional analysis, other related metaphors are used to illuminate certain aspects and dimensions of organizing creativity.

Processes: 'Continuously ... Over Time'

The use of 'continuously' and 'over time' proposed in the *sensitizing conception* earlier indicates a process perspective. Process theory in general assumes that reality is not composed of discrete events, but constantly transforming and evolving. The metaphor of a flowing river is commonly used to illustrate the central idea of a process perspective. Rather than conceiving of reality as static, the river metaphor suggests that reality is constantly in motion and changes all the time. In fact, one of the major distinctions discussed in research on creativity is between a variance perspective and a process perspective (Mohr, 1982).

A variance perspective aims to explain and measure precisely how different independent variables affect an outcome such as creativity. The assumption that drives variance perspectives on creativity is that the value of the causal variable will always predict the value of the outcome variable. For example, a variance model may propose that if someone manipulates the variable of a creative personality, a complex job, and non-controlling managers, an organization will produce more creative outcomes (see Oldham and Cummings, 1996). Variance research seeks to isolate specific factors and assess their effect on an outcome. The aim of variance research is to provide definitive explanations, and it is inspired by natural science research philosophies and an objectivist research philosophy.

In contrast to a variance perspective, a process perspective allows people to understand and, to some extent, explain creativity by considering how it develops over time. Studying processes allows researchers to account for and understand how important factors contribute to creativity and how those factors may connect and interact with each other in specific contexts and situations. Process theory cannot deliver definite answers, but it can provide probabilistic explanations—that is, an understanding of what might be probable explanations for creativity. Even though most scholars agree that creativity is highly complex, a process perspective is fairly uncommon, presumably because of the dominance of the objectivist approach to organizational creativity research (Fortwengel et al., 2017). As mentioned earlier, in this book I apply a process perspective, meaning that the aim is to account for how creative processes unfold over time and what role temporalities play in organizing creativity.

Practices: 'Generate, Develop, and Evaluate'

Lastly, the sensitizing concept of creativity draws attention to practices of generating, developing, and evaluating ideas. A practice is a recurrent pattern of activity that incorporates and integrates several related elements, such as the body, knowledge, language, symbols, things, emotions, and contexts (Reckwitz, 2002). For example, the practice of generating an idea may involve drawing (body) a technical diagram (knowledge and symbolic language) with a pen (tool) at a workspace (context).

Most practices are routines, which are acquired repetitive practices that help people cope successfully with different situations (Feldman, 2000). For that reason, individuals tend to repeat them almost mechanically. While routines lead to predictability and consistency, they are also prone to erroneous behaviour. Take the practice of evaluating wine. Scholars have found that wine experts judge white wine that has been coloured with a red substance based on flavours that they expect from red wine. In other words, the experts relied on routines and previous practices of assuming a certain flavour profile from a wine with the colour red (Morrot et al., 2001). Imagine, however, if the experts had been served orange wine. Very likely, they would have started to contemplate what that means. Has the wine gone bad? Is it an experiment with new grapes? Hence not all practices are mindless routines; they can become deliberate and contemplative, especially when problems with the routines arise (Heidegger, 1927). As I will show throughout the book, deliberate contemplations of practices and routines underpin the seed for new ideas and alternative ways of solving problems.

Furthermore, how to handle problems in routines and practices illustrates the importance of interpretation, which is a way of understanding and explaining the meaning of a given situation and indicating how one should act. In routines, interpretations are almost automatic; people readily understand the meaning of a situation and act accordingly. With a view to the wine example above, the colour red is automatically interpreted as red wine and its associated tastes. In more complex, ambiguous, and novel social situations, individuals may lack ready-made interpretations of what they mean and how they should act. An orange colour in wine leads to a new situation which calls for more deliberate, reflective interpretation and a creative change of practices. As shall be seen throughout this book, organizing creativity requires ongoing interpretation and enactment of practices which may lead to the generation and development of transformative ideas.

Outline of the Book

To structure the argument, the book distinguishes and discusses key aspects of organizing creativity in five separate chapters and a concluding chapter. These aspects are framed as specific activities when organizing creativity: theorizing (Chapter 2), generating and developing ideas (Chapter 3), evaluating ideas (Chapter 4), organizing (Chapter 5), and reflecting (Chapter 6). Apart from Chapter 2, each chapter is structured based on the triangle model suggested in Figure 1.1—that is, each chapter discusses context, process, and practice with regard to the key aspect and practice that is focused on. Moreover, throughout the book, practical examples and key research findings will be used to illuminate and deepen the discussions. Since these features highlight specific examples and aspects, they are called *Spotlight on Practice* and *Spotlight on Research* respectively.

To provide a theoretical background to how organizational creativity has been discussed, Chapter 2 provides an overview of different conceptions of organizational creativity. To structure the theoretical discussion, four metaphors of organization—*organism, brain, culture*, and *transformation and flux*—are used. Based on these metaphoric interpretations of organization, I will discuss conceptions such as interactionists' models of organizational creativity, design thinking, culture, and process perspectives. The overall objective of the chapter is to establish a theoretical basis for a richer and deeper understanding of the discussions in following chapters. While an array of theories will be discussed in Chapter 2, cultural and process theories are the main theoretical source of inspiration for the analysis.

Chapter 3 focuses on the first aspect of organizing creativity—generating and developing ideas. The first section of the chapter suggests four different contexts—*routine, loose coupling, weak ties*, and *organized anarchy*—that influence the generation and development of ideas based on the strength of the situation and the nature of the problem. This is followed by a discussion of the notion of time relevant to processes of generating and developing ideas. The first section focuses on a discussion of time based on the metaphor of a *chordal triad* of past, present, and future, which is then used to illuminate key process dimensions of organizing creativity, such as knowledge, motivation, attention, and imagination. The discussion of process dimensions will then expand to the role of other individuals when generating and developing ideas, as well as the use and function of objects. The last section of Chapter 3 distinguishes between cognitive and interactive practices of generating and developing ideas, and presents and discusses selected and systematically researched findings.

In Chapter 4, I will dive deeper into aspects of evaluating ideas. To understand what influences the value of ideas, the concept *orders of worth* is central to the discussion of evaluation contexts. I will then distinguish seven orders of worth—*inspiration, market, domestic, industrial, fame, civic, green*—that provide different values and forms of justification when evaluating ideas. This will be followed by a discussion of how processes of evaluation may unfold, and their possible outcomes, such as rejection, acceptance, or friction. The notion of friction will be discussed in more detail as an effective prerequisite for transformative ideas. From the discussion of evaluation processes, the chapter transitions to the discussion of evaluation practices. To evaluate an idea, it must be pitched first. Thus some space will be devoted to examining practices of pitching ideas. Subsequently, I distinguish between transactional and transformative evaluation practices. The former assumes that the value of an idea can be exchanged, much like a transaction of goods, while the latter argues that evaluation is situational and is transformed in interactions with others.

Chapter 5 shifts perspective to how people may structure activities and processes when organizing creativity. The main focus of this chapter is on processes and practices of organizing creativity—the conception and context of an organization is discussed at length in Chapter 2. The main part of the chapter is devoted to critically discussing four modes and practices of coordination and their relevance to organizing creativity: management, leadership, teams, and networks. All modes of coordination play an important role when organizing creativity, which means that contradictions and paradoxes are an inherent part of the process. Hence this chapter will discuss how *paradoxes* influence the process of organizing creativity and how organizations and practitioners may deal productively with them.

Chapter 6 takes a step back in the analysis by critically reflecting on some of the ingrained assumptions of organizational creativity research. In the first section, organizing creativity is discussed and linked to the broader social and economic context. Based on the aforementioned humanist and instrumentalist camps of creativity research, this discussion distinguishes their related outcomes of creativity and examines each of them. The chapter then outlines a different approach and practice referred to as *radical transformative creativity*. This seeks to problematize an unreflective pursuit of instrumentalist creativity and instead aims for a pluralistic creativity process and ideas that contribute to social economic and ecological sustainability.

Finally, Chapter 7 concludes this book by recapitulating the main argument and providing a reflection on the implications for research and practices of organizing creativity.

2

Theorizing Organizational Creativity

This chapter explores the question of how organizational scholars have conceptualized creativity and creative processes. The purpose of the chapter is twofold. First, it serves as a general and systematic overview of research on organizational creativity and related critiques. Second, it provides a necessary theoretical backdrop for the arguments made throughout the rest of the book, which are mainly based on cultural and processual perspectives. The overview is structured around four metaphors of organization: organism, brain, culture, and transformation and flux. These metaphors were chosen because they are the most dominant when theorizing organizational creativity.

Arguably, the most influential metaphor is the organization as organism. Linked to the human relations movement, which emerged in the first half of the twentieth century, the organism metaphor highlights the central aspect of needs. Individuals thrive creatively in organizations that consider their needs, and organizations are most effective and creative in environments to which they are most effectively and efficiently adapted and which fulfil their needs. In particular, the work by Teresa Amabile is of interest here (Amabile, 1988, 1997b; Amabile and Pratt, 2016).

Another influential metaphor for organization is the brain, which is linked to the scholarship of James March and Herbert Simon (March and Simon, 1958). The brain metaphor emphasizes the central function of seeking, evaluating, and processing information, as well as making decisions in organizations. With regard to organizational creativity, the brain metaphor underpins the popular notion of design thinking which will be discussed in detail later in the chapter.

The culture metaphor shifts the perspective to the symbols and values of an organization and how interpretations and meanings influence behaviour. The discussion draws on this perspective to classify different cultures and their implications for organizing creativity.

Lastly, the transformation and flux metaphor is linked to process theories of organization that have gained popularity in recent decades. Process theory highlights how organizations are not static entities, and that organization is an activity. Thus, organization should not be discussed as 'being', but as 'becoming' (Tsoukas and Chia, 2002). 'Becoming' refers to how organization is an ongoing process that never stops but needs to be constantly achieved. Organizational creativity should not be seen as an outcome of a system, but as inherent in ongoing organizational processes. Hence the perspective shifts from organizational creativity as a noun to an understanding of organizing creativity as a verb connoting an activity. With regard to process approaches, this chapter further distinguishes between moderate and strong process views and their implications for organizational creativity (Fortwengel et al., 2017). The cultural and processual perspectives are linked to the subjectivist research approach discussed in Chapter 1 and thus constitute the ontological and epistemological foundation of the book.

Organizing Creativity. Stephan M. Schaefer, Oxford University Press. © Stephan M. Schaefer (2023).
DOI: 10.1093/oso/9780198893509.003.0002

Metaphors of Organization

Defining an organization and delimiting it from other social groups, such as families or societies, is not straightforward (Silverman, 1970). There are some distinguishing features, however (see Daft et al., 2020). An organization is a social entity, which means that it comprises a collection of people. An organization usually has a goal that it would like to achieve, whether it is to sell a new product, educate students, or care for patients. To achieve these goals, an organization must coordinate, perform, and control activities. To perform these activities, it is necessary to decide who is doing what, as well as when and where they are to do it. These decisions usually result in organizational structures. An organizational structure describes and prescribes the relationships between people or groups of people. The combination of different organizational structures into a coherent entity is called an organizational design, which is visualized in an organizational chart—typically a diagram with boxes and arrows.

However, just because there is an organizational design, that does not mean that organization happens according to the intended structure. People must act on organizational structures—organizations do not organize; people organize. Yet people have different motivations, values, and goals, and those individual goals may or may not always align with the organization's own goals. Therefore, one additional organizational concern is how to align individual and organizational goals. This could happen by force, by negotiation, or by manipulation of people and groups. Moreover, although the goals of an organization may be fulfilled, this could have come at a high social and environmental cost. Hence people, goals, structures, relationships, processes, values, power, and authority, as well as social and environmental impacts, are all basic elements of an organization. Consequently, organizations are complex, multidimensional social entities and if all of these elements are important, how can people make sense of what an organization really is?

The organizational researcher Gareth Morgan suggested using metaphors to capture the diversity of perspectives on organizations (Morgan, 1997). Generally, people use metaphors 'whenever we attempt to understand one element of experience in terms of another' (Morgan, 1997: 4). For example, people say that creativity is like a river when they attempt to understand it in terms of its processual and flowing nature. Metaphors unlock different perspectives of experiences and are a powerful way of framing theories of organizations. Metaphors are also *generative*, which means that they prompt new ways of thinking, new ideas, and new solutions, making them valuable tools for activating creative ways of thinking about organizations (Schön, 1979). Chapter 3 discusses the use and function of metaphors in more detail. For now, it is fitting for a book on creativity to use metaphors' generative potential to highlight diverse aspects of organizational creativity and organizing creativity. In contrast to the aspiration for precise technical explanations, metaphors are a creative tool to make sense of elusive phenomena such as organizational creativity.

In total, Morgan proposed eight metaphors for organizations: machines, organisms, brains, cultures, political systems, psychic prisons, transformation and flux, and instruments of domination. These metaphors draw analogies to other disciplines or non-organization theories: machines to engineering, organisms and brains to biology, cultures to anthropology, political systems to political sciences, psychic prisons to psychoanalysis, transformation and flux to process philosophy, and instruments of domination to critical theory. All metaphors highlight a specific perspective on organizations and the role of creativity within those organizations. Table 2.1 provides an overview of the eight metaphors, including a short summary, their original discipline, dominant theories and concepts, and how creativity features in these theories of organization.

Table 2.1 Metaphors of organizations and their implications for organizational creativity

Metaphor	Central idea	Key works and reviews	Perspective on creativity
Machine	Organization consists of mechanically interrelated parts.	Scientific management (e.g. Taylor, 1911); bureaucracy (e.g. Weber, 1978).	Creativity is deviation, but necessary for predefining an organizational design.
Organism	Individuals and organizations must satisfy needs and adapt to their environments.	Human relations movement (e.g. Roethlisberger and Dickson, 1939; Trist and Bamforth, 1951); contingency theory (e.g. Burns and Stalker, 1961; Lawrence and Lorsch, 1967); population ecology (e.g. Hannan and Freeman, 1977).	Creativity is a human need which must be fulfilled, and is necessary for adapting to external environments.
Brain	An organization is constantly processing, learning, and memorizing information and making decisions.	Decision-making theories (e.g. March and Simon, 1958; Cohen et al., 1972); organizational learning (e.g. Argyris and Schön, 1978).	Limited ability to process information (bounded rationality) potentially limits creativity, while constant learning facilitates creativity.
Culture	An organization is guided by individual and collective values, beliefs, norms, and rituals.	Conceptions of organizational culture (e.g. Smircich, 1983; Alvesson, 2013b).	Creativity is facilitated by a shared sense of meaning and potentially obstructed by fragmented meaning systems.
Political system	An organization is characterized by different interests, conflict, and the use of power to further interests.	Resource dependence theory (e.g. Pfeffer and Salancik, 1978); power and resistance (Fleming and Spicer, 2014).	Creativity becomes an object of bargaining, negotiation, and power.
Psychic prison	People in an organization become entrapped in conscious and unconscious ways of thinking.	Psychodynamics (e.g. Gabriel and Carr 2002, de Vries and Miller, 1984); groupthink (Janis, 1982)	Creativity is hindered by not accepting or considering other ways of thinking or perspectives
Transformation and flux	Organizations are in constant motion and flux.	Sensemaking (Weick, 1995); process theory (Langley et al., 2013; Hernes, 2014).	Creativity is an inherent part of organizational processes.
Instrument of domination	Organizations are sites of exploitation, alienation, and inequality.	Critical management studies (Alvesson and Willmott, 1992; Fournier and Grey, 2000)	Creativity can become a tool of the elite for domination and exploitation.

It is beyond the scope of this book to discuss all eight metaphors in detail. Therefore, the following discussion focuses on four of the most influential metaphors in organizational theory and the organizational creativity literature: organisms, brains, cultures, and transformation and flux.

Contingency and Interactionist Models

It is rather difficult to imagine the experience of mining coal before all of the convenient technologies and tools existed. Back then, it was necessary to work in a group, equipped with a shovel, deep down in the ground in a dimly lit and dusty mineshaft. In this environment miners needed to know exactly what they were doing, relying on each other and keeping each other safe. This group effort most likely led to strong bonds between miners. Since there was no possibility of rapid communication as exists today, miners had a significant degree of autonomy when making decisions. This is how the workers of a coal mine in Durham, UK experienced their work during the 1940s, just before management decided to introduce a new technology called long wall mining. This method mechanized the mining process, removing much of the autonomy, skill, and team spirit from the miners. The result was that they felt anxious and alienated, and they lost their sense of belonging and responsibility (Trist and Bamforth, 1951).

Trist and Bamforth's influential study of coal miners not only drew attention to how technology impacts individual and social behaviour, but also flagged the importance of individuals' needs in organizations. To create effective and efficient organizations, it is essential to consider how an organization meets individual and group needs. Conversely, it is also important to assess how changes in the organizational environment impact individuals and groups, as in the case of the miners and the introduction of new technologies. The realization of the negative impact of Tayloristic work regimes on workers' motivation and well-being highlighted the essential role of individual and group needs for organizations, which became the central leitmotif of the organism metaphor of organizations and an interactionist perspective on organizational creativity.

The guiding principle suggested by the organism metaphor is that to function well and possibly even survive, individuals, groups, and entire organizations must see how their respective environments meet their needs. To put it very simply, an organism adapted to the cold would not thrive or even survive for very long in a desert. For example, the miners felt that their need for autonomy and the feeling of belonging to a close group of co-workers were met. But the automatization of mining changed their work environment, which did not meet their needs any more, and they lost their sense of meaning and belonging. Accordingly, the environment and the individuals within it must fit together to accomplish the most efficient and effective method of organizing. The question of how people can achieve the best fit between environment, organization, and individual is referred to as the *contingency perspective* in organization studies (Burns and Stalker, 1961; Lawrence and Lorsch, 1967).

Organization scholars Tom Burns and Richard Stalker put the contingency perspective on the map with their landmark study on organizational innovation and creativity. They were interested in how organizations adapt to different environments that were either stable or unstable (Burns and Stalker, 1961). They found that in stable environments, organizations adopt a bureaucratic or *mechanistic* management system, which means that there is a high degree of formalization, less autonomy, and more hierarchy. In contrast, in turbulent environments, organizations have what they called an *organic* management system that enables them to be more creative. An organic management system has a low degree of formalization and allows for a high degree of autonomy and flexibility to react to sudden changes in the environment. Organic management systems must generate more creative ideas because the organization is pressed to find ways to continuously adapt to new challenges and problems. The organic management system was thus the first attempt to conceptualize a fitting organizational structure for creativity considering the relationship between external environment and organizational structure.

Creativity researchers have continued to work with a contingency perspective and the question of how individuals and environments may be best fitted to produce creative outcomes. They have emphasized the relationship between individual, group, and organizational environment and tried to capture some of the dynamic aspects of how an environment influences individuals and groups in their efforts to be creative. Instead of contingency, organizational creativity scholars have used the label *interactionist* to denote the dynamic aspect of establishing a fit between individual, group, and environment (for a description of interactional psychology, see Terborg, 1981). Yet, similar to a contingency perspective, the central question of an interactionist approach is how to produce the optimal fit between an individual or group and their organizational environment that will eventually lead to creative outcomes. Interactionist models have become the most influential approach to studying organizational creativity. In what follows, I discuss two of the foundational models of the field: the componential theory of innovation (Amabile, 1988) and the multilevelled interactionist model (Woodman et al., 1993).

Componential Theory of Creativity and Innovation

In 1988, Harvard professor Teresa Amabile published a book chapter in which she reported the findings of a qualitative study on a group of R&D scientists (Amabile, 1988). Based on her interviews, Amabile proposed a set of theoretical propositions, which would go on to become arguably the most influential theory in the field of organizational creativity. She called it the 'Componential Theory of Innovation and Creativity'. Amabile's theory aimed to capture how work environment and individual creativity are closely interlocked systems. In other words, she argued that an organization must find the right fit between its internal work environment and individual or group creative processes.

Amabile distinguished between two levels which interact: individual or group creativity and organizational innovation. The level of individual or group creativity includes three components. The first component is *skills in the task domain*. A domain contains the knowledge of a specific subject or discipline. Hence an important aspect of creativity is possessing knowledge in a specific domain, such as engineering, chemistry, marketing, and so on. The second component is *creativity-relevant processes*. The assumption here is that creativity is based on specific behaviours and cognitive styles of individuals, such as the ability to think divergently or to be able to cope with paradoxes. Lastly, Amabile listed *intrinsic motivation* as an essential component. Intrinsic motivation, she argued, stimulates more individual creativity than external rewards, and thus has a significant influence on individual or group creativity.

In the spirit of an interactionist perspective, however, Amabile further postulated that individual creativity is not enough and proposed that to successfully implement ideas—that is, to generate innovation—three organizational-level components are essential. First, there is the *motivation to innovate*, which refers to the attitudes and vision of top management and how much it aspires to be creative. This must be complemented by allocating *resources in the task domain*. This includes all kinds of resources, ranging from subscriptions to scientific publications to materials for prototyping, but also resources to boost networking. Additionally, *skills in innovation management* are an important factor, which includes management techniques and principles such as appropriate goal-setting, the right work assignments, or communication skills.

Both levels interact with each other, which means that the organizational environment influences individual or group creativity, which in turn feeds into organizational innovation. The optimal set-up for generating innovation is 'when an intrinsically motivated person with high domain expertise and high skill in creative thinking works in an environment high in supports for creativity' (Amabile, 2011: n.p.). According to Amabile this set-up allows an individual to combine their expertise knowledge and the ability to deviate from ingrained modes of reasoning with an intrinsic drive to explore new ideas, which increases the likelihood for creativity and innovation to occur.

Recently, Amabile's theory has been updated to consider new research findings (Amabile and Pratt, 2016). The main amendments to the model include a consideration of the complex factors that drive individual motivation, the essential role of affect and emotions, and the assumption that all components—motivation, domain knowledge, and creativity skills—must be present to generate creative outcomes. Despite the model's updates, the contingency approach inherent in the organism metaphor has remained the key underlying assumption as the model assumes that individual creative processes need to be fitted to a conducive work environment.

Shortly after Amabile's original chapter on the componential theory, another influential article was published which proposed how creativity may be possible within a complex social system such as an organization (Woodman et al., 1993). Woodman et al.'s ambition was to summarize previous findings in the literature to provide an overview of the most common relationships between sets of variables and their impact on creativity. They proposed a multilevel approach to creativity in which individual, group, and organizational processes are analysed in a complex system of interactions. Woodman et al. suggested an input-transformation-output model in which creative input is made up of an array of different dimensions at the individual, group, and organization level, which cover many aspects, such as intrinsic motivation, knowledge, personality, and cognitive abilities. Group characteristics include norms, cohesiveness, size, diversity, roles, task, and problem-solving approaches, while organizational characteristics comprise culture, resources, rewards, strategy, structure, and technology. These characteristics impact the transformation processes and establish a creative situation that interacts with creative behaviour. The initiated creative processes then lead to creative outcomes in the form of new products or ideas.

Objectivist and Subjectivist Assumptions

Interactionist models inspired by an organic metaphor of organizations have made valuable and important contributions. First, they flagged the importance of creativity for organizations, previously firmly in the domain of psychology. Second, they captured and combined different levels of analysis—individual, group, and organizational—rather than merely focusing on individual creativity. By linking different levels of organizational creativity, researchers tried to model the complexity of organizational creativity. Third, they emphasized the importance of context and its influence on creative behaviour and outcomes. The complexity of creativity and the importance of context are two essential dimensions discussed in this book.

However, organic models of organizational creativity can be generally considered objectivist. The introduction to this book already discussed objectivism, but it is worth briefly recapping its assumptions. Objectivist research in the social sciences strives to emulate research philosophy and methodologies of the natural sciences. An objectivist approach assumes that the world exists as an objective, external reality, independent of an observer or people's interpretations. Reality is ordered and structured, which means that it is assumed that creativity follows somewhat ordered and discrete patterns. It is those patterns and factors that objectivist creativity research strives to explain. The goal of objectivist research is to generalize findings and seek universally valid inferences. Objectivism is therefore traditionally linked to quantitative research methodologies leaning on statistical methods. Amabile's and Woodman et al.'s conceptions are objectivist perspectives, as they aimed to model and explain causal relationships based on ordered relationships between different sets of variables and concepts.

Objectivist research on organizational creativity and its assumptions have been discussed critically. The critique can perhaps be best illustrated by using a simple example. Suppose someone tries to investigate why an organization does not produce any creative ideas. They analyse the situation and notice that the company does not mention creativity in its strategy, nor does it seem to have a reward system that triggers intrinsic motivation. Thus, since the input (strategy and reward system) is missing, they assume that individuals are not prompted to generate ideas (process), which will not lead to creative outcomes (output). They therefore suggest having a strategy focused on creativity and implementing a reward system aimed at influencing intrinsic motivation. Intuitively, these measures make sense, as a strategy and a reward system appear to fulfil important functions when trying to increase creativity.

Yet there are some problems with this rationale. First, it is unknown whether there is a causal relationship between input and process. The problem here is the assumption that individual creativity processes are *triggered* by certain characteristics. However, human behaviour seems to be more complicated than that. Just because there is a strategy that spells out creativity does not mean that people become more creative. Moreover, reward systems may have different effects on different individuals. This does not mean that they do not have any effect at all, but linear cause-and-effect assumptions and oversimplifications must be treated with caution. Lastly, the question of how to define creative output arises. Does it include all ideas, only ideas evaluated as creative by managers, or only formalized ideas such as patents? In other words, it seems difficult to generalize what counts as creative. This makes organizing creativity inherently more difficult and even paradoxical as we shall see in chapter 5.

An alternative to objectivist approaches addresses the complexity of human behaviour based on individual and collective interpretation. This alternative perspective is referred to as subjectivist. The main assumption of a subjectivist approach is that reality is socially constructed through the way people have assigned meanings to their actions and environments, including organizational creativity (see Spotlight on Research: Social Constructionism). As seen in the Introduction, the aim of a subjectivist approach is to explore how individuals understand and make sense of organizational creativity. If someone samples some opinions of what counts as creative, they will surely find that there are distinct differences in the way individuals make sense of creativity. Some may think that creativity includes radical ideas, while others see creativity as incremental problem solving (see for example Storey and Salaman, 2005). Moreover, organizational members perceive their contexts differently, which may lead to different interpretations. For example, for engineers ideas need to be technically advanced while for the marketing department they should be aesthetically appealing (Dougherty, 1992). Furthermore, some may feel that their ideas are valued, while others do not dare articulate their ideas because they perceive their environment as hostile or are afraid of being ridiculed (Edmondson, 1999).

Figure 2.1 provides a simple schematic based on a model by Silverman (1970) which illustrates a subjectivist approach to organizing and which informs the general approach taken in this book. It shows how context, interpretation, and action are interrelated and influence each other. Interpretations influence actions, while consequences of actions also influence interpretations. Similarly, context influences interpretations, while interpretations may also change beliefs about the context. Silverman's model is linked to the triangular conception of context, process, and practice that was discussed in the Introduction. A context has no static influence on action or interpretations, but all three dimensions are mutually dependent and embedded in a constant, yet sometimes inert, process of change.

Objectivist models inspired by an organism metaphor have been the most influential perspectives on organizational creativity (Rickards and De Cock, 2012). The reasons may be that creativity research has its roots in psychology, which is traditionally influenced by the natural sciences, and a desire to explain and control creative processes. Overall, these models have provided valuable contributions and insights into the influence of context and different levels on creative outcomes, yet they only tell a fragment of the story about organizational creativity. To expand the perspectives and achieve a holistic understanding of organizational creativity, it is necessary to draw inspiration from different disciplines, methodologies, and ontological assumptions (Styhre and Sundgren, 2005). To that end, this book draws on a subjectivist conception of organizing creativity to complement objectivist understandings. The first step is to discuss the brain metaphor and the concept of design thinking, which addresses the importance of understanding context and the complexity of creative problems.

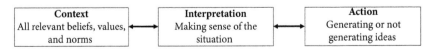

Figure 2.1 A subjectivist model of organizing creativity

Spotlight on Research: Social Constructionism

One of the most influential and seminal sociological studies of the twentieth century is called *The Social Construction of Reality*, penned by the sociologists Peter Berger and Thomas Luckmann (Berger and Luckmann, 1966). In their book, Berger and Luckmann explore the nature and formation of knowledge of everyday life. Their key argument is that reality is subjectively constructed but objectively experienced. To substantiate this claim, they unpacked three basic observations: society is a human product, society is an objective reality, and man is a social product.

Their first claim refers to how society is produced by social interaction, in which people use typifications of others with whom they interact. They may use broad or narrow categories to label and classify others as *creatives*, *nerds*, *German*, *extrovert*, and so on. These typifications can be very detailed for a person who someone knows very well (*my German friend Otto*) or very broad if someone has only heard about that person (*the German*). People also typify the nature of the interaction. If interactions occur frequently, they turn into habits and establish common actions and meanings concerning a situation. Think about a small start-up company. In the beginning, it is chaotic as people start interacting with each other. After a while, however, these interactions become somewhat typified and habitualized. John is mostly taking care of the finances, Sarah is fiddling with the products and Kevin is talking to the customers. John, Sarah, and Kevin continue to interact closely with each other and share their respective knowledge, but each slowly starts carving out their own defined spaces in the interaction.

Berger and Luckmann call these recurring interactions and the emergence of a common meaning structure *externalization*. This means that individuals make their intentions and actions explicit so that common meanings emerge that guide their interactions. Over time, these interactions may become even more stable. Employees always refer to Kevin when a customer is calling or forward the latest request for financial data to John. When the organization grows further, it creates a common stock of knowledge about how to deal with certain situations. It might create databases to store such knowledge. It might formulate job descriptions for people who are hired. It might set up and define common rules and conventions. This process of formalizing and stabilizing is what Berger and Luckmann refer to as *institutionalization*. This means that loose interactions have turned into a system of stable patterns of social interaction. In this example, it means that the organization turns from a loose band of humans trying to build their start-up into a system of stable, abstracted typifications with commonly accepted norms and conventions. This means people do not have to reflect much on how to categorize and deal with others, but draw on the formalized and stabilized typifications and interactions that have been established previously.

Their second claim—that society is an objective fact—refers to the outcomes of institutionalization. Institutions may reach a state where they are perceived as objective fact, in a process that Berger and Luckmann refer to as *objectivization*. This occurs when institutions are legitimized to the point that people forget they have been based on social interactions. For example, people tend to take for granted the structure and processes in organizations. They must have different departments for human resources (HR), marketing, and so on. These functions and structures have become an objective fact that people do not tend to question. The subjective production of an objective reality creates a paradox: humans themselves produce social reality through institutionalization and abstracted typifications which is ultimately perceived as objective and consequently non-human.

In a last step, humans internalize their institutions (*man is a social product*). This happens by way of socialization. New members of an organization, for example, accept the prevailing institutional order and act according to its norms and conventions. They are taught the knowledge of how the organization works and how they must behave. The institutions are rarely questioned, but accepted as fact.

Externalization, objectivization, and internalization according to Berger and Luckmann are ongoing dialectical processes. People are most likely familiar with the famous dialectical triad: thesis – antithesis = synthesis. The same dynamic, according to Berger and Luckmann, is happening in their model. There is a continuous process of challenging (antithesis) established institutions (thesis), which may lead to their transformation (synthesis). This means that new objective realities could be constantly constructed through subjective actions, but—of course—some institutions are so ingrained that they are not easily challenged.

It is precisely this dialectical perspective that is very interesting for understanding creative processes. In general terms, a change to and of an institution is a creative act. The philosopher Ian Hacking (1999) provided a useful set of questions to assess the perceived objectivity of facts. According to Hacking, people should ask themselves whether the current situation may be taken for granted as a natural fact. They may then discover that the current situation does not have to have the form that it has, and that it may not be determined by natural causes. If whether the situation is actually considered to be quite bad for people is further reflected on, consideration might be given to how the situation could be improved by altering institutions.

Design Thinking

Back in 2012, when riding a commuter bus in Seoul, South Korea, many commuters experienced a new form of advertising. During a bus ride in the past, they had frequently had to listen to advertising jingles, but now Dunkin' Donuts, the coffeehouse chain, added another sensory layer to their advertisements. At first, their jingle appeared to conform to the regular format, playing a conversation between a woman and a man in which the woman enthusiastically gives the man a coffee after which he excitedly asks where she got that delicious coffee, to which she replies: 'Dunkin' Donuts'. So far, this was nothing unusual. Yet while the jingle was playing, a device sprayed the scent of coffee into the bus. The commuters were now not only exposed to the message, but also to the smell of fresh coffee. The combination of auditory (listening) and olfactory (smelling) components was supposed to stimulate the commuters to grab a coffee when getting off the bus, where a Dunkin' Donuts was conveniently located (Garber, 2012).

The Dunkin' Donuts advertisement illustrates the notion of design thinking, which links to the brain metaphor of organization. Generally, the brain metaphor highlights aspects of information processing and decision-making in organizations. Much like the human brain, organizations take in and evaluate information, make decisions based on established neural pathways or routines, and may create new neuronal connections to learn. Specifically, the concept of design thinking focuses on how designers accumulate information, then use this information to solve problems and learn in the process. The ad agency for Dunkin' Donuts collected and evaluated all kinds of information about the coffee drinking habits of commuters in Seoul and used it to design an effective advert to sell more Dunkin' Donuts coffee by triggering a craving for coffee during the commute. The design of the Dunkin' Donuts ad will serve as an illustrative example to highlight various aspects of design thinking in more depth in the following section.

Theoretical Perspectives

An explicit interest in studying design thinking did not clearly emerge until the end of the 1980s, when researchers began to systematically join the terms 'design' and 'thinking'. However, conceptualizing design thinking proved to be difficult, as Kimbell (2011: 288) noted: 'it's hard enough understanding design and thinking, let alone design thinking'. Thus, this section approaches the topic of design thinking first from a theoretical perspective and then from a management practice perspective.

Two theoretical perspectives on design thinking can be distinguished: one that focuses on the individual designer, and another which looks at the broader system linked to design. *Designer-oriented* conceptualizations study individual designers and their ways of solving problems. The level of analysis is the single designer and their practice. An influential conception was proposed by Donald Schön, who is well known for his concept of the 'reflective practitioner' (Schön, 1983). Based on a comprehensive study of how professionals carry out their work, Schön argued that practitioners were either 'reflecting-in-action' or 'reflecting-on-action'. 'Reflecting-in-action' refers to how, in the process of doing something, practitioners tackle problems as they emerge. Following Schön's reasoning, it is unlikely that the designers of the Dunkin' Donuts ad, for example, mapped out the entire design beforehand and then merely executed it. Instead, they probably started working on some ideas and solutions, but in the process of working on them, encountered problems which led to the revision of their practices and, ultimately, their solution. For example, this may have included technical issues with the scent machine or getting the permission to spray scent in the bus. 'Reflecting-on-action' means that practitioners contemplate what they did some time after they finished the task. In the case of the Dunkin' Donuts advertisement, designers may have gathered information after running the ad to take stock of the project and reflect on what they did, how they did it, and what they might learn from the entire process.

Similarly, Lawson (2006) studied closely what designers were actually doing, and—based on his numerous examples—he argued that designers are typically confronted with ill-defined and ambiguous problems which tend to have no clear solution. This may sound trivial, but it led him to the conclusion that designers focus on suggesting solutions rather than analysing the problem in depth. In other words, designers are more likely to think on their feet. This indicates a difference between how scientists and designers solve problems. Designers tend to be more constructive, which means that they try different solutions to a problem. Scientists, on the other hand, are more analytical, which means that they analyse data in depth and approach problems more systematically. So a scientist who created an ad for Dunkin' Donuts would have perhaps analysed available data concerning the behaviour of commuters, proposed hypotheses, and then run statistics on what the best ad design would be. In contrast, since designers work more intuitively with what could work, they would have perhaps experimented with various ideas and ultimately chosen to try adding the smell of fresh coffee when playing the jingle. The significance of the distinction between a scientific approach and a design approach is that the latter tends to produce pragmatic solutions rather than trying to understand problems in depth before rationally solving them.

Design-oriented conceptualization broadens the focus from the specific practice of a designer to a generalized theory to facilitate the application of design thinking to other domains. In other words, design-oriented concepts aim to make design practices more generally applicable and integrate the work of different design professionals. According to Buchanan (1992), design is not specific to objects, but influences life in four important domains. Design is essential for creating visual and graphic communication (e.g. logos for companies), it plays an important role in creating objects (e.g. tangible products), it influences how actions may unfold (e.g. efficient logistics), and it determines how people integrate different elements of a complex system (e.g. urban planning). Consider again the Dunkin' Donuts ad. The design solution has multiple dimensions. For instance, it involves communicating a message with the jingle, designing the action of spraying a scent in the bus at the most appropriate moment, and determining how the ad fits into the complex system of early morning commutes in a big city. Hence, all kinds of design domains have been involved in creating the ad. According to Buchanan, it is therefore important not to think about design by separating professional design domains, but to consider the interaction and integration of different design domains.

The integration of design domains is especially important, since the purpose of design is to 'tame wicked problems' (Buchanan, 1992). Generally, problem solving is considered a linear process. People identify the problem and all necessary aspects, propose a solution to it, and then solve it. For example, when someone is tired in the morning, they solve the problem by drinking a cup of coffee or tea because they contain stimulating substances. However, according to Buchanan, this neat sequence of problem solving is not what designers are usually confronted with. They must 'tame wicked' problems. The use of 'tame' suggests that the problem cannot be solved conclusively, but it emphasizes the ability to take the edge off some aspects of the problem. Yet, while it may be possible to attenuate the severity of a problem, new ones may emerge. The adjective 'wicked' evokes the messy, ambiguous, and ill-defined nature of problems.

Wicked problems lack clear conditions or limits. If a problem does not have clear limits and conditions, there is no obvious solution. For that reason, design thinking is about generating a satisfying solution for these wicked problems out of multiple other options. Consider the problem of stimulating commuters to drink more coffee. There are essentially few limits to this problem: people have different tastes when it comes to coffee, they tend to drink their coffee at home and not on the way to work, they are in a hurry and need to get to work, they may have free coffee at the office, and so on. Consequently, this problem is not clearly delineated, which means that there are numerous possible solutions to stimulate commuters to buy Dunkin' Donuts coffee. In this case, the solution was to spray scent into the bus to activate people's natural reaction to scents and create a subconscious desire for coffee.

Theories on design thinking have flagged important aspects that have been similarly discussed in the field of organizational creativity. First, design scholars have distinguished between two levels of design thinking—the individual and the system. Design thinking is not only at play when a designer works on a design problem; it is a system-wide mode of integrating different design domains and their ideas. Similarly, organizational creativity scholars have argued for the integration of ideas from different domains and industries (Hargadon and Sutton, 1997). Second, design thinking challenges the understanding of linear problem solving by highlighting the ill-defined, wicked nature of problems that prevents a clear-cut solution. This overlaps to some extent with the notion of open and closed problems in creativity research, which are discussed in more detail in Chapter 3. Third, theories on design thinking have highlighted the idea of thinking on one's feet. If there are no obvious solutions to wicked problems, a design may as well just be based on intuitive and constructive solutions rather than a comprehensive analysis of the problem and a search for a single solution. This suggests that problems or pressing issues may be solved more readily since there is less time spent on a systematic, rational analysis of the problem that may not lead to more clarity. Analogously, creativity researchers have discussed the critical role of intuition and experimentation as opposed to rational thinking in organizational creativity (Lee et al., 2004). Therefore, it does not come as a surprise that design thinking as an approach to facilitate creativity has become one of the most popular and influential management concepts to emerge in the last decades, and so the discussion here turns now to the key ideas of design thinking management practices.

Spotlight on Research: The Principle of 'Less is More'

Imagine that a toddler needs help with building a bridge out of LEGO pieces. She points to two pillars of the unfinished bridge: one consists of three pieces, and the other of two pieces. She wants them level so that she can connect the bridge. How can the problem be solved? Most likely, the person helping will add a piece to the shorter pillar to make the bridge level, rather than take one away. The observation that people are likely to add components rather than subtract them when solving a problem or designing new ideas intrigued a team of researchers, who tested their observation systematically in a series of experiments (Adams et al., 2021). Their study confirmed people's automatic tendency to make *additive changes* to ideas, designs, and solutions rather than *subtractive changes* if they are not explicitly reminded that subtractive changes are possible and should be considered.

For one experiment, the researchers recruited college students on a busy campus and asked them to change a LEGO structure. The LEGO structure consisted of a roof that was held up by only one pillar. Under this roof, an action figurine was placed. The task was to change the LEGO structure in such a way that the roof would not squash the action figurine. The researchers divided the students into two groups and told one group that adding pieces would cost 10 cents. The other group was told that adding pieces was 10 cents, but they were also given the extra information that subtracting pieces was free. In the first group, only forty of the ninety-eight participants subtracted the LEGO piece, while sixty out of the ninety participants in the second group removed the LEGO piece to stabilize the roof. The results of this study indicate that even when additive changes come at a cost, individuals may add components. Only when individuals are explicitly made aware of the possibility of subtracting components will they be more likely to do so. The study suggests that people's default behaviour when designing things or solving problems is to add components. This may be why so many designs are overloaded with functions and additional components that may not be useful. A focus on a 'less is more' attitude, however, may lead to designs that are equally, if not more, effective.

Management Approaches

The aim of the management approach to design thinking is to teach practitioners the 'how to' knowledge (Johansson-Sköldberg et al., 2013). Thus, instead of analysing designers' thought processes or theorizing systematic patterns of design, management approaches seek an understanding of successful cases of design thinking to learn from them. Similar to the theoretical perspective, the management literature includes different contributions on how to practise design thinking. Most contributions include a focus on concrete activities and practices, different thinking styles, and the mentality with which design problems are approached (Hassi and Laakso, 2011). Two contributions and recommendations on how to practise design thinking have become especially influential.

One of the enduring contributions to the management literature emerged from the successful work by the design agency IDEO. In a hugely popular *Harvard Business Review* article, IDEO's chairman, Tim Brown, laid out the principles that IDEO applies in its design projects (Brown, 2008). He argued that successful design thinking produces a product or service based on a profitable and viable technological solution that meets people's needs. According to him, three components are vital for the process: inspiration, ideation, and implementation. An extended version of Brown's three principles underpins the curriculum of the School of Design at Stanford, California, which was established by IDEO founder David Kelley. The faculty teaches design based on *five modes*: empathize, define, ideate, prototype, and test. The first mode refers to activities that explore what users need and—possibly—want. Based on the findings from this mode, the define stage aims to identify possibilities emerging from the needs and wants of the users. These possibilities should inspire concepts and ideas during the ideate mode, which should then be translated into physical or visual form in the prototype stage and finally tested. The most important practical implication of the IDEO model is that it links the identification of the needs and wants of individuals to an experimental design process of generating and concretizing technologically feasible and potentially profitable ideas that are continuously tested with consumers.

Another influential contribution to the management literature on design thinking is based on the work of Roger Martin, who was involved with IDEO but later developed his own design thinking practices (Martin, 2009). Martin analysed interviews with managers who were successful in managing their organizations and concluded that '[t]he best of what I see in the best business people is the same as what I see in designers at their best' (Dunne and Martin, 2006: 513). Accordingly, Martin argued that to be successful, organizations should work like design shops. Notice the difference here. Martin argued for the design of organizations like design shops and not specific design practices like the aforementioned IDEO method. A design shop, in contrast to a traditional company, seeks to solve wicked problems rather than merely managing big budgets and staff, as many organizations are wont to do.

Moreover, perhaps most important in his approach is the integration of abductive, inductive, and deductive thinking. To Martin, thinking abductively means the ability to think about *what might be*—to put it more simply, to generate ideas. Deductive thinking, according to Martin, refers to *what should be* (e.g. the expectations of actions), and inductive thinking refers to *what is* (e.g. the actual developments). The integration of abductive, deductive, and inductive thinking characterizes successful design shops and should therefore also guide thinking processes in traditional organizations if they want to be able to compete. Integrative thinking should be complemented with a high degree of collaboration as well as iterative thinking, which means that people constantly test, change, and improve solutions.

Overall, management approaches to design thinking have mostly drawn inspiration from design practices and transferred those into propositions for managing the creative process and structuring organizations. Translating practices into best practices is tricky, though, as each design situation may be different from the next. Another interesting and relevant question that emerges from linking research to management practice is who and how someone profits from its diffusion and commercialization. Many researchers are, of course, interested in disseminating their findings to improve existing conditions in organizations—for example, medical research that helps cure diseases or engineering science that is useful for building infrastructure. However, the dissemination of research becomes problematic when it is entangled with financial interests or a demand for quick fixes.

In the field of management and organization studies, it has become common for researchers to act as consultants for organizations or teach executives and get paid for their advice. Consulting on how to organize creativity is no exception. In other words, research gets commercialized and is sold to a receptive audience. This is, of course, not a matter of immediate concern, but it may support an attitude to not complicate the message and to suppress alternative interpretations that the audience may not want to hear. With regard to design thinking, there are certainly financial interests at stake—for example, recruiting students to design thinking programmes or selling design thinking advice to companies. Thus, people should be attentive to the content and form of advice given under the label of design thinking, while asking critical questions of what it means and who profits (for a critical discussion of design thinking, see Vinsel, 2018).

Design Thinking and Pragmatism

Design and design thinking are productive concepts to stimulate reflections on practices of organizing creativity. As ideas in design and creativity overlap to a high degree, there is an opportunity to learn from each. Most importantly, design thinking challenges the static linearity and causality of creativity models discussed in the earlier section on interactionist models. Furthermore, design thinking questions the notion of a simplified linear sequence of finding, analysing, and solving problems by emphasizing the *taming of wicked problems* through experimentation, intuitive thinking, and continuous adaptation of solutions (reflection-in-action).

Yet it is still necessary to acknowledge that researchers do not have a clear understanding of design thinking. Instead, they have numerous understandings based on different philosophical or theoretical traditions. Different perspectives and understandings of the nature of design thinking naturally complicate *generalized* prescriptions on 'how to do' design thinking because it appears that successful design thinking is context-dependent. Johansson-Sköldberg et al. (2013) compared a designer to a musician to highlight the problematic aspect of providing prescriptions for practice. People would never think about a musician without referring to their style and instrument. Similarly, they should not refer to a designer without referring to their genre. The existence of different 'genres' of design thinking means there is a need to 'look for where and how the concept is used in different situations, both theoretical and practical, and what meaning is given to the concept' (Johansson-Sköldberg et al., 2013: 132).

Kimbell (2011) argued in a similar vein, urging readers to consider the situation and context of design practices and how people can learn from them within a specific context rather than taking them out of context. Thus, design thinking is not about following a script on how to think like a designer, but about being sensitive and responsive to situations, emergences, and transformations. Both authors point their readers to a *pragmatist perspective on design thinking* as a productive lens to make sense of and use the concept (Dalsgaard, 2014).

Imagine an argument about what it means to chase a squirrel moving around a tree at a constant pace, always remaining out of sight. The question is whether the pursuer is going around the squirrel. If by 'going around' it is meant that the pursuer is north, east, south, and west of the squirrel, then they are going around the squirrel. However, if it means surrounding the squirrel from the front, the side, the back, and the other side, then the answer is no; the pursuer is not going around the squirrel. Does it matter? No, not really. The pursuer is still chasing the squirrel around the tree. This story of the squirrel was used by William James to illustrate one of the basic tenets of pragmatism—that practical consequences matter, not theoretical disputes (James, 1907). In other words, it does not matter whether or not the pursuer believes they are running around the squirrel, as the practical consequences are still the same: they are still running around the tree chasing the squirrel. With this and other ideas, William James and his friend Charles Peirce laid the foundation for pragmatism, which has since become an influential philosophical movement. In organization and management studies, pragmatism has influenced process theories of organization as well as Karl Weick's sensemaking perspective (Weick, 1995), which will be discussed in more detail later in the chapter. Here, I briefly outline the main tenets of pragmatism and their link to design thinking.

Pragmatism focuses on action and consequences. In contrast to so-called dualist philosophies, which separate mind and body, pragmatism argues that mind and body are inseparable. This means that knowledge and rational thinking do not come from the mind alone (the body simply being a 'shell'); instead, practical knowledge derives from engaging the world with all five senses. For pragmatists, theory and practice are not two distinct spheres, as theories guide practices. To put it metaphorically, theories are the tools used for practices. Yet theories that guide practices are not generally valid, but must be proven and possibly adapted to the situations that are encountered. This is because pragmatists do not understand the world as inherently stable, but as constantly emergent and—therefore—open to change. Moreover, people do not passively experience given situations; they are active creators who determine how they make sense of situations. In this way, people may try to stabilize some situations by establishing routines and habits, but experience other situations as much more open and ambiguous. Hence people may strive to transform an uncertain and ambiguous situation into a more stable and certain one. This can be accomplished by drawing on certain means and tools, such as language (Dalsgaard, 2014).

It may already be rather apparent how pragmatism and design thinking are linked, but it would be beneficial to consider the Dunkin' Donuts example again for illustration. The agency's task was to create an advertisement to stimulate individuals to buy more of Dunkin' Donuts' coffee. Based on this problem, the designers aimed to make sense of the situation. Their theory was that commuters were in a hurry to get to work and craved coffee for stimulation, but were also somewhat indifferent about where the coffee came from. Moreover, they drew on theories that combined visual and olfactory stimulation to arouse a craving for coffee. These theories guided their practices to turn the somewhat ambiguous situation into a stable situation to facilitate the choice of Dunkin' Donuts coffee. The designers explored possible technologies and constructed the spraying device that was activated at the right time when the bus approached a Dunkin' Donuts. Hence the design transformed the commuter situation. While it seemed to increase consumers' desire for Dunkin' Donuts coffee, it also transformed the commuting situations for everyone on the bus. In particular, everyone on the bus was not only exposed to the sound of the jingle, but also the scent of coffee, and some people may not have been pleased with this intrusion to their senses. So while it may have turned some individuals on to Dunkin' Donuts coffee, it probably also angered others who felt harassed by the unwanted smell. Overall the Dunkin' Donuts example illustrates how design thinking may work in practice, by drawing attention to how designers experimented with different ideas based on their intuition and thus tackled the wicked problem of nudging people to purchase Dunkin' Donuts coffee instead of any other available coffee brand. Yet it also shows that while the design may have solved a problem for Dunkin' Donuts and their consumers, it created new problems for others.

In conclusion, a pragmatist perspective stresses the situated, emergent, and transformative nature of design thinking. This means that designers try to make sense of ambiguous situations surrounding *wicked problems* by drawing on applicable theories. In most cases, they may be able to get a better grip of what is going on in a situation, but occasionally they do not. In any case, they endeavour to find possible solutions. Depending on the wickedness of the situation, the designer will experience emergent problems, new situations, and unexpected outcomes in the process. This means that the process is transformative in the sense that situations may change, but also that designers learn and adapt their theories. In the end, however, it is not important whether they go around the squirrel, but what practical, transformative consequences their design has for users.

Spotlight on Practice: PlayPump©

Access to drinking water is still a problem in many parts of the world, especially the most arid regions. In 1989, mechanical engineer Ronnie Stuiver from South Africa invented a mechanism for a different sort of water pump. He combined it with a merry-go-round, a common installation on playgrounds. The principle of his pump was intuitively simple: children would spin the merry-go-round, which would pump clean water from underground into a tank 7 metres above ground. From this tank, people could draw fresh water through a tap. In addition, the tank would be used as a billboard for advertisements to generate income. Stuiver's idea was snatched up by Trevor Field, who purchased Stuiver's patent and the marketing rights. Field began producing what he trademarked as PlayPumps and gained the attention of donors. He received money from the US government and was endorsed by celebrities such as Jay-Z. By 2009, about 700 pumps had been installed throughout South Africa, Mozambique, and Swaziland (March, 2009). However, by 2009, PlayPump announced that it would hand over its technology to the non-profit organization Water for Life. In its announcement, Play-Pump wrote 'that delivering safe water is humbling work, and that ongoing operations and maintenance is a challenge for most players involved in the delivery of solutions. We must continue to innovate to find models that can ensure sustainability' (Edson, 2009). This sounded like defeat, so what had happened to this seemingly ingenious idea?

There seemed to be many reasons for the failure of PlayPump. One of the main reasons was the discrepancy between its design and its use. While it seemed ingenious to combine work and play, the play was not enough to do the work. In areas where there was a high demand for water, children had to pump continuously for hours to fill the tank. For example, in some areas in Mozambique, it took up to four hours to fill the 2,500-litre tank with fresh water and meet local demand. Play threatened to turn into exploitative labour. In many cases where children lost interest and were not forced to play, women from the village had to spin the merry-go-round, which was particularly annoying for them as it was harder and slower than regular pumps. Moreover, PlayPumps were more expensive to install and harder to maintain than regular pumps (UNICEF, 2007). In hindsight, a representative of an NGO commented that PlayPump's marketing may have been perfect but that their product just did not work (Chambers, 2009).

The failure of PlayPump highlights the 'wicked' problem of supplying fresh water where it is needed. To begin with, how to supply water is very specific to the environment and situation of a community. While in some situations the PlayPump might have worked, in others it became a problem rather than a solution. Additionally, a design is only as good as its practical consequences. While design thinking must consider the situation, it must also cope with emergent and unexpected problems, such as that users may not behave as anticipated. Analysing how design transforms users' experiences both positively and negatively should prompt learning and, if possible, adaptations. The case of the PlayPump furthermore illustrates the tendency to impose Western design solutions on other cultural contexts without sufficiently taking account of ideas from local designers and creatives. This relates to the important point made in the text, that design solutions are situational and context-dependent. A design solution is never finalized but needs to be evaluated based on its use and consequences.

Organizational Culture

The chief technology officer or CTO of the high technology company that I was studying in one of my research projects was very passionate when he talked about offices and travel policies in his organization. He told me that he has 'the same room and it is not any bigger than the rest of the engineers. My room is outside the toilets. It is true. And we don't have any company cars. Our CEO goes tourist class when he travels.' Apparently, management had the same office size, no say in office location (his was next to the toilet), and no preferred treatment when travelling. Now this may all just be taken as a literal description of office sizes and locations and the company's travel policy. Yet his statement was also intended to reveal a deeper meaning of what it means to work for this organization. In his statement, he conveyed the company's values of flat structures and the lack of status hierarchies connected to offices, cars, or flights. The office set-up and policies were symbolic of the organization's values and beliefs, and constantly reminded employees of these.

Meanings and symbols are cornerstones for organizational cultures. While organizational culture appears to have a decisive influence on creative behaviour, it is difficult to decipher. Hence it is necessary to first unpack culture's essential components and subsequently focus on its functions and outcomes. Based on this discussion, culture will be related to organizational creativity along two dimensions: the strength of culture and the inclination to take risks or not. These two dimensions render four ideal types of creativity culture that I call *progressive, small wins, maverick,* and *fragmented.* These four types of culture will be discussed in the last section.

'Webs of Significance'

There are so many definitions and conceptions of culture that Alvesson (2013b) argued that there is a pervasive tendency to frame almost every aspect of organizations as culture or cultural. Therefore, it is important to work out some of the essential features of what constitutes a culture to delimit it from other concepts. One often cited definition comes from the cultural anthropologist Clifford Geertz, who claimed that 'man is an animal suspended in webs of significance, that he himself [sic] has spun. I take culture to be those webs ...' (Geertz, 1973: 5). His definition includes important propositions that allow for a deeper examination of some of organizational culture's characteristics.

First, Geertz discussed 'man as an animal'. He thereby highlighted that humans are first and foremost biological creatures. However, they are different from other animals, as they do not act based only on their instincts. The philosopher Friedrich Nietzsche referred to humans as 'non-fixed animals' (*nicht festgestelltes Tier*), which highlights their ability to think, imagine, and base their actions—at least partly—on a free will, which begs the question of what people do with their 'non-fixed' nature. According to Geertz, they 'suspend [themselves] in webs of significance'. That means that people endow other people, objects, and events with meanings that provide cues for interpreting objects, individuals, and events and stimulate attitudes, feelings, and (inter)actions. Objects, individuals, and events are thereby turned into symbols, which can be understood as objects, individuals, or processes that confer other meanings to people (Edelman, 1964).

Symbols evoke attitudes, arouse feelings, and stimulate behaviours. Symbols can also represent a clear relationship. For example, when someone claims that 4 > 2, '>' is a symbol that means something is greater than something else. However, often the meanings of symbols are not as clear-cut and can lead to multiple interpretations that deviate from the intended one. For example, consider a tree. A tree as a symbol may carry different meanings. It may be meaningful as a resource, a place of rest, a sacred place, a reminder of home, and so on. Alternatively, consider the example of the company's office space and travel policy, which carried meanings about equality and humility. However, having an office close to the toilet could also mean that the individual does not have to go far when the need arises. If meanings and symbols become important, useful, and desirable for individuals and groups, they may then turn into values, which influence people's interpretations, behaviours, and interactions.

Moreover, Geertz's definition of culture draws attention to how human beings actively spin the webs that he considered to comprise culture itself. Culture, in other words, is not static, but meanings and symbols are socially constructed. Geertz highlighted individual and social agency and the ability of individuals to create, maintain, and transform culture. This ability may be referred to as 'symbolic work' (Schaefer, 2019), which entails that people constantly try to create, maintain, or change meanings of symbols to order social relationships and evoke favourable interpretations. Organizations are constantly engaged in symbolic work to convey important values and beliefs to their employees and other stakeholders. For example, organizations may communicate their contributions to charities to flag their social commitments, or top management may walk around factories once a week to convey the value of approachability.

Lastly, Geertz evoked the image of webs, which draws attention to the complex structures and relationships of a culture. While a web is a complex structure, it also provides order. Analogously, a culture is highly complex, yet it provides stability to relationships between people and objects. Of course, webs have different properties and characteristics. While some webs are strong and supportive, others may be fragile and weak. We will return to the distinction between strong and weak cultures later in the chapter.

All in all, a culture is based on meaningful symbols that provide shared values which influence people's interpretations and actions. Cultures are complex structures that provide order while changing over time. They influence interpretations and actions in ways that people are mostly unaware of. The realization of how culture influences individual actions exposes an important aspect—that each organization *is* a unique organizational culture, which means that every organization has produced different meanings, symbols, and values that contribute to its coordinated success. Such a perspective stands in contrast to assumptions that culture is a manipulable variable that organizations *have* (for a discussion of different conceptions of organizational culture, see Smircich, 1983). Assuming that an organization *is* a culture also suggests that changing an organization is more difficult than merely changing a variable (see also the 'Spotlight on Practice: 3M and Six Sigma').

The distinction between *being a culture* and *having a culture* is crucial. Essentially, it means that there is no outside of culture but that each act in an organization is influenced—at least in part—by cultural values.

A Typology of Creative Organizational Cultures

What, then, are the function and outcomes of organizational culture and its link to organizational creativity? It is possible to distinguish *four functions of culture* in organizations: control, emotional regulation, direction, and integration. First, culture may be used to control people's behaviour. If an organization has a set of pervasive symbols with strong, socially shared meanings and values, this will create a set of norms that people will gladly follow, even when they are not supervised. Thus the meanings and values govern the behaviour and feelings of employees and turn into a form of social control (O'Reilly, 1989) or normative control (Kunda, 1992). Considering organizational creativity, the control function highlights how a strong organizational culture may increase motivation for generating creative ideas for the benefit of the organization. This may be especially important when considering some of the negative effects of direct control on creative behaviour (Amabile, 1997b). In particular, the regulation of employees' feelings is an important function of organizational culture because an emotional bond creates a stronger identification with the organization. Regulating employees' feelings and behaviours through strong values may also create an atmosphere of consistency, reliability, and trust. Consequently, culture can function as a compass (Alvesson, 2013b), which helps someone establish their bearings by asking where they are and where they want to go. A compass thus charts possible courses of action and allows people to travel in a desired direction. At the same time, a compass sets a boundary about possible courses. In an organization, the compass highlights the function of a meaning and value system which provides direction for everyone. Culture then enables people to navigate the organization and its employees in the desired direction. For example, an organizational culture may indicate whether or not new ideas are desirable.

Another function of organizational culture is integration. Organizational culture integrates people and departments by means of a common set of values. This is especially important with a view to organizational creativity processes. Naturally, all organizations have different subcultures that have developed their own idiosyncratic norms and values— for example, think about the differences between marketing and engineering. This is not surprising given the different tasks and objectives of different departments. It becomes a problem, however, if these different group cultures inhibit cooperation and integration because the differing value sets are not synthesized (Dougherty, 1992). A common organizational culture can provide a sense of unity in which different opinions, values, and meanings are treated respectfully with the aim to benefit the organization as a whole and not only the specific subgroup.

An organization's culture may be useful for controlling the behaviour of its members, providing a sense of direction and purpose to its members, integrating groups and departments within and across the organization, and producing strong emotional commitment from its members. Table 2.2 provides an overview of the four dimensions and their respective features of organizational cultures that tend to be stronger or weaker. Please note that the distinction should be used merely as an indication of a positive and negative

Table 2.2 Strong and weak cultures

	Strong culture	Weak culture
Regulation and control	Members tend to act in the interest of the organization	Members act in their own interest if given the opportunity
Direction	Members have a sense of a common direction and purpose	Members have no understanding of what the organization wants and needs
Integration	Groups and departments share a common set of values	Groups and departments are not integrated and act according to their own interests
Impact on emotions	Members have trust and feel safe	Members feel suspicious and cynical

tendency towards cultural strength. They are—as is the case with all abstractions—meant to provide ideal types.

A *strong organizational culture* tends to be able to regulate behaviours so that employees act in the interest of the organization. Organizational members share a sense of a common direction and know what the organization strives to achieve. Departments aim to collaborate, and the common feeling is one of safety and trust. In *weak organizational cultures*, members tend to act in their own interests. Members have only a vague understanding of what the organization stands for and how its future should look like. Groups are more likely to stick to their own values rather than work from a set of shared values, and members feel cynical about and disconnected from the organization and distrust others.

With a view to organizational creativity, an organizational culture must generate specific norms that make them more likely to generate transformative ideas. One essential norm that facilitates creativity is the attitude towards *risk taking and risk aversion*. O'Reilly (1989) specified norms of risk taking and included the freedom to experiment and fail, a genuine dialogue about ideas, the possibility of questioning and challenging the status quo, a focus on the long term, and a general openness to change. Risk-taking norms raise the probability of producing creative ideas. In contrast, an organization that is not inclined to take risks and plays it safe has a lower probability of producing transformative ideas. Norms of risk aversion involve a conservative attitude regarding the status quo, no serious engagement with ideas, a focus on the short term, and a negative attitude towards substantive change (Rehn, 2019). All in all, norms of risk taking and risk aversion indicate how organizational members behave regarding the generation, articulation, and discussion of new ideas.

Based on a combination of strong and weak organizational cultures and norms of risk taking and risk aversion, it is possible to generate four ideal-typical cultural contexts that influence the potential for organizational creativity. Figure 2.2 depicts four cultural contexts that have low, high, and medium potential for creative ideas.

An organization which is *ready to take risks and has a strong organizational culture* will have a high potential for creative ideas. Organizational members and groups are willing to experiment, but also feel committed to the organization. They have a sense of direction and trust. Moreover, departments, groups, and individuals tend not to focus on their own interests, but aim to collaborate and share new ideas to benefit the organization overall. Strong, risk-taking cultures may be referred to as *progressive*, which denotes challenging the status quo based on a strong commitment from members.

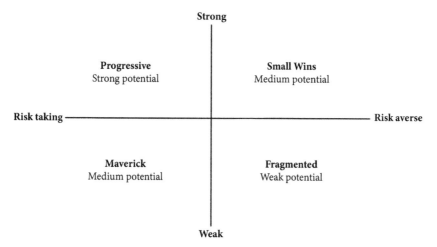

Figure 2.2 A typology of creative organizational cultures

The company W. L. Gore & Associates, for example, is known for its unique organizational culture and creative products, the most famous one being the fabric called Gore-Tex. However, Gore is not only well known for its fabrics; it has successfully experimented with other products, such as guitar strings and dental floss. Gore's company structure resembles a lattice, meaning that relationships and communication are lateral rather than hierarchical. People are connected to each other in multiple ways, and teams are formed based on people's connection and reach. To support a lattice structure, Gore's organizational culture must be based on strong values of individual responsibility, a clear sense of direction, commitment, and trust that employees will act in the interest of the organization. To support the development of new ideas, each employee is given time to experiment with their ideas (dabble time). For example, the guitar strings that Gore developed started in dabble time, when an engineer used Gore-Tex coating for his mountain bike cables and realized that it could be used for guitar strings as well. The engineer pitched his ideas and assembled a team of interested associates to work on his experiment. Some years later, they produced a guitar string that they baptized 'Elixir' and that held its tone three times longer than the average string (Hamel and Breen, 2007). Overall, Gore's strong organizational culture and people's identification with its mission and goals are linked to allowing risk-taking behaviour (dabble time) which may result in transformative ideas.

An organization that is *risk averse and has a weak organizational culture* has a low potential for organizational creativity. Organizational members and groups have no sense of direction and would rather protect their own or their group's interest than act in the interest of the organization. Employees do not feel that they can take risks or articulate new ideas without being met with indifference or even hostility because the culture has produced mistrust and an attitude of self-preservation. Such a weak, risk-averse culture may be referred to as *fragmented*, pointing to the lack of integration and direction within the organization and its ignorance about the need for new ideas to keep the organization going in the long run. This means that a fragmented organizational culture does not support the production of profitable new ideas that are needed to sustain the organization, as the case of the company Research in Motion (RIM) illustrates.

RIM developed and launched the BlackBerry in 1999. The BlackBerry was a small hand-held device with a physical keyboard with which the user could access emails (it was the forerunner of the smartphone). However, RIM reacted too late and too inconsequentially as competitive products appeared, such as the iPhone or the Android operating systems. One of the reasons that RIM was unable to keep up with the competition and develop new innovative products appeared to be its organizational culture. In an open letter to the CEO that was allegedly written by a high-level employee, the employee blamed the culture of RIM for lagging behind its competitors. The letter drew attention to feelings of anxiety about raising new ideas: 'You have many smart employees, many that have great ideas for the future, but unfortunately the culture at RIM does not allow us to speak openly without having to worry about the career-limiting effect.' The letter went on to describe a sense of disorientation: 'Teams still aren't talking together properly, no one is making or can make critical decisions, all the while everyone is working crazy hours and still far behind. We are demotivated.' Overall, employees seemed to be apprehensive to challenge the status quo and initiate changes in products: 'The truth is, no one in RIM dares to tell management how bad our tools still are' (Geller, 2011). The fragmentation within RIM eventually led to its failure to keep up with the developments on the mobile phone market. The example of RIM illustrates a fragmented culture in which groups did not cooperate for the good of the company but rather stuck to their own subgroups. At the same time, RIM's culture also discouraged risk taking which might have led to new ideas. This eventually led to its demise.

An organization that has *a strong culture but is risk averse* has a medium potential for organizational creativity. People feel a sense of direction and are committed to the goals of the organization. Yet the organization is risk averse, which means that it is hesitant to fundamentally change its processes, structures, products, or services. This may be the case for highly structured organizations that are not dependent on regularly generating trans-formative ideas but which are dependent on routines. Yet, as we will discuss in more detail in Chapter 3, routines may also change in small ways over time but maybe not in an overly disruptive manner.

Consider in this regard the case of an organic supermarket chain studied by Endrissat et al. (2015). Working in a supermarket is highly routinized and does not allow for much risk taking or novel ideas. However, it appears that even if there is little room for experimen-tation, work in a supermarket can be considered what the authors call 'enchanting'. This 'enchanting work' refers to a meaningful experience, in which employees develop a feeling of trust, a sense of participation, and close bonds to their co-workers, managers, and cus-tomers, all of which indicate a strong culture. In addition, the supermarket chain employs what they call 'store artists', who are supposed to create in-store artistic work. While store artists also do routine tasks at the checkout or by stacking shelves, they are free to use their creativity for small changes. For example, store artists often create signs for products which contain creative motifs. For this work, they have the liberty to be more creative than merely writing text. Hence, although the organization is not engaging in transformative changes, it allows for small acts of creativity. This strong and risk-averse culture may be referred to as one of *small wins*. The idea of a small wins culture is inspired by Karl Weick's idea of how organizations develop through what he calls 'micro-innovation' (Weick, 1984). Rather than grand experiments and disruption, small creative acts allow the organization to stand out and compete. These accumulated small acts over time keep the organization competitive in the long run.

An organization that has a *weak culture combined with high risk-taking behaviour* instils little common sense of direction, no integration between groups or individuals, and little trust. However, employees are challenging the status quo constantly, working on their own ideas and projects. Such an organizational culture has a medium potential for creativity since ideas may emerge that could benefit the organization. A weak, risk-taking culture bears resemblance to the figure of a *maverick*. During the time of large cattle herding in the US, a calf that was not branded—that is, with a mark in the skin—was called a maverick to denote its status as separate from the herd and owner. Similarly, a weak, risk-taking culture consists of independent individuals and groups who act in their own interests, challenging existing arrangements, and working on their own projects and ideas. This means that maverick cultures may produce successful transformative ideas, but those ideas are first and foremost in the interest of single individuals or groups and may not align with the organization's mission and goals.

Consider the story of Nobel laureate Kary Mullis, who earned his PhD at the University of California, Berkeley in 1973. He was an eccentric who produced his own hallucinogenic drugs and wrote scientific articles that explained the cosmos from beginning to end. After he left the university, a friend landed him a job at a biotech company called Cetus. While Mullis was a highly creative and capable engineer, he was also a maverick because he quarrelled constantly with his colleagues and did not seem to care much about following company norms. Mullis later recalled that '[Cetus management] said 10 percent of your time you should do whatever you want to do.' Yet for Mullis, it seemed 'hard for them to measure what 10 percent of my time is. So I can use as much of my time as I want to for my own curiosity' (McDonald, 2019). Mullis did not align with the norms and values of the company culture and decided to set his own rules. In 1983, during a drive through the hills of Mendocino, he was struck by the idea of replicating DNA, which would later be known as polymerase chain reaction (PCR). Initially, however, he was met with scepticism at Cetus, not least because of his erratic behaviours and his tendency to cause strife among his co-workers. Eventually, his friend provided him time and space to try his idea. It turned out that PCR worked. In 1986, Mullis left Cetus, who gave him a $100,000 bonus—selling the PCR patent would later earn the company $300 billion. In 1993, Mullis was awarded the Nobel Prize. Mullis continued being a controversial figure celebrated by some and rejected by others. His short stint working for an organization illustrates how his maverick behaviour, linked to a weak organizational culture, led to a truly transformative idea. This was only made possible, however, through his friend protecting him and providing him with the necessary resources.

Spotlight on Practice: 3M and Six Sigma

The company 3M often serves as the quintessential example of a creative organization. It is mostly known for the development of Post-it notes, but it has continued to invent new products, resulting in over 100,000 registered patents (see www.3m.com). 3M's success has been ascribed to its strong organizational culture, which is based on an entrepreneurial spirit, freedom to experiment with new ideas, tolerance for failures, and a willingness for collaboration. It seems that 3M has a truly progressive organizational culture. During the late 1990s, the height of the age of the new economy, there was a growing concern with 3M's profitability compared to other high-tech companies. Therefore, for the first time in 3M's history, an external CEO, James McNerney from GE, was hired in 2001. He intended to implement some drastic changes. GE had adopted the performance management system Six Sigma during the 1990s, and it had become a central management tool. McNerney had similar plans for 3M.

Six Sigma consists of numerous, mainly statistical, tools and practices which are used to increase efficiency and process predictability. It involves setting up clearly defined goals, closely monitoring and controlling processes through key metrics, and improving the processes based on the received feedback. Six Sigma was diametrically opposed to the practices that existed at 3M in 2001, which were mainly based on intuition, experimentation, and rough estimates. Thus 3M underwent a radical change to its progressive organizational culture when Six Sigma was rolled out companywide in 2001.

The principles of measuring, controlling, and eliminating appeared to be welcomed at first, as they led to some positive experiences. For example, a product manager commented, 'In my area, we used it [Six Sigma] to support merchandising, packaging, website design. We applied it to the back-end activities of sales and marketing, and it gave us amazing results' (all citations are taken from Canato et al., 2013). Yet, after some years, the organization started to perceive a real threat to its core values as well as a decrease in innovative ideas. An operations manager commented that the organization had lost its unique values: 'The two fundamental principles of 3M used to be tolerance for mistakes and entrepreneurial spirit. This is not true anymore.' Another product manager put it more drastically: 'Six Sigma killed entrepreneurship, which was one of the fundamental traits of 3M. The rush to rationality killed what made our company great—that is innovation at all levels, the capacity to find new ways.'

The growing dissatisfaction and the absence of radical new ideas changed things around. In 2005, McNerney left 3M, and a new CEO was hired who abandoned the strong focus on Six Sigma and its principles. But 3M did not merely bounce back to its old organizational culture based on high levels of experimentation and intuition. The implementation of Six Sigma had led to reflections on how 3M could improve some processes without changing its underlying core values. Six Sigma had allowed organizational members to communicate more effectively across divisions, formulate goals, and structure processes better. As a consequence, 3M retained some Six Sigma practices which they thought would help them develop new products. Hence Six Sigma offered a comprehensive mode of experimentation with a new way of organizing 3M, and it had seriously challenged the company's status quo and strengthened its culture.

Notably, organizational culture plays an essential role in organizing creativity. However, it is important to bear in mind the negative implications of strong cultures. While individuals and groups are less influenced by weak organizational cultures and mostly act in accordance with their own or their group's values and beliefs, strong organizational cultures 'win the hearts and minds of the employees' (Willmott, 1993: 516). If employees devote their hearts and minds to the organization, a strong organizational culture may exert a pervasive, even insidious, form of control over people's behaviour. An organization which holds such sway over its employees bears the risk of leading to conformity and even blind obedience. With such a strong influence comes the responsibility of allowing employees to challenge the status quo, as was discussed in the context of progressive cultures. Note here the importance that a progressive organizational culture should not only extend to experimentation with new product or service ideas, but also include the possibility of experimenting and questioning processes and structures of the organization as such. In progressive cultures, there may not only be norms and values that strengthen the efficiency and effectiveness of an organization and facilitate the generation of ideas. A progressive organizational culture must include *metanorms*, which can be described as norms about norms. One metanorm should allow individuals to question and challenge existing norms and values (Robertson and Swan, 2003). The notion of metanorms is more thoroughly examined in Chapter 6.

Culture, however, is dynamic rather than static. While conscious efforts to change a culture may only seldom work, values and meanings do change incrementally through interaction between organizational members. Moreover, a culture may indicate why and how people act without explicitly focusing on how these actions unfold and what the consequences may be. However, it is not only important to understand the values and norms driving creativity, but also how these values and norms play out in organizational life. The next section will therefore take a closer look at the unfolding of organizational processes, and highlight and discuss their importance to organizing creativity.

Flux, Transformation, and Organizational Creativity Practices

Imagine a person on the bus to work, which, gets stuck in traffic. Their crutch for killing time in those frustrating moments, their mobile phone, has run out of battery. Without anything else to do, they start chatting with their neighbour, who happens to work at the same company, but—for some reason—they have never met. The person starts talking about a problem at work, and they realize that the other person may know someone who can help. This person ends up in an engaged discussion about the issue that has bugged them for so long. Happily, the co-workers part ways in front of the main building of their workplace when the bus finally arrives. Their chance encounter has finally solved the problem for one of them.

The imagined encounter on the bus is what organizational creativity researchers have referred to as a 'fleeting moment' (Hargadon and Bechky, 2006). Fleeting moments are those unique situations during which people generate and evaluate ideas. These moments are also seldom repeated because they emerge out of unique situations. It is like hitting a billiard ball with a white cue ball; the constellation of billiard balls on the table will differ each time. Similarly, the traffic during the commute, the empty battery, and the person's seat next to their co-worker on the bus created a unique situation which will most likely not happen again. Fleeting moments, unique situations, and constant changes are some of the characteristics of a process approach. The central assumption of a process approach is that people should consider the world and organizations not as static, but as constantly evolving. Rather than speaking about organizations as a noun, people speak about organizing as an activity (Weick, 1995). A process approach thus fundamentally challenges the notion of organizational creativity as static—a characteristic commonly linked to the organism metaphor—by conceptualizing creativity as an unfolding activity.

Now, it seems that not everything is open to constant change. The bus runs on a schedule (most of the time at least) and everyone has a workplace to go to (for now at least). Hence it seems that people have a certain stability and routine in their experiences. In other words, there appear to be different degrees of change and stability. Indeed, Fortwengel et al. (2017), who reviewed the process literature on organizational creativity, recognized different assumptions about how much and how often organizations change. Based on their findings, they divided process perspectives on organizational creativity into *strong and moderate approaches*. A strong approach assumes that there is little to no stability and that everything is constantly changing. Just as the billiard balls end up in a unique constellation each time, organizations consist of unique situations. A moderate approach, on the other hand, supposes that there is some stability, but that stability is amendable with small steps over time. Hence, while a strong process approach suggests that creativity happens all the time in each of our interactions, a moderate process approach argues that creativity processes can be structured but that those structures are themselves subject to (inert) change over time. The two conceptions have different implications for how to facilitate creativity.

This section unpacks and discusses the relevance, distinctions, and concepts related to strong and moderate process approaches to organizing for creativity. A process approach has become more popular among organizational creativity researchers over recent years because it acknowledges the complexity of the subject. As such it avoids the simplifications of previous models and provides a more complex insight into how creativity unfolds in an organizational context.

Strong Process Approach

An appropriate metaphor for understanding a strong process approach is the ginger plant. Ginger has a quite irregular structure consisting of root nodes and knobs with no visible stem or regular forms. The ginger root structure is a subterranean stem of a plant, referred to as a rhizome. While the rhizome may initially seem to be a peculiar image for discussing a strong process approach and creativity, the image of the rhizome has gained widespread popularity based on an influential post-structuralist philosophical treatise by Félix Guattari and Gilles Deleuze (Guattari and Deleuze, 1987). Their ideas have also inspired organizational creativity scholars (Styhre and Sundgren, 2003). When looking at a rhizome, it is noticeable that there is no centre. Its structure is random, as buds and roots spread in various directions. New connections do not emerge from a single stem, but from all kinds of directions. As such, the rhizome is a flat structure that lacks a clear hierarchy and principle for developing and growing. Such a non-hierarchical structure based on emerging and random connections, no higher ordering principle, and the constant creation and transformation of new combinations is the hallmark of a strong process approach to organizational creativity.

A strong process perspective assumes that organizations are constantly transforming. This transformation, however, is not governed by a higher order principle. Just like a rhizome, an organization has no stable centre or context from which its structure develops. Organization is the result of an ongoing activity that constantly connects interpretations of past experiences, present circumstances, and future expectations (Hernes, 2014). Like the rhizome, the connections of past, present, and future can lead to very different structures and outcomes. This unpredictability means that there is an *inherent indeterminacy in actions and interactions* since it is impossible to know how emerging constellations will turn out. To put it simply, people can never know what will happen when they act or inter-act with something or someone, but they know it will be different from before. Consider the encounter on the bus again. The conversation may or may not happen; just as one cannot know how the rhizome will grow, one cannot know what their commute to work may lead to. For that reason, 'the rhizome offers unlimited opportunities for connections and there-fore for the creation of new ideas' (Styhre and Sundgren, 2003: 426). The upshot is that a strong process approach suggests that all actions and interactions of individuals in orga-nizations are potentially transformative as new people and groups make new connections, ideas are exchanged in interactions, people change their perspectives based on conversa-tions, and so on. Just like the ginger root, the encounters between people in organizations can take any direction; they are indeterminate.

A strong process perspective has mainly spread in the field of organization and manage-ment studies based on the early work of Karl Weick, who has become a highly influential scholar in the field (see Spotlight on Research: Karl Weick's 'Sensemaking' Concept). For example, Drazin et al. (1999) used a process perspective inspired by Weick's work for a land-mark contribution to the organizational creativity literature. Drazin et al. (1999) challenged the extant literature on organizational creativity by arguing that it reduced the complexity of creativity too much. Their alternative concept used a strong process approach by attend-ing closely to how 'individuals attempt to orient themselves to, and take creative action in, situations or events that are complex, ambiguous and ill defined' (Drazin et al., 1999: 287). Consider how their notion of creativity highlights how creativity is a volatile and ambigu-ous process. People *attempt* to be creative and seek *orientation*. Seeking orientation refers to a lack of a clear ordering principle that guides creativity, but suggests an ambiguous and ill-defined situation that does not provide clear direction. The ambiguity of the situation only allows attempts to be creative and offers no clear, straightforward action. Here, the strong process approach overlaps to some extent with design thinking, which also postu-lates that people are only able to tame wicked problems and deal with emerging situations. In most situations, individuals have few insights into what a situation involves and how it may evolve. This means that creative ideas emerge through the way people make sense of and act in ambiguous situations. Drazin et al. prompted readers to think about orga-nizational creativity as a constantly ongoing and collective sensemaking activity that may produce transformative ideas. Chapter 4 will return to their ideas in more detail when it discusses the process of evaluation.

A strong process perspective is a long way from the cause-and-effect models discussed earlier, which were based on clear and simple principles and causal relationships. In con-trast, a strong process approach argues that the generalization of cause and effect is not possible as all situations are unique and thus their outcomes are not predictable. Fur-thermore, a strong process approach challenges many of the existing models of managing creativity, which are based on trying to control, or at least influence, the process. Accord-ingly, Styhre and Sundgren (2003: 426) argued that a strong process approach or the 'rhizome model emphasises that all inventive and creative activities are always fluid and fluxing, essentially escaping such [managerial] practices aimed at control'. This is what transpires when thinking about the rhizome: people cannot control its growth, but they may somehow be able to channel it carefully. Chapter 5 discusses some concrete practices for how to cope with the fluidity of creativity by elaborating the concept of improvisation and how it helps address the indeterminacy of management in general and creativity in particular.

Spotlight on Research: Karl Weick's 'Sensemaking' Concept

Imagine that someone enters a dark room full of unfamiliar objects and people. The only thing they have at their disposal is a flashlight. To orient themselves, they can shine a light on the things around them. When they direct the light, they may see a couple of chairs, a table, the door, and so on, but they will never see the whole room. However, they will slowly be able to piece together a mental image of the room. Depending on the level of darkness and the person's mental image, they may be able to move around easily or inch towards the middle of the room. They will take each step first and discover what they have done afterwards. They may also tell others about what they think the room looks like or inquire about how they might navigate the room. Yet if the set-up of the room suddenly changes, they must revisit their mental image and adjust it accordingly.

The metaphor of the dark room and the flashlight, which is borrowed from Taylor and Van Every (2000), is useful to illustrate the basic notions of the sensemaking perspective, which was developed and popularized by Karl Weick's work. The central question of a sensemaking approach is how individuals interpret and act in an ambiguous environment, and how that affects organizations. According to Weick (1995), sensemaking has seven essential properties. First, it concerns *identity*, which denotes how people refer sensemaking to their interpretation of who they think they are—that is, the identity they adopt. Second, sensemaking is *retrospective*, which means that people make sense of their actions after they have carried them out. Third, people actively *enact* their environments by making distinctions and giving meaning to objects and people. Fourth, this process is inherently *social*, as all sensemaking happens in relation to others and not in isolation. Fifth, sensemaking is constantly *ongoing* and does not have a beginning or end. Sixth, while making sense, people *extract cues* that are familiar from the environment to make sense of their surroundings. Seventh, people seek *plausibility* and not accuracy by creating plausible stories for themselves.

Now consider the dark room and flashlight again. The dark room represents an unstructured and ambiguous environment, and the flashlight an individual's mental processes. The individual entering the room has a certain understanding of themselves—for example, as cautious or adventurous—which will influence how they approach the exploration of the room and shine their flashlight (identity). They then take some steps into the room, but only after they have moved forward can they can make sense of what happened, what their new location is, and how the environment has changed when taking the steps (retrospection). Once they move around a bit, the person creates a mental image of the environment (enactment) that makes sense to them, but which cannot be entirely accurate (plausibility). To move around further or to make sense of emerging obstacles, the person uses their knowledge of things and constellations that they are familiar with (extraction of cues). During their exploration of the room, they also seek or help others, perhaps telling them about features or listening to their accounts of the room (social). However, since they never know what awaits or develops in the darkness, the exploration of the room will never really stop (ongoing).

The exploration of the room with a flashlight highlights how individuals create what Weick refers to as 'intrasubjective meanings'—for instance, individual mental maps of the room. Organizations, on the other hand, are characterized by the ongoing creation of 'intersubjective meanings'—for instance, a common understanding of the room. Weick defined organization as 'a consensually validated grammar for reducing equivocality by means of sensible interlocked behaviors' (Weick, 1979: 3). Organizations are, to return to the metaphor, commonly agreed upon explanations (consensually validated grammar) of how the dark room looks (reducing equivocality) and how people should move within it and use it (sensible interlocked behaviour). Hence from making personal sense of the room, people create a shared sense of the room for others. If this shared sense becomes a norm, it develops into an organizational structure that provides a stable description of the room that guides behaviours. The trouble is that such stability is almost impossible in a complex, ambiguous, and volatile environment characterized by innumerable intrasubjective and intersubjective meanings. Patterns of collective sensemaking are constantly challenged and changing, which provides the ground for creative transformations.

Overall, sensemaking is an intriguing perspective from which to discuss organizational creativity. However, it is important to bear in mind that the 'sensemaking perspective is a frame of mind about frames of mind that is best treated as a heuristic than as an algorithm' (Weick, 1995: xii). In other words, much like the strong process approach, the sensemaking perspective should not be seen as a definite theory, but to stimulate reflections about how organizations and organizational creativity are based on ongoing processes of sensemaking.

Moderate Process Approach

Moving day on university campuses tends to be chaotic, as it means that thousands of eager new students move into their new residences. It tends to produce traffic chaos, angry parents, and exhausted students. The organizational researcher Martha Feldman was intrigued by how the housing department at her university handled moving day and other issues, and for over four years she studied departmental routines (Feldman, 2000). She found that to alleviate the chaos of moving day, the housing department started liaising with the local police to direct traffic flows and reduce traffic jams. Moreover, the university department assigned spaces for vendors, who tried to sell stuff to the new students and tended to clog the entrance halls, creating even more chaos. One year, however, the athletics department scheduled a football game on moving day, which would have led to even more chaotic traffic situations. This prompted the housing organization to change their fixed moving date and coordinate with the athletic department in future to avoid scheduling clashes. The shifting routines around moving day are an example that illustrates how routines are not immutable, but change incrementally over time. Feldman referred to these as 'performative routines'. Routines, according to her, are not simply executed, but performed. That means routines are not mere patterns of repetitive and rigid behaviour, but enacted by people, and this enactment involves a range of different emotions, thoughts, interpretations, and actions—much like an actor on stage would not simply read the lines of a play, but actively perform the assigned lines out of the script (see also Feldman and Pentland, 2003).

Feldman's findings are interesting because they cut right to the heart of one of the major issues of the social sciences in general, and organizing creativity in particular: the structure–agency problem. Suggesting how to solve the structure–agency problem is, as will be seen in the following section, the central issue of the moderate process approach for organizational creativity. Thus it is necessary to begin by outlining the structure–agency dilemma and how organizational creativity may be related to it. Then the conversation shifts to what I call the *creativity-as-practice* approach, linked to a moderate process perspective of creativity.

The most vexing questions of the social sciences ask what determines individual and collective behaviour, whether individuals have the power to act on their own will, and whether individual and collective action is determined by underlying laws and structures. In the latter case, it is assumed that social structures and rules are so strong that individuals seem to have no will of their own, and that individuals and collectives merely respond to social rules. This may be referred to as a deterministic perspective on social behaviour. The other extreme is to claim that individuals exercise their free will and act without being influenced by social structures. This could be referred to as the voluntaristic perspective on social behaviour.

Both views are extreme in that they highlight either the power of structures or the power of individuals in shaping society, organizations, and organizational creativity. The models inspired by an organism metaphor discussed earlier build on a deterministic perspective in which structures and contexts trigger individual creativity. For example, there is an underlying assumption that if organizations provide intrinsic motivators, individuals will be more creative. Such cause-and-effect conceptions of creativity, however, leave little room for how individuals make sense of the situation. A voluntaristic perspective, on the other hand, would analyse the intentions and actions of individuals. It is interested in how individuals interpret and make sense of the creativity strategy, hierarchy, and informal processes of the organization and places a significant amount of emphasis on an individual's ability to seize unique situations for creative encounters. For example, the conception of emerging moments of creativity discussed earlier is based on the assumption that individuals and groups seize the opportunity based on their interpretation and actions in a unique situation (Hargadon and Bechky, 2006).

Considering the two sides of the spectrum—structure and agency—both seem somewhat plausible. Certainly, creativity is influenced by social structures, yet individuals also seem to act based on their own interpretations. So is it possible to combine these two conceptions somehow? This is the leading question of a moderate approach to organizational creativity, which tries to understand organizational creativity through the combined influence of structure and agency. Moreover, it is the logic that underlines the triangular context, process, and practice approach to organizing creativity applied in this book as it links a somewhat stable context to the indeterminate unfolding of processes and the practices of individuals and groups.

One of the most influential sociological approaches seeking to strike a balance between structure and agency is the structuration theory by the sociologist Anthony Giddens. As part of this theory, Giddens expounded the 'duality of structure' (Giddens, 1984), by which he meant that social structures simultaneously contain deterministic and voluntaristic qualities. According to Giddens, social structures guide human behaviour and tell people what to do, while at the same time an agent has—when they act—the possibility of changing the structure. In other words, a social structure is a medium for, as well as an outcome of, action. That means that a structure guides behaviour (medium), but the structure is also reproduced and possibly transformed in that behaviour (outcome).

To make more sense of his ideas, it would be beneficial to return to Martha Feldman's study on routines, in which she explicitly referred to Giddens's theory of structuration. She found that the routines of the housing department were neither fixed to determine behaviour nor completely at the will of the individuals. Routines structured behaviour (medium) but were also incrementally changing over time (outcome). Her findings are significant to organizing creativity because they show that routines and creativity are not mutually exclusive, but that the enactment of routines may lead to transformative changes of the very same routines. Sonenshein (2016), for example, argued that routines and creativity are not two separate processes; they are intertwined. He found that employees in a boutique store would not simply follow rules on how to set up displays, but worked actively with the rules to lend the displays their personal touch. Hartmann (2014) similarly demonstrated that organizations based on strict routines and hierarchies, such as the military and police, seem to be informed by creative acts that are necessary to perform their routines. Even the replication of routines seems to have innovative effects, as Schmidt et al. (2019) illustrated in a study on new venture creation.

These studies flag up a highly important issue—that organizational creativity is performed based on the structures and routines of an organization which enable and constrain creativity at the same time. One of the key questions that a moderate process approach addresses is therefore what individuals in an organization do when they are creative within the constraints set by the rules and routines of that organization. In other words, it seeks to understand not what people ought to do when being creative in theory, but what they do and how their actions impact organizational creativity. Based on these ideas, it is possible to outline a creativity-as-practice approach.

Practices have become a popular level of analysis in organization and management studies—especially in fields such as strategy, technology, and organizational learning (Rennstam and Lundholm, 2020). Yet a practice perspective has seldom been applied to understanding organizational creativity processes (for exceptions, see Garud et al., 2011; Sonenshein, 2016). Now a practice perspective may be confused with a psychological perspective that focuses on cognitive processes and the execution of creativity skills proposed, for example, as one dimension of the Componential Theory of Creativity (Amabile, 1988). In contrast, a creativity-as-practice approach is sociological because it seeks to address how individuals and groups are creative within the social structures and contexts of the organization. As such, it combines the macro level and micro level in the spirit of striking a balance between structure and agency. Creativity-as-practice is inspired by a similar perspective on strategy (Whittington, 2006) and recent work in organizational creativity research on 'idea work' by Håkonsen Coldevin et al. (2019). It comprises three components. The first is *creative praxis*, which means the actual creative practices of individuals and groups. Second, *creative practice* refers to the institution or organization's routines and beliefs concerning creativity. Third is *creative practitioners*, which encompasses the individuals who are enacting creativity.

concrete example may shed more light on the interplay between these three dimensions. Garud et al. (2011) studied 3M and how it sustained creative practices over time. They provided multiple examples of such organizational creativity practices. One popular practice that 3M applies is the 15 per cent rule, which means that employees can work on their own ideas and projects for up to 15 per cent of their time. This is what, in the context of the creativity-as-practice approach, would be considered an organizational creative practice based on a distinct rule. However, Garud et al. showed how this organizational rule was performed in various ways: some used more than 15 per cent, while others used less. The 15 per cent rule was thus interpreted and enacted differently from 3M's original intentions. Essentially, the exact rule and number was not as important as 'the intended message ... that 3M employees had the discretion to use their time and the company's slack resources to explore new ideas' (Garud et al., 2011: 757). In other words, praxis was inspired by practice but not determined by it. This is an important insight, as the rule provided direction without determining people's actions. Conversely, people could not simply do whatever they liked, but were restricted by the availability of resources and the existing slack, and guided by the rough figure of 15 per cent.

Feldman (2000: 614) described this indeterminate nature of praxis and practice very well:

> Routines are performed by people who think and feel and care. Their reactions are situated in institutional, organizational and personal contexts. Their actions are motivated by will and intention. They create, resist, engage in conflict, acquiesce to domination. All of these forces influence the enactment of organizational routines and create in them a tremendous potential for change.

Feldman reiterates the notion of performativity by referring to how context and individual intermesh in the enactment of routines, which provides the possibility for transformation and creativity. Linked to the performativity of routines, a creativity-as-practice approach helps make sense of how organizational practices influence and support creativity while at the same time exploring how those practices are enacted, who enacts them, and how practices may change over time. The creative potential of organizational routines will be explored further in Chapter 3.

All in all, a process approach changes people's perspective on organizational creativity by assuming that *time matters all of the time*. Hence, in contrast to a system view where time only matters when switching from one phase to the other—for instance, switching from gathering resources to generating ideas—a process approach, whether strong or moderate, makes time an inherent part of the analysis of organizational creativity. The image of a river may be helpful to explain the difference. Obviously, a river does not flow in stages from one point to the other but it is constantly flowing. Analogously, a process approach focuses attention on the constant flow of events and how past, present, and future shape activities in the flow. For that reason, attention shifts from understanding the static orga-nization of creativity (an entity) to the flow of organizing creativity (an activity). Precisely this tension between 'being' and 'becoming' (Tsoukas and Chia, 2002) is one of the cen-tral questions of process research on organizational creativity. A moderate approach seeks to balance being and becoming by juxtaposing and analysing stable routines and actual practices, while a strong process approach focuses entirely on how creativity emerges in activities. Such process thinking and its contextual embeddedness will be most frequently drawn upon throughout the rest of this book.

Conclusion

This chapter has discussed various theories, models, and concepts that seek to make sense of context, process, and practices of organizational creativity. To structure the discussion, different metaphors were used. Based on the work by Gareth Morgan, eight metaphors of organizations were described with regard to the general aspects that they highlight about organizations and, specifically, the role that organizational creativity plays. Four of these metaphors are especially dominant in making sense of organizations: organism, brain, cul-ture, and transformation and flux. These four metaphors were therefore chosen to frame the subsequent discussion.

First, this chapter presented and critically reflected on contingency and interaction-ist models inspired by the organism metaphor. Interactionist researchers have suggested models of organizational creativity that integrate individual, group, and organization lev-els. They have proposed that it is necessary to seek an optimal fit between an individual or group and their organizational environment to foster creative outcomes. One of the main accomplishments of interactionist models is emphasizing the crucial role of context in organizational creativity, which challenges the dominant psychological perspectives. Inter-actionist models are based on objectivist assumptions, which were discussed critically and it was suggested that to complement and augment perspectives on organizational creativity, a subjectivist perspective is fruitful.

The rest of the chapter was devoted to applying a subjectivist perspective and discussing the three remaining metaphors and their link to organizational creativity research, start-ing with design thinking linked to the brain metaphor. Design thinking is a concept that has not been conclusively defined. One of the central characteristics of a design thinking approach is how individuals and groups use and apply information and their knowledge to tackle or tame wicked problems. The popularity of design thinking stems in part from its pragmatic approach. A pragmatic approach on design thinking highlights how actors are not passive bystanders of the world, but actively engaged in forming it. A distinct focus is on the consequences of actions. If a design works, that may be good enough, yet if it becomes problematic, actors must engage and take further actions. This creates a constant engagement with design solutions and their consequences. As such, design thinking has been useful by highlighting the crucial role of practices and emergence in organizational creativity.

From design thinking, the chapter transitioned to the crucial role of culture in orga-nizations. Culture stresses the influence of norms, values, and beliefs on organizational creativity. Norms, values, and beliefs imbue symbols with meanings to guide people's interpretations and actions that they are mostly unaware of. As such, organizational culture provides direction for people and seeks to integrate the diverse values of individuals and groups in the organization. Based on two dimensions, strength and the propensity to take risks, four ideal types of organizational culture with a specific bearing on organizational creativity were suggested: progressive (strong, risk taking), fragmented (weak, risk averse), maverick (weak, risk taking), and small wins (strong, risk averse). A cultural perspective on organizational creativity highlights the importance of context—in particular, the subconscious, largely unnoticed influence of values and norms that govern creativity. Moreover, it shows how meaningful, value-laden symbols influence and are influenced by interpretations and practices.

Lastly, the chapter discussed a process perspective of organizational creativity that explicitly shifted focus from organizational creativity as a noun to organizational creativity as an ongoing activity. A central element of a process perspective is how organizations are constantly changing and evolving. Yet scholars have discussed the rate of change differently. Strong process approaches assume that there is no stability and that organizations are constantly becoming. Moderate process approaches, in contrast, identify a certain inertia in change and argue that structures stabilize and routinize organizational action but are subject to change over time. The moderate approach thus emphasizes how structures may facilitate but not determine creativity processes by providing direction while a strong approach views creative outcomes as indeterminate, which makes their facilitation problematic.

Across the varying conceptions of organizational creativity discussed in this chapter, the three overarching core dimensions of the triangular framework can be identified. *Context* was specifically highlighted as an important influence in interactionist approaches, organizational culture, and stabilizing structures in moderate process approaches. *Process* and emergence was the central element in the process perspective but also played a pronounced role in design thinking, which highlighted the ongoing engagement with arising problems in designs. Lastly, concrete *practices* played a significant role in design thinking but were also a central element in the suggested creativity-as-practice approach linked to a moderate process perspective.

In the next chapters, the three core aspects—context, process, and practice—will be used to systematically analyse key aspects of organizing creativity. Note that again this will involve a shift from conceptualizing organizational creativity primarily as a noun to an emphasis on organizing creativity as an ongoing activity. The next chapter initiates the detailed examination of different aspects of organizing creativity by focusing on generating and developing ideas and examining closely different contexts, process dimensions, and popularized practices.

3

Generating and Developing Ideas

There are so many ways to use the word *idea*. For example, 'he had no idea' means that he has no knowledge and is clueless. It can also mean that he may not have expected an outcome to happen the way that it did ('he had NO idea that this would happen ...'). It is also possible to say 'she is full of ideas', which means that she may be interested, knowledge-able, and energetic in trying out and thinking about new things. Or one can exclaim that 'sometimes, he has ideas', which emphasizes beliefs and values. Thus, the connotations and meanings of 'idea' are, as with creativity, extensive and have been the cause of confusion in studies on organizing creativity (Hua et al., 2022). It is therefore important to unpack the notion of an idea.

To get a grasp of what an idea is and how it is considered in this book more systematically, it is useful to start with a philosopher. In his essay 'Concerning Human Understanding', published in 1690, John Locke thought that an idea 'stand[s] for whatsoever is the object of the understanding when a man [sic] thinks; I have used it to express whatever is meant by phantasm, notion, species, or whatever it is which the mind can be employed about in thinking ...' Locke mentioned 'several ideas, such as are those expressed by the words, Whiteness, Hardness, Sweetness, Thinking, Motion, Man, Elephant, Army, Drunkenness, and others' (Nidditch, 1975: I.i.8). For Locke, ideas can contain everything from fantasies to concrete objects. He also believed that humans initially resemble empty containers, but are filled with ideas from birth through their experiences—as opposed to other philoso-phers, such as Plato, who thought that ideas already exist within people and only need to be developed.

John Locke further distinguished between simple and complex ideas. Simple ideas are basic perceptions, such as colours, tastes, and noises. For Locke, simple ideas arise passively to the mind, which reflects on them and presents them to the individual. These ideas, how-ever, are not something that can be forced by will; they simply are, and they arise with experience. Yet of course, people do have ideas that are more complex. Locke therefore argued that people combine simple ideas to generate a complex set of ideas based on their experiences and knowledge. Although John Locke did not have today's tools and knowledge to understand how the brain works, his main concept of what an idea is remains intriguing, especially his distinction between simple and complex ideas—the latter being the mainstay of creative transformations and the essence of what Håkonsen Coldevin et al. (2019) call 'idea work'.

Another aspect of an idea worth considering is its collective nature. The Romantic notion of the lone genius or artist coming up with an amazing idea has been a common view, and this may certainly be the case for some artists. Most ideas, however, are generated and developed by a collective of people. This is especially true for a social entity, such as an organization. The Russian thinker Bakhtin discussed the 'dialogic nature of an idea', by which he meant that an idea is a 'live event' which plays out between individuals instead of within an individual. An idea, according to Bakhtin, 'wants to be heard, understood,

Organizing Creativity. Stephan M. Schaefer, Oxford University Press. © Stephan M. Schaefer (2023).
DOI: 10.1093/oso/9780198893509.003.0003

and "answered" by other voices from other positions' (Bakhtin, 1984: 88). Hence, Bakhtin pointed to another common observation—that ideas must be discussed with others to flourish. They may be conceived by individuals but developed by many. Hence, ideas are commonly collective rather than individual achievements.

These different philosophical notions of an idea are good starting points because they highlight some important issues that will be discussed in this chapter: simple ideas arising in the mind, and the subsequent practice of generating and developing complex ideas through compiling, combining, and 'working on ideas' (Håkonsen Coldevin et al., 2019). Locke's reference to the importance of experiences for generating and developing ideas and the significance of others in idea generation will also be part of the discussion in this chapter. All of these notions inform a working definition of ideas that Hua et al. (2022: 8) suggested namely that '[i]deas are provisional and communicable representations'. Similarly, ideas can be understood as simply arising or intentionally produced representations. Such ideas can be simple but also combined to generate more complex ideas in an intentional effort by an individual or a collective of people. However, ideas are provisional, as they may change in the process of being produced or communicated. This leads to the act of generating but also developing ideas, which alludes to the provisional nature of initially generated ideas that are communicated and worked on over time.

In what follows, I will expound the context, process, and practice of generating and developing ideas by first discussing a typology of idea generation contexts. This will be followed by a more close examination of dimensions of idea generation and development processes with special consideration for its temporal perspectives. Then follows an exploration of idea generation and development practices that have been systematically researched.

A Typology of Idea Generation Contexts

In August 1949, a wildfire broke out in the Mann Gulch, which is a valley in Montana. Fifteen firefighters were deployed to parachute into the area and extinguish the flames. After a turbulent plane ride, they landed safely atop the hill but with a broken radio and their equipment scattered. Once they landed, the foreman of the crew, Dodge, told his men to advance to the river and try to get closer to the flanks of the fire to fight it from there. Dodge met the fire prevention guard, who were on the ground when they arrived. Together, they went up the ridge to eat while the men did as ordered and headed down into the valley. From the top of the hill, Dodge noticed how the fire was suddenly getting more intense. He ran after his men to warn them, and, once he reached them, the fire blew up. The flames and heat became so intense that it was impossible to reach the river in the valley. Dodge told his men to race back up the steep hill to the top of the ridge. He also told them to drop their heavy tools immediately to be quicker. Most men refused to let go of their tools, which were weighing them down in their scramble for the top of the hill. The fire, however, was quickly catching up to the men, and it became clear that they would not be able to reach the safety of the hilltop. In this critical moment, Dodge lit a fire just in front of them. His motivation was to create an escape fire, which would burn an area that the approaching real fire would spare, as there would be no fuel that it could feed on. Such an escape fire would therefore create a safe zone for the entire team. He told his men to follow him into the safe zone of the escape fire, but they did not obey and kept scrambling up the hill. Most could not outrun the fire, and twelve of the firefighters did not make it out alive, as the flames caught up with them. Dodge survived in the safe ground of the escape fire, and two other firefighters made it to a safe place on the steep hill (Rothermel, 1993).

The events that unfolded at Mann Gulch illustrate one of the most important aspects of organizational contexts: how well the interactions between organizational members are governed by rules or values. In general, firefighters must be able to rely on each other in extreme situations. In a fire, one of the key aspects is establishing responsibilities on the ground, a functioning chain of command, and clear tasks for each person. Crews must be briefed and told how and when to execute the tasks they are given. Everyone must also have undergone extensive training to be able to execute these tasks well. Furthermore, the incident commander on the ground must monitor the progress of the operation, and ensure that information flows are handled appropriately and that operating officers on the ground do not have to deal with too many complex issues and information at once.

Ideally, a successful firefighting operation is based on smooth and efficient deployment and clear organization. The Mann Gulch wildfire shows, however, how organizations that are supposed to be based on well-known procedures and clear instructions can unravel in a sudden loss of meaning. Commands are misunderstood and not obeyed, as the ambiguity of the situation leaves people unsure of what to do. In the Mann Gulch, fire team members mistrusted the actions of their commander, whom they barely knew, and they suddenly missed a clear direction of what to do. Though there are conflicting accounts of what transpired in the Mann Gulch case, it generally illustrates how values and structures may not have been strong enough to govern a joint action of the team (Weick, 1993). It illustrates the significance of values and norms as well as rules for the functioning of organizations which has a bearing on organizing creativity as well.

Organizational theorists and social psychologists have referred to the influence of values, norms, and rules on individual behaviour as the *relative strength of an organizational context* (Snyder and Ickes, 1985), which is reminiscent of what was discussed as strong cultural contexts in Chapter 2, the difference being that it not only includes values and norms but also routines and structures. Contexts can be strong, which means that individuals know exactly what is expected of them and how to act in a given situation. Everyone knows the appropriate behaviour and can identify the relevant cues from the environment. For example, a red traffic light is a strong context in which everyone knows to stop. It can also be expected that others will stop. In a weak context, on the other hand, there is ambiguity about how to act, what is appropriate to do, and what the actions of others and superiors mean. Individuals in weak contexts have difficulties encoding the situation and knowing which behaviour is expected of them, and what effects these behaviours will have on others (Mischel, 1977). The relative strength of a context allows an analysis of how well people are able to comply with and navigate any context.

As mentioned above, the relative strength of organizational contexts is mainly influenced by cultural values and institutional rules and regulations, which impact people's expectations, actions, and interactions. For example, highly bureaucratic organizations strive to establish strong situations in which there are apparent and obvious rules on how people should act, which are complemented by beliefs in the efficiency of this form of organization. In contrast, organizations that operate in complex and turbulent environments, which Henry Mintzberg calls 'adhocracies', may find that they have no specific rules established for how to act or what is expected from each team member (Mintzberg, 1980). Neither organizational form is superior but each may work better in certain environments than others, as we have discussed with a view to contingency theories in Chapter 2. How the strength of context influences creativity will be discussed in more detail later in this chapter.

Spotlight on Practice: The Fire at Notre Dame

On 15 April 2019 at 7 p.m., thick smoke rose from the attic of the Notre Dame cathedral in Paris. Around this time, the first firefighters arrived on the scene. On their arrival, they immediately plugged their hoses into the standing pipes and began pumping water onto the flames. One small team of firefighters started climbing towards the attic of the cathedral, where the flames were bursting through the roof. The team included 27-year-old Myriam Chudzinski, who was familiar with the building because she had trained at Notre Dame a couple of months earlier. She knew the layout and that the attic did not have any firewalls which would prevent the fire from spreading through the dry wooden beams. She took lead of the team and started pouring water on the flames, which continued raging, eventually setting the wooden beams on fire. After an hour, the team heard a thundering noise as the cathedral spire collapsed. The generals on the ground saw that the attic was lost and called all teams to retreat to safe ground.

Safely on the ground, the teams relayed the information that the fire was eating away at the north tower, including the wooden structure that held eight bells. The collapse of the bell structure would most likely destroy the entire north tower. This was a critical piece of information that would change the course of the events. The commanding general, Jean-Claude Gallet, ordered the firefighters to focus all of their energy on saving the tower. From a temporary outpost on the square next to the cathedral, General Gallet's deputy, General Jean-Marie Gontier, coordinated the front-line actions surrounded by whiteboards and maps of the advancing fire. Time was of the essence, and decisions had to be made quickly. Then, Master Sgt. Rémi Lemaire had an idea. He suggested fighting the fire in the north tower by climbing up the south tower and plugging hoses into fire trucks next to the tower, compensating for some of the low pressure in the pipes along the church. From the south tower, firefighters could enter the north tower to fight the fire close up. It was clearly a risky strategy, but it was approved. Lemaire and his team climbed up the south tower and dropped onto a platform between the two towers. They slowly moved into the tower and eventually tamed the flames enough to prevent the church bells from collapsing. By 11 p.m. the fire was under control. Myriam Chudzinski, the team commander, commented afterwards that she did not realize the 'huge team effort' until she saw the damage and what they had achieved with their coordinated efforts (Peltier et al., 2019). The firefighting operation at Notre Dame is, in contrast to the Mann Gulch case, an apt example of a highly structured operation and the influence of strong norms and meanings on the successful outcome of the firefighters' efforts.

Another important dimension specifically regarding idea generation and development is the *nature of the problems* that people encounter in an organizational context

(Unsworth, 2001). Imagine a creative painting class. In the first lesson, the instructor teaches painting techniques, such as how to use perspective, colour, and so on. In the second lesson, the instructor places an apple at the front of the room and tells the students to paint the apple. The students use all that they have learned in the previous lesson to paint the apple. In the third class, the instructor lays out forty different objects in front of the class: apples, pears, glasses, bowls, stuffed animals, and other items. Then, the students are instructed to arrange the objects however they like and paint them. In the fourth and final class, the students are told that they are supposed to sit in front of the white canvas and paint anything that comes to mind. As this example illustrates, problems vary by context. In the second art lesson (painting the apple), students are presented with a clearly outlined problem that they can solve with the solutions they have been taught. These types of problems are 'presented-problem situations', or—more simply—*closed problems* (Getzels, 1975). A problem is closed because it is given, and solutions to solve it are usually known. A typical example of a closed problem is a maths exercise in school. The problem is given and solutions to solve the problem are known but they need to be applied in the right way to solve the problem.

In contrast, the third and fourth art classes present another kind of problem. As opposed to clearly outlined problems, the students are asked to think about what they want to paint. The problem here is not defined, and the aspiring painters must discover what possible problems and solutions there are. These moments are referred to as 'discovered-problem situations', or *open problems* (Dillon, 1982). Open problems do not have a predefined solution. They may not even be known as problems yet. So, in some situations, individuals must imagine problems, as in the art class. The individual is then prompted to dig deeper, to envision and formulate problems and, in another step, to find possible solutions.

People in organizations must make decisions on a daily basis that concern either closed or open problems, not least regarding idea generation and development (Unsworth, 2001). One of the enduring insights about organization that has transpired from research and practice is that humans do not act like machines or merely execute predefined actions. Rather, individuals in organizations must constantly deal with different problem situations that may perhaps only require the application of a known solution or may be ambiguous—that is, situations in which problems are not as clear-cut, even if they seem routine (Bernstein, 2012). Note, however, that the distinction between open and closed problems is analytical. This means that the distinction is valuable for a thorough analysis of contexts but in empirical situations problems are complex and can contain multiple open and closed problem elements.

Put together, the strength of situations and the nature of the problem create four ideal-typical organizational contexts with specific opportunities and constraints for idea generation and development, as shown in Figure 3.1. Each context links to an influential concept in organization theory—*routines, loose coupling, weak ties,* and *organized anarchy,* which will be expounded in the following discussions.

Before embarking on the discussion of each quadrant of Figure 3.1, a few caveats are necessary. First, an organization does not consist of one unified context. Take, for example, an organization that produces video games. Video game production requires many different skills. Designers come up with storylines and rules for the game, artists sketch figures and landscapes, and programmers produce the code for the game. These groups all work in

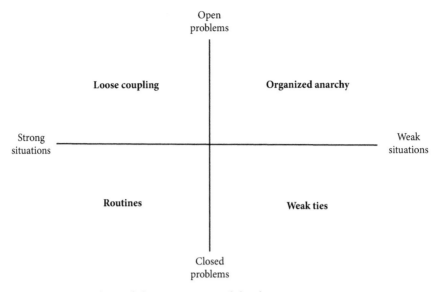

Figure 3.1 A typology of idea generation and development contexts

very different contexts. Designers may predominantly deal with open problems and weak contexts, while coders use programming languages to produce the game, and thus primarily deal with closed problems. Therefore, there are different contexts with varying features in one single organization. Second, contexts are dynamic. This means that they may change over time from weak to strong or from strong to weak, from primarily open to closed problems, and so on. Furthermore, an organization undergoes constant changes of varying size. Some contexts, however, are, as discussed regarding a moderate process perspective (see Chapter 2), more inert than others. For example, the routines in a manufacturing plant may change less often than the work of an architect. Third, contexts are of course more complex and not only characterized by their strength and the nature of problems. Yet those two dimensions are influential in generating and developing ideas and thus are important to consider when organizing creativity.

Routines

Strong situations with mostly closed problems can be described as routine contexts. Routines were already discussed in Chapter 2, but for the development of the argument in this section it is worth recapitulating and expanding on the previous discussion. Routines are 'repeated patterns of behaviour that are bound by rules and customs and that do not change very much from one iteration to another' (Feldman, 2000: 611). Hence, in routine contexts, there are clear rules and values for how to carry out tasks. Each problem has a known solution written down in a manual or other instructions. For example, when assembling a car, workers execute the same behaviour for each car and, should a problem arise, they will react according to a standard procedure that they have learned. Another example is calling a support line and expecting that the employees there know how to fix the problems in a standardized manner. Intuitively, people do not associate routine contexts with generating transformative ideas at all. In other words, doing the same thing repeatedly with clearly defined rules does not lead to innovation or transformation.

Some of the metaphors and associated theories on organizations' routines and creativity may indeed be opposed to each other. From a machine perspective—a common metaphor for organization—deviating from a routine would be considered inefficient and inappropriate. The machine would simply not work without each part doing what it was assigned to do. Similarly, the organism metaphor discussed in Chapter 2 assumes that if the needs of an organization are met, it will be satisfied. For example, people in stable environments do not need to deviate from their routines and be innovative because they do not have to react to changes in the environment (Burns and Stalker, 1961). In contrast, in a turbulent environment, routines would not be an effective structure for organizations and hence they should adopt a more organic approach that allows for more flexibility and creativity.

Nevertheless, considering a process perspective on organizations, the relationships between routine and idea generation may start to look different, as has already been discussed in Chapter 2. Organizations in this perspective are not static entities, and people are not machines that only execute predefined tasks. Moreover, foreseeing every problem and solution is close to impossible in most situations, as there are so many influences that could impact work processes. Rather, it is appropriate to look at organizations as ongoing accomplishments in which people's actions lead to small and large transformations. Seemingly stable routines may buzz with life, which means that the routines are carried out by human actors, thereby involving emotions, decisions, a variety of possible actions and outcomes—whether or not they were intended. Routines are performative and involve emotions, thoughts, and actions, which may or may not change the previous routine (Feldman and Pentland, 2003). The upshot is that routine and creativity are not mutually exclusive.

Consider, for example, how employees in a clothing boutique decorate windows and tables. Commonly, clothing boutiques may have a visual merchandise manual describing how clothes should be arranged on the display tables. The manual acts as a guide to solving the known problem of decorating a table, based on clear rules and expectations. Looking closely at how employees actually go about decorating tables, however, reveals a more complicated pattern. Some may strictly follow the guidelines to the letter, while others may choose to fold the clothes in a way that is not predefined, or arrange the colours of the clothes in different ways (Sonenshein, 2016). Simply put, they perform the routine of decorating the table differently. Alternatively, consider an assembly line in a factory in China in which there were strict rules about how to put together pieces of equipment for various Western firms. This context seems to have clearly defined rules and known solutions to problems. However, employees found 'all sorts of "better ways" of accomplishing tasks by their peers—a "ton of little tricks" that "kept production going" or enabled "faster, easier, and/or safer production"' (Bernstein, 2012: 188). Thus while the production was governed by strict routines, incremental, creative adoptions were necessary to improve efficiency.

Overall, routine contexts may appear to be less conducive to generating and developing transformative ideas. Yet, considering the performativity of routines, even individuals and groups in routine contexts generate and develop transformative ideas. This stands in contrast to the received wisdom and common assumption that routines are by their very nature uncreative.

Spotlight on Research: Idea Generation and Development in Bureaucracies

Can the police and military be creative, or is their bureaucratic, rule-based organization the antithesis of creativity? This question intrigued the researchers Mia Koss Hartmann and Rasmus Koss Hartmann, so they decided to take a closer look at whether and how police officers and soldiers are creative (Hartmann and Hartmann, 2023). For their study, they spent two and a half years conducting ethnographic research with members of the police force and military. They followed police officers and soldiers in their day-to-day activities and observed their actions closely. This method is called 'shadowing' and highlights the constant presence of the researchers in all activities—like a shadow. What they found was that, contrary to the common notion of highly bureaucratic organizations, police officers and soldiers were highly creative and generated many transformative ideas and solutions. In fact, the participants told the researchers that their organizations were so bureaucratic that they had no choice but to develop creative ideas of their own.

Indeed, the research team recorded 110 creative solutions that they observed during their study. To develop these solutions, police officers or soldiers would either use discarded materials from their own organizations or try to acquire them through informal channels within their respective organizations. For example, a police officer developed a tool for breaking car windows after an experience in which he had been a first responder to a car accident and had to get two injured passengers out as fast as possible, but struggled to break the window for a long time. In another example, a police officer got help from his mother to sew a belt that he used to carry his equipment when working in plain clothes, as the regular belts were too noticeable. In another case, soldiers changed the electric wiring in their vehicles so that they could charge laptop computers directly in the vehicle and did not have to wait to get back to camp. These ideas facilitated and simplified the work, but they were not ordered by superiors.

These findings challenge the widespread belief that strong contexts with closed problem solving, such as bureaucracies, are not creative. Rather, it appears that the enactment of bureaucracies, which means the *performing of bureaucratic rules*, may lead to creative acts. Thus, a bureaucratic system as such may not approve of creative processes since management would not approve of changes to rules. Yet a detailed look at how members of the bureaucracy perform rules reveals that in many instances they may change them without approval from management. Hartmann and Hartmann's study also draws attention to the fact that research into creativity benefits from detailed observations of creative processes to reveal their complexity.

Loose Coupling

A common perception of an organization is that it is based on clear intentions, the fulfilment of commonly agreed upon goals, and rational actions, similar to the assumptions about routine contexts. This idea of what an organization is assumes that its goals and intentions link tightly to its actions. For example, in this perception of organizations, it would be assumed that when an organization introduces a new digitalization strategy, it will adopt information technology (IT) systems to pursue this strategy. The employees of the organization then use these IT systems, which will lead to fulfilling the strategic goals. Or, consider that an organization has grown so much that it has implemented an HR department, which has been given the sole responsibility for searching for and recruiting new employees for all departments in the organization. In both examples, the organization's goals and intentions are tightly coupled to practices: the digitalization strategy is coupled to the IT system, which is coupled to the actions of employees, and the HR department's task is clearly linked to searching for and recruiting new employees for the entire organization. Assuming a tight link between intention and action is common in organization and management studies based on a rational approach which explains organizational actions on the assumption that they will apply the best possible solutions to achieve their goals.

However, some organizational theorists have questioned this assumption of tight linkages between elements in organizations and the rationality and intentionality that it implies. As an alternative conception, they have suggested 'loose coupling' (Weick, 1976), which highlights that in an organization, goals, intentions, and practices are not necessarily as tightly linked to each other as originally assumed. For instance, in the case of the IT system, the organization may intend to link its strategy and actions, but employees may not adopt the system as planned because they are not capable of doing so, or they continue using other systems that they think are better. The HR department may have the task of searching for candidates, but the managers of the R&D division may find it more effective to recruit students who worked for them part time during their summer holidays. The role of HR should then just be to approve them as new employees.

In other words, organizations may strive for tight couplings between goals and actions, but they also need to account for all of the factors that disturb them. So there is an obvious contradiction in how to manage organizations: they must function rationally and efficiently, but they must also allow for disturbances and indeterminacy. After all, people are not machines.

Essentially, the notion of loose couplings in an organization suggests that there is a connection or responsiveness between elements, but this connection allows the coupled elements to possess their own identities and logics or distinctiveness. The essence of loose coupling is well captured in Figure 3.2, which shows traffic at a busy intersection. There is responsiveness of all traffic participants—otherwise, they would hurt each other—but there is also clearly a distinctiveness of road users acting independently without seeming to adhere to the rules too much. Thus, while the intersection obviously does not have a rational system, which would be the most sensible solution to regulate the traffic through for example traffic lights, it does not descend into total chaos—the different traffic participants manage to establish a flow.

For the context of idea generation and development, the general observation that *two elements in the same context can be distinct from each other but at the same time be responsive* is the central notion. This type of loose coupling usually manifests in strong contexts linked with open problems or opportunity discovery, because in those contexts action is guided by the norms, values, and rules of a strong context and emerging problems are solved by using those existing norms, values, and rules. Open problems are therefore decoupled from

Figure 3.2 Loose coupling at a traffic junction

problem solving based on the norms, values, and rules inherent in the existing context. In other words, people may be involved in a core task guided by strong rules and regulations while simultaneously engaged in a loosely coupled or even decoupled task—pondering problems and ideas not necessarily connected to the core task.

One example of how loosely coupled elements at work may lead to new ideas is the notion of daydreaming or 'mind wandering' (Baer et al., 2020). Many people have experienced their thoughts starting to wander during a meeting. Wandering thoughts are then loosely coupled to, or even decoupled from, the task at hand, which however is still executed. Such mind wandering is frequent in individuals (Killingsworth and Gilbert, 2010), and—in general—organization and management researchers have argued that mind wandering is bad for performance and considered it as undesirable for an organization. However, mind wandering can involve all sorts of different ideas and thoughts. Therefore, one important aspect to consider is the content of episodes of mind wandering. It may involve rich imagination and playful possibilities that lead to new creative ideas. This is referred to as 'imaginative mind wandering' (Dane, 2018). Hence, regarding idea generation and development, imaginative mind wandering, or even boredom, can facilitate the generation and development of transformative ideas (Park et al., 2019).

The creativity researchers Kimberley Elsbach and Andrew Hargadon have even argued that a loose coupling between the core task and mind wandering should be part of designing a workplace for professionals. To facilitate the generation of new ideas and allow for mind wandering, organizations may consider periods of 'mindless work', which includes tasks that are 'low in cognitive difficulty and performance pressures' (Elsbach and Hargadon, 2006: 475). Mindless work allows individuals to let their mind wander while still executing their tasks, which may stimulate new transformative ideas.

Spotlight on Research: Walking and Idea Generation

Wandering and idea generation are not only reducible to thoughts. The German philosopher Friedrich Nietzsche once wrote, 'Sit as little as possible; do not believe any idea that was not born in the open air and of free movement—in which the muscles do not also revel.' Indeed, Nietzsche had the habit of walking up to eight hours a day. His routine of walking was less of an exercise than an activity during which he conceived most of his transformative philosophical ideas (Gros, 2014). Likewise, Steve Jobs was an avid walker who would go on long hikes to deliberate on his ideas (Isaacson, 2011).

Research has found that walking may increase idea generation. In an experimental study, researchers divided students into three groups: one that was seated, and others that were either exercising on a treadmill or strolling through the park outside. During their activities, the groups were asked to complete a creativity test. What the researchers concluded was that walking outside had the most visible effect on coming up with ideas that were not targeted at solving a closed problem (Oppezzo and Schwartz, 2014). In another study, researchers found that prolonged immersion in nature leads to better performance in creativity-related tasks. In this study, the researchers had groups of individuals hike for four days in the remote wilderness of Alaska, Maine, and Colorado and then complete a creativity test on which the hiking groups scored better than a group that was about to start their hike. The researchers conjectured that the positive relationships between hiking and creativity may be due to the disconnectedness from the abundance of stimuli from modern technology, the positive and gentle stimulating effects of natural environments, and the ability to contemplate without interruptions (Atchley et al., 2012).

While experimental research on creativity is not without problems because it necessarily needs to reduce the influence of variables in a controlled environment, qualitative research among academics has also pointed to the positive benefits of walking on new ideas and thinking (Keinänen, 2016). While research tries to systematically prove a connection between idea generation and walking, this might also be a good environment for self-study. How many ideas can people come up with when they take a hike in the woods?

Weak Ties

Consider three situations. First, imagine an IT employee who must report their performance regularly to their manager. Their performance is assessed by key performance indicators that are used to make decisions about salary and promotions, and the employee uses them to make decisions about their team's promotions. Second, imagine a freelancer who offers IT services to customers. The freelancer receives compensation for the work they do, and their contract is renewed if the customer is satisfied—if not, they will choose someone else. The freelancer must therefore acquire customers constantly. Third, imagine someone who is part of an IT team which collaborates regularly on projects for customers with whom that person has developed a long-term relationship. For each project, the person teams up with different people who they either already know or have been recommended to by others.

These three situations include different types of relationships or, in the parlance of social scientists, *ties*. In the first case, the IT employee works in a highly structured, strong context, where they are part of a clearly defined hierarchy in which ties between individuals are vertical, internal, and impersonal. This is commonly referred to as a *bureaucratic organization*. The second context is defined by market exchanges, in which the freelancer has external, transactional—rather than personal or hierarchical—relationships with customers. This is referred to as a *market-based organization*. The third case is somewhere in between. The person does not work in a well-defined hierarchical (strong) context, but changes teams every so often. Yet they have developed some closer relationships with their customers and some team members. In this case, ties are embedded, which means that relationships are personal, mutual, and horizontal. This is what researchers have called *network-based organization* (Uzzi, 1996). In contrast to bureaucracies as strong and regulated contexts and markets as impersonal and transaction-based, network-based organization consists of interpersonal ties that involve informal socializing across formal boundaries (Powell, 1990). However, networks can contain different types of ties, and—regarding idea generation and development—the nature and strength of their ties are important.

In 1973, the sociologist Mark Granovetter made a groundbreaking contribution to the field of sociology and network theory. His article was entitled 'The Strength of Weak Ties' (Granovetter, 1973). This title seems puzzling at first, since strength is not necessarily related to weakness. Granovetter (1973: 1361) defined the strength of a tie as 'a (probably linear) combination of the amount of time, the emotional intensity, the intimacy (mutual confiding), and the reciprocal services which characterize the tie'. Taking this definition as a point of departure, he distinguished between strong ties and weak ties. A strong tie develops when people spend a considerable amount of time with someone, build trustful and intimate relationships, and can rely on mutual support. In other words, strong ties are very close relationships in which the people involved know each other very well, and share preferences and values—like a friendship, for example. A weak tie, on the other hand, may be an acquaintance that someone occasionally meets and talks about the latest issues with, but would not call if they had a serious personal problem.

Based on the distinction between strong and weak ties, Granovetter makes an intriguing point with a bearing on idea generation and development processes: a weak tie will generally expose people to more diverse impressions and ideas than strong ties, and therefore may be more beneficial in various activities, including generating and developing transformative ideas. For example, close friends may listen to the same music, like the same bars, watch the same movies, and have the same political opinions. These common interests and values will not provide inspiration for many new ideas. Weak ties, however, are not as involved with each other and may challenge world views and opinions. A context of weak ties may therefore stimulate ideas because it exposes people to new and unknown knowledge and perspectives, allows critique of their own ideas, and by sheer quantity of acquaintances increases the chance of encounters with other people's knowledge and perspectives. Figure 3.3 provides an illustration of weak and strong ties. It shows how a weak tie allows people to tap into the knowledge of other groups with strong ties.

In a network-based context characterized by weak ties, individuals and groups usually depart from defined problems within their organization—though, of course, weak ties can

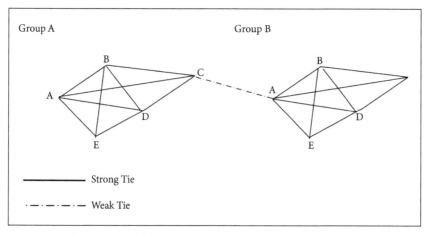

Figure 3.3 The structure of weak ties

also lead to discovering opportunities. Ideas related to solving problems are generated and developed by using the weak ties to tap into the expertise of relevant networks. In a study on the design company IDEO, Andrew Hargadon and Robert Sutton found that design teams would regularly consult their extensive networks to search for solutions to their design problems for their customers. They demonstrated that IDEO was connected to a broad variety of different networks that it could tap into and extract knowledge from. This exploitation of weak ties led to many different innovative solutions for clients because it allowed the designers to connect concepts from different industries to generate and develop ideas (Hargadon and Sutton, 1997).

Thus, weak tie situations may be beneficial to idea generation and development if individuals and organizations manage to obtain input from various sources across their networks for solving problems that they are currently working on. Chapter 5 will return to and elaborate on the notion of weak ties when discussing networks as a mode of coordination.

Organized Anarchies

Anarchy tends to be understood as the absence of order and authority and the dissolution of rules. Anarchy may therefore appear to be the antithesis of organization, which relies on authority and order. So how would those two contrary concepts be linked? In a widely influential contribution to the field of organization studies, Michael Cohen, James March, and Johan Olsen elaborated their concept of 'organized anarchy' and explored how decisions are made in those contexts (Cohen et al., 1972). To clarify the concept of organized anarchy, they listed three attributes: problematic preferences, unclear technologies, and fluid participation. The first means that in organized anarchies, people do not know in advance what they want and need—they act first and then declare a preference. The second attribute, unclear technologies, refers to the ambiguity of activities in the organization. Organizational members do not know precisely how things work, and much is based on trial and error and the unpredictable outcomes of actions. Lastly, an organized anarchy is characterized by different levels of involvement, which means that people's time and commitment to activities vary and that there are frequent changes of who does what and when. Thus, an organized anarchy truly is a weakly defined context as it does not provide much guidance or order for people.

As one might imagine, in organized anarchies, the decision-making process does not follow a sequence that is deemed logical and rational—such as identifying a problem or relevant issues, examining alternatives, proposing a solution, and making a decision to solve it. In contrast, Cohen et al. (1972) argued that decision-making in organized anarchies is comparable to a 'garbage can'. To understand the garbage can decision model better, an example is helpful (the terms in parentheses are those used by Cohen et al.). Consider how an organization may make a decision about a new software solution. Some time ago, Developer X had some extra overtime and developed a software solution for processing demographic data, which he thought was an opportunity to make the process more efficient. Developer X showed his solution to Manager A, who was not interested. None of his colleagues seemed to need this software either (solution without closed problem). Developer X therefore stored it on his computer for the time being. A few months later, some employees became frustrated because their way of processing demographic data was too slow, and they were constantly behind schedule (identified problem without a solution). By then, however, Developer X and Manager A had left the company, and Manager B was now in charge (fluid participation). As the delays in processing data became more urgent, Vice President C called for a meeting (choice opportunity). She wanted to discuss how to process demographic data more efficiently, as top management had been pressuring her to keep to the schedules. In this meeting, someone remembered the software that Developer X had developed. However, since Developer X and Manager A had left the organization, the solution was not known to anyone, and other software had to be purchased, meaning that Developer X's solution was left unused.

This example highlights how solutions, problems, and participants are disposed independently in a (metaphorical) garbage can. The software solution, the identified efficiency problem, and all individuals involved are not clearly connected, but they exist independently in the garbage can. Yet, in the garbage can, solutions, participants, and problems may or may not be connected at an appropriate choice opportunity. In the example, the solution to the problem may be chosen by the participants, or problem and solution may not be connected at all. The upshot is that decision-making becomes random, as solutions, problems, and participants exist independently and are not rationally linked (as the rational decision-making model would suggest)—only a choice opportunity might bring them together. Therefore, an organized anarchy is 'a collection of choices looking for problems, issues and feelings looking for decision situations in which they might be aired, solutions looking for issues to which they might be the answer, and decision makers looking for work' (Cohen et al., 1972: 2).

The consequence of garbage can decision-making in organized anarchies is that solutions may exist without closely defined problems and vice versa—problems exist without any solutions. In anarchic contexts, ideas are generated without a defined problem, and rules and regulations are missing that would guide its purpose. Hence, ideas are not generated in response to a problem, but may end up in a metaphorical garbage can, where they may or may not be linked to a specific problem in a choice situation. Thus the generation and development of ideas depend on an appropriate choice opportunity in which problem and solution may be combined to generate and develop a transformative idea.

All in all, the typology proposed in this chapter draws attention to contexts character-ized by different degrees of clarity regarding guidelines and norms and the nature of the problem being either open or closed. It provides a starting point for analysing some of the enabling and constraining factors that influence idea generation and development pro-cesses. The next section turns to process aspects involved in generating and developing ideas: temporality, interaction, and objects.

Temporality, Interactions, and Objects

As seen in the previous section, people can carry out routines by executing them accord-ing to a preconceived plan—for example, a manual or some other guidelines. Alternatively, people can actively try new features that they have imagined and thought about before, thereby deviating from the manual or routine in various ways. In the first case, individuals depersonalize the routine. This means that they do not choose to be personally involved in their work tasks. In the second case, people choose an active 'personalization strategy' (Sonenshein, 2016). In this case, the context influences idea generation and development, but it does not determine it. That means that the context alone does not lead to idea genera-tion, but that people exert influence on the context as well. The ability to act individually in certain contexts is referred to as *agency*, though the term has been used broadly and widely across different disciplines with varying meanings.

The following discussion links agency to *time* when generating and developing ideas. Most models of the idea generation and development process do not consider the influence of past, present, and future explicitly. In fact, there is a tendency to view an organization as an 'atemporal entity composed of social actors, mediated by technologies and surrounded by a neutral, external environment' (Hernes, 2014: 12). What Hernes means is that organi-zation research does not clearly consider how time *shapes* processes of organizing. Rather than looking at models that describe static relationships, the perspective should be shifted to how organizing happens over time. Similarly, regarding the idea generation and devel-opment process, it is important to reflect on how ideas are shaped by the history of the organization, (unexpected) events in the present, and imagination of the future possibili-ties of ideas. This varied influence and manifestation of past, present, and future on idea generation and development processes can be linked to *memory, attention, motivation, and projection* as important process dimensions of generating and developing ideas. Moreover, relationships with others and objects play an essential role in processes of generating and developing ideas. Yet, before turning to all of these important dimensions, a more nuanced discussion of agency and its inherently temporal nature is needed.

The Chordal Triad of Past, Present, and Future

Processes of idea generation and development in specific contexts concern the flow of activities *over time*, which means that processes of idea generation and development are 'informed by the past (in its habitual aspect), but also oriented toward the future (as a capacity to imagine alternative possibilities) and toward the present (as a capacity to contextualize past habits and future projects within the contingencies of the moment)' (Emirbayer and Mische, 1998: 963). Emirbayer and Mische alluded to the constant interplay of past, present, and future in human activity. To further conceptualize agency, they used the image of a chordal triad to illustrate the link between time and agency. Generally, a musical chord consists of three notes that, when struck, sound simultaneously. Similarly, past, present, and future are always struck together in a given moment. Past actions, present experience, and future possibilities are simultaneously present in all activities.

However, in most cases, there may be one note that is more dominant than the others. This means that in the given moment, either memories of the past, ruminations about the future, or full attention to the present dominate, while the other temporal dimensions fade to the background. Furthermore, there are often disharmonies. That could mean that people experience a loss of meaning because past, present, and future do not fit together. Things that people thought they knew do not apply, or expectations are not met. Take as an example the case of the Mann Gulch fire discussed earlier in this chapter. Recall how the team of firefighters suddenly could not make sense of the situation based on their experience and training. Moreover, they did not expect that an escape fire could save them (Weick, 1993). Past, present, and future were experienced as disharmonious and chaotic.

The image of the chordal triad illustrates how past, present, and future are interwoven in idea generation and development processes. For example, loose coupling and mind wandering mean that in the present moment, people execute habits based on past behaviour without thinking about it. At the same time, people may be involved in imagining future possibilities while having to be responsive to the present if problems occur with their task or they are called to attention. The following sections discuss selected process dimensions that are linked to different temporal orientations that have received systematic attention from organizational researchers: memory (past), motivation and attention (present), and imagination (future).

Memory and Knowledge

Most activities are based on mindless, automatic behaviour. The memory involved in automatic behaviour makes life much easier and more efficient. Like individuals, organizations must be able to consistently coordinate their activities and rely on and repeat past experiences to be efficient. Individual memory refers to the ability to retain and recall past knowledge. Similarly, organizational memory describes how past knowledge is retained, conserved, and retrieved in organizations. Organizational memory, however, is not only the sum of individual memories. While an organizational memory is dependent on individual memories, it goes beyond them as well because, even if individuals (and their memories) have left the organization, in the ideal case it still needs to remember how to run its operations and execute certain processes (Levitt and March, 1988).

Knowledge is a crucial component in individual and organizational memory. One important approach distinguishes between two types of knowledge: *Tacit knowledge and explicit knowledge*. The distinction between these two types of knowledge has ramifications for how people can share and retain knowledge in an organization and build an organizational memory (Hislop et al., 2018). Explicit knowledge can be articulated, written down, and accessed by everyone. The ability to share explicit knowledge means that people can use a 'people-to-document' approach in which individuals codify and transfer knowledge to documents that can be accessed by others (Hansen et al., 1999). Explicit knowledge may also be linked to what scholars have called 'declarative organizational memory' (Moorman and Miner, 1998). Declarative memory refers to the 'know what', including facts about the production line, customer preferences, manuals for routines, and so on. Explicit knowledge can also be shared through physical artefacts, such as prototypes or other technical objects that people have collected.

Tacit knowledge, on the other hand, is difficult to transmit to others. It is 'sticky' and hard to articulate. It comprises people's beliefs and mental frames of how to act, as well as knowledge about how to do things that is difficult to codify (the classic example is riding a bike). Tacit knowledge resides with the knower—that is, the person who has the knowledge. Hence, tacit knowledge may be conserved in routines, beliefs, and values as well as within people's practices in the organization. The importance of social interaction for sharing knowledge makes it a 'people-to-people' approach, which can be linked to 'procedural memory', which itself describes how an organization 'proceeds' with processes and activities (Moorman and Miner, 1998). Procedural memory encompasses all practical knowledge on how to do things in an organization. This means procedural knowledge tends to be best shared through interactions between people, which involves showing others how to do things or support them when they do them.

For idea generation and development, individual and organizational memory and their link to knowledge is crucial. First, memory and knowledge are important raw materials for the idea generation process. Individuals and organizations must have some expertise and knowledge in the domain they are working in (Amabile, 1988). Second, to effectively generate and develop ideas, individuals and organizations must be able to build on previous ideas and knowledge. The image of a sponge might be helpful to understand this argument. Similar to a sponge, an individual or organization can absorb new knowledge and impressions based on the 'absorptive capacity' that is its pre-existing knowledge (Cohen and Levinthal, 1990). For example, an individual who does not know the basics of how a car works will not be able to absorb and assimilate new ideas and knowledge about cars because they cannot link it to a pre-existing knowledge structure. Third, as will be discussed later, using and extending previous knowledge is the crucial pillar on which practices such as generative metaphor or divergent thinking operate (Ward, 2004). However, memory can also prevent new ideas from emerging because previous knowledge becomes so dominant that no one dares to challenge it; this is mainly linked to the values and beliefs of an organization—as seen in the discussion of organizational culture in Chapter 2. This means new ideas which challenge the dominant knowledge tend to be regularly rejected (this will be discussed in more detail in Chapter 4).

Motivation

The creativity researcher Teresa Amabile explored the role of *intrinsic motivation* in organizational creativity for decades. Intrinsic motivation means doing an activity for the sake of doing it because it is enjoyable, while extrinsic motivation drives actions for the sake of an external outcome or reward (Ryan and Deci, 2000). Amabile used the metaphor of finding a way out of a maze to describe the role that motivation plays in generating new ideas and solutions:

> Someone who is extrinsically motivated is motivated primarily by something outside of the maze, the extrinsic goal. Since that goal can only be achieved once the maze has been exited, the best strategy for the extrinsically motivated person is to take the safest, surest and fastest way out of the maze; the well-worn pathway, the uncreative route.
>
> (Amabile, 1988: 144)

In this metaphor, the motivation to engage in generating and developing new ideas is based on the passion and drive to explore aspects that are not demanded or rewarded by the organization. It is about struggling inside the maze for a while and not trying to exit it at all costs via the safest route. However, the relationship between intrinsic and extrinsic motivation and its link to generating and developing ideas is more complex than this image highlights.

One persistent assumption in the literature is a 'hydraulic conception' of extrinsic and intrinsic motivation (Amabile, 1988). Basically, this metaphor highlights how extrinsic motivation forces out intrinsic motivation like liquid in a tube flowing from one side to the other. So, the assumption is that stimulating extrinsic motivation decreases intrinsic motivation and vice versa (Lepper and Greene, 2015). However, in recent years this hydraulic conception of intrinsic and extrinsic motivation has been challenged and given further nuance. Researchers have argued that there is a distinction between controlling people's efforts and giving them informational feedback (both extrinsic motivators). Controlling undermines intrinsic motivation, while information may have no impact—or even a positive impact—on creativity (Amabile, 1997a). To return to the maze metaphor, it may be counterproductive to control whether people get out of the maze in the fastest and safest way possible, but it may help to provide supportive information about whether they are on the right track and leave it up to people to use the information to find a way out.

Moreover, as seen in the discussion of the typology of idea generation and development contexts, a purely controlling environment based on rules may also stimulate creativity. In these environments, individuals may come up with solutions to cope with the tight organizational rules, to be more efficient. Hence, in addition to the difference between intrinsic and extrinsic motivation to generate ideas, there may also be a link between these two types of motivation and the nature of the problem discussed at length in the previous section (see also Unsworth, 2001). Unsworth argued that—based on the distinction between intrinsic and extrinsic motivation and the nature of the problems, open or closed—there may be four types of creativity in organization. First, there is *responsive creativity*, which refers to dealing with closed problems based on external motivation. Examples here are required solutions to defined problems. *Contributory creativity* materializes when there are closed problems and intrinsic motivation. For example, this occurs if someone suggests an idea for a project that they are not part of. *Expected creativity*, on the other hand, links to open problems and extrinsic motivation. Here, ideas emerge in response to required solutions for problems that must still be discovered. Lastly, *proactive creativity* is based on open problems and intrinsic motivation. Here, unprompted ideas may be suggested for discovered problems. Unsworth's conception extends the discussion on extrinsic and intrinsic motivation further by nuancing different forms of creativity in which either form of motivation plays a role. It is an important conception because, similar to the discussion on routines, it challenges the simplified assumption that intrinsic motivation has a positive and extrinsic motivation a negative effect on creativity.

All in all, motivation is crucial for stimulating engagement in generating and developing ideas in organization. The role of motivation is, however, complicated because it depends on the nature of the problem at hand as well as the structure of rewards provided by the organization. But essentially, it appears obvious that the more that people are driven by passion, curiosity, and self-determination, the more they will use their energy to generate and develop new ideas.

Serendipity and Attention

The microbiologist Thomas D. Brock is mostly known for the discovery of one of the key ingredients—a heat-resistant microorganism—in the process of DNA replication. Brock discovered and extracted this microorganism from the hot springs in Yellowstone National Park in the United States. However, before his discovery, Brock was never really interested in visiting the oldest national park in the US, which he thought was more of an amusement park than a nature reserve. However, by chance, he took a detour through the park on his way to the Western US and was intrigued by the colours in the hot springs. He started taking samples, isolated the organism, and started researching into it. What he found changed the science of DNA replication fundamentally, and the work led to the Nobel Prize (Brock, 1995).

This story is one of many in which a discovery was made by chance, leading to a new transformative idea. It shows how generating and developing ideas may hinge on the ability and opportunity to expose oneself to new situations and, at the same time, pay close attention to them, as unexpected experiences may lead individuals to new ideas. Such an occurrence of unanticipated events or experiences that prompts a new idea is referred to as *serendipity*. Serendipity includes three important aspects. First, it is an unexpected experience or observation. Second, it challenges previous understandings, which arouses curiosity. Third, it requires an individual to act on that curiosity (Gabriel et al., 2014). Serendipity is thus not something that merely happens to people as passive recipients, but something that requires individual agency and attention (de Rond, 2014). In the above example, Brock had an unexpected experience (he came to Yellowstone), which aroused his curiosity (the colours in the hot springs), which prompted him to act (take samples and do research on them).

Research has shown that people often do not pay attention to their unexpected and potentially transformative experiences. Instead, they are wired to stick to routines and habitual ways of doing things. This form of 'inattentional blindness' was tested in an interesting experiment (Simons and Chabris, 1999). Participants watched a video of people passing a basketball to each other. The participants were instructed to keep count of the number of passes between the players in the video and write it down after the video finished. The video, however, was altered so that after a while, a woman holding an umbrella or dressed as a gorilla walked across the screen. Absorbed in the task of counting passes, most participants failed to notice the woman with the umbrella or the gorilla. These, and other studies, provide evidence of the confirmation bias, which describes how people tend to cling to their beliefs and expectations and seek confirmatory evidence, even in the face of contradictory evidence (Nickerson, 1998). Inattentional blindness and confirmation bias may prevent individuals and organizations from generating and developing ideas.

Organizations have realized these tendencies and thought about different ways of influencing serendipity. For example, on an individual level, weak ties are an important aspect of accidental and unexpected discoveries. While strong ties mainly provide people with confirmation of what they like, know, and think, weak ties potentially provide new insights, arguments, and issues that challenge previous understandings and may prompt the exploration of divergent ideas (Hargadon and Sutton, 1997). On an organizational level, the capability to exploit potential unexpected and puzzling observations may be reflected in how much *slack* the organization offers. Organizational slack simply means that the organization provides extra resources and time for activities that are not related to producing its usual output so that people have extra resources to pursue explorative activities (Cyert and March, 1963). Common practices include providing extra time for new project ideas or additional resources that are not directly related to the organization's production processes, thereby potentially stimulating serendipitous encounters. However, with today's tendencies towards just-in-time production and the maximization of efficiency, organizational slack is seldom deliberately facilitated. Moreover, it seems that too much slack may have a negative impact on organizational performance and innovation, because a lack of economic constraints may not translate into value-adding projects but rather aimless exploration (Nohria and Gulati, 1996). It is therefore important to find the right amount of slack for creativity.

Imagination

Many of people's thoughts and activities are concerned with the future. Indeed, existentialist and pragmatist philosophers—among others—have argued that human beings' existence is always directed towards the future. The philosopher Martin Heidegger, for example, claimed that to exist as a human being means to be constantly engaged in future-directed activities. For him, a universal aspect of human nature is to 'care' about and for the future (Heidegger, 1927. Pragmatists, such as John Dewey, have equally argued that, for individuals, the primary element in life is anticipation and prospective activities (Dewey, 1981). Similarly, organizations engage in extensive planning and strategic thinking to anticipate and hypothesize how the future may look. Emirbayer and Mische (1998: 984) called this the 'imaginative engagement of the future', which is an important dimension in processes of idea generation and development. In fact, imagination and creativity have been used synonymously, before the notion of creativity became a frequently used term (Weiner, 2012). Hence, it is important to demarcate how imagination and idea generation and development are linked to each other and how imagination is used in organizations.

The notion of imagination or imagining is so broad and slippery that it is not possible to provide an inclusive definition (Walton, 1990). For the purposes of this book, imagination is referred to as a conception of some thing or event that is not immediately present to all of the human senses, but constructed by the mind. For example, I see a dog in front of me that I can smell, pat, hear, and take out on a leash. I engage with it with most of my senses, and it is present to me in this moment, and thus not an imagination. In contrast, I can create an image of a dog in my mind. This image is not something directly perceived by my senses, and it may take any shape that I want. Here, it is possible to refer to 'imaginative mind wandering', which has been discussed previously (Dane, 2018). The content of the imagination differs: from thinking about a nice beach, to the upcoming elections, to simply bizarre ideas. For example, imagining a dog lets me ponder my friend's dog in more detail, or how I would take care of a dog, or simply amend my image of a dog at will, giving it pink fur or six legs. The upshot is that imagination can generate endless possible scenarios, images, and outcomes which are crucial for idea generation and development.

Idea generation and development in organizations usually involves an active and intentional imagining of future possibilities. Imagination, then, concerns how people actively envision how their ideas may change the course of future events or how they may impact, for instance, their work processes or product development. This intentional act of imagination may involve different alternatives or conjuring up mental pictures of a certain outcome. For example, it has become common in organizations to use simulation models and techniques that provide predictions of how a technology or idea would turn out (Dodgson et al., 2006). Imagination in idea generation and development has a similar function— to simulate in one's mind how an idea may turn out in practice and what impact it may have on the organization. It concerns 'the generation of hypotheses about how the world might be: how the future might look and act' (Gartner, 2007: 624). An important activity of individuals and groups is (self-)reflection by stepping back from previous beliefs and practices to ponder questions such as 'what if we …?' or 'what would happen if X is removed/changed/added …?' The significance of such activity lies in its potential to stimulate reflection on alternative scenarios and possibilities for change, that may be missed if we simply continue to do what we do.

Spotlight on Research: Flow—the Effortless Process of Creativity

In 2019, Alex Honnold climbed the famous rock formation El Capitan in Yosemite National Park. What made this rather common event particularly newsworthy was the fact that he had no ropes or other auxiliary means when he did it. A wrong step or misguided grip meant certain death. When a reporter asked him why he climbs, he answered, 'You could say that no person has ever answered this question well. Why not ask a monk why they meditate. Why does anyone have a hobby or passion? It's because I find meaning and fulfilment in it, it's beautiful, and I enjoy it' (Synnott, 2015). It is precisely this notion of passion and strong meaning related to acts of creation which has intrigued the creativity researcher Mihaly Csikszentmihalyi for decades. Based on his extensive studies of creative individuals, he proposed the concept of the 'flow of creativity', which, he argued, underpins all creative processes—from rock climbers to scientists. Csikszentmihalyi (1996: 108) mused that 'chess players, rock climbers, dancers, and composers devoted many hours a week to their avocations. Why were they doing it?' Pursuing this question, he found that it was the experience of their activity that made them so dedicated. The positive feelings attached to their activities were not there when they took drugs or alcohol or simply relaxed. Surprisingly, these activities were often strenuous, painful, and risky. Moreover, they involved new discoveries and ideas. Csikszentmihalyi referred to these experiences as 'flow'. For him, flow depicts a focused, effortless, and rewarding feeling when executing an activity, which often leads to new discoveries.

In his research, Csikszentmihalyi explored the dimensions that enabled a creative flow experience. He found that there must be clear goals so that the individual knows what they must do next. There should also be immediate feedback to their actions. Moreover, a person's actions should match their skills, which means that they do not experience something as flowing when it is either too difficult or too boring. In addition, there must be true involvement in the task at hand, which means no distracting thoughts that draw attention away from that task. Therefore, people do not start worrying about failure when they are in the flow, but simply do what they do, which also means that their self-awareness disappears and that they are not consciously aware of how they appear to others. An individual's sense of time becomes distorted as they experience time flying by, and the task becomes an end in itself rather than a means to an end. These characteristics of flow make it a unique experience that enables creative actions to unfold.

Using Csikszentmihalyi's findings, it is not difficult to see how Alex Honnold experienced his free climb as a flow experience. He had clear goals of what to do based on his year-long sketching and planning of the route up the rock. Each step also gave immediate feedback to his activity—in the worst-case scenario, a false step meant a fatal plummet. Hence, he had no choice but to concentrate fully on the task at hand, as it was a matter of life and death. Distractions or daydreaming had no place in his endeavour, and the stakes certainly did not make it a boring task. He was also intensely concentrated on his task. On his way up, he encountered a few people—a group was dangling in a tent from the wall. One spectator there was wearing a unicorn costume—something that was certainly eye-catching. However, Honnold failed to notice this costume, as he was so concentrated on what he was doing. Honnold was also not overly concerned with how he appeared to others while he climbed the wall, nor did he do it as a means to achieve reputation or fame. Finally, when asked why he climbs, he answered, 'I like the movement, I like swinging, it all feels kinda playful and fun' (Wollastan, 2019). His experience alludes to the joyful experience of flow linked to the ability to fully concentrate and act in the present. It illustrates how in flow experience past, present, and future exist simultaneously.

According to Csikszentmihalyi, flow experiences are crucial to sustaining creativity and keeping transformative ideas flowing. They certainly appear to be valid for many activities, such as Honnold's rock climbing experience. Flow also contains many of the aspects discussed with regard to past, present, and future, such as the necessity of knowledge and memory, the deep engagement and attention to the present moment, and future planning based on goals.

Interactions and Objects

In 1968, Spencer Silver, a senior chemist, joined 3M to develop strong adhesives for the aerospace industry. In one experiment, he discovered that his mixture stuck to a surface while remaining easy to peel off. He was astonished by this discovery, but it did not have any aeronautical applications, as he needed stronger adhesives. Silver had an intuition that this discovery had potential, but he was unsure how to realize it. He started using 3M's technical forums to spread his discovery and hoped that it would spark further ideas from others. One of the people who attended Silver's seminars was Arthur Fry, a chemical engineer working at a department that developed Scotch tape. In his free time, Fry liked to sing in a choir. One of the problems that he struggled with was that the bookmarks in his notes kept falling out. While he was at choir practice, Fry remembered Silver's presentation and pondered whether the adhesive that he had invented could be used to make the bookmark stick. Fry tinkered with Silver's mixture and produced an adhesive that kept the bookmark firmly in place while remaining easy to remove. Fry, satisfied with his solution, left it at that for a while. However, one day he was writing a report to his manager, and he ripped part of the bookmark off and stuck it on the front of the report with a question scribbled on it. The manager took the paper, wrote an answer, and stuck it back on the paper. At this point, Fry experienced what he described as a 'Eureka moment'—the birth of the Post-it note. The development of the Post-it note illustrates *the role of relationships and interactions* in the generation and development of ideas. Silver communicated and shared his findings in the forum of 3M, but others did not know what to make of them. Fry picked up on Silver's idea and used it at his choir practice and eventually also in correspondence with his manager. Generating and developing the idea for the Post-it involved continuous relationships and interactions with others.

A central issue regarding the characteristics of these relationships in the idea generation and development process is whether relationships serve to work on and develop distinct ideas or whether ideas emerge in the process of relating to others. Regarding these two sets of characteristics, the story of the Post-it leaves room for two interpretations. First, Silver passed on his discovery of the adhesive as a distinct, identifiable concept to Fry, who snatched it up, developed it further—first in the choir practice, and then in the interaction with his manager. Second, Silver may have had only a vague notion of his initial discovery of the adhesive, and during his interactions in the forum he may have received more input regarding his initial idea, which led to a joint development of his inchoate idea. In later interactions, Silver and Fry may have had further discussions about changes to the mixture and possible uses of the adhesive, which may have transformed but also sharpened the idea. The final touch may have come through the episode involving his manager, in which they discussed how they could develop the adhesive bookmark further. These two possible interpretations of how relationships shaped the idea of the Post-it link to what Hua et al. (2022) called a 'particle' and a 'wave' conception of ideas. These metaphors draw on the famous wave–*particle* duality discussion in quantum physics. In brief, wave–particle duality states that physical entities can simultaneously be waves and particles, which are considered two mutually exclusive states of being (Davis, 2012).

A particle is a concrete, finite object that can be located in time and space. Applying the particle analogy to the conception of ideas, they can also be understood as 'identifiable, discrete entities' (Hua et al., 2022: 22), such as concrete concepts, models, or patent proposals. Related to the role of interactions in generating and developing processes, conceiving ideas as particles means that individuals can transfer distinct ideas from them to others. Moreover, creatorship of ideas or input to ideas is determinable, as people can identify the individuals who shared the idea.

In contrast to a particle, it is not possible to localize a wave concretely. Waves spread out over an area and may move through or interfere with each other, yet they also disappear into each other. As such, the wave metaphor highlights ideas as processual—that is, emergent and moving rather than having a concrete, identifiable location and status. Here, creatorship of ideas is collective because it is assumed that the generation and development of ideas is always inherently collective and relational, and not focused on a few exceptional, concretely identifiable ideas and individuals (Hargadon and Bechky, 2006; Håkonsen Coldevin et al., 2019). In brief, ideas do not exist as independent entities, but emerge in the ideation process in specific contexts and interactions.

Notably, the wave–particle duality conception harks back to the discussion of the process approach in Chapter 2. Indeed, Hatch (2011) applied the metaphor of wave–particle duality to describe organizations as either a noun (organization) or an activity (organizing). This is mirrored in the discussion of different models in Chapter 2. Generally, the particle perspective informs interactionist models, while a wave perspective adheres to a process perspective. For the discussion here, it is important to bear in mind that interactions in idea generation and development processes involve both conceptions at the same time: concretely identifiable as well as emerging ideas. For example, ideas may be concrete in the form of patent applications or other formalized idea descriptions but those concrete ideas may also over time become emergent as they are discussed, changed, and reformulated in interactions with others. As Hua et al. (2022) argued, the particle and wave conceptions of ideas, though based on mutually exclusive ontologies and research traditions, complement each other; they are both needed for a holistic understanding of idea generation and development processes, as will be seen in Chapter 4 for evaluation processes.

With regard to the wave–particle duality, objects play an essential role. Objects can be concrete, physical things, but also representations, such as concepts or PowerPoint slides. As such, they seem to be related to the particle perspective. Yet, other scholars have argued that objects are not merely passive entities in organizational processes, but afford various interpretations which make their use indeterminate (Prasad, 1993). In other words, what an object means to someone and how the person will use it is not predetermined but based on their interpretative discretion. This perspective relates to a wave perspective on ideas. To further discuss the dual role that objects may play in idea generation and development processes, it is helpful to distinguish three types of objects: boundary, epistemic, and technical (Ewenstein and Whyte, 2009; Nicolini et al., 2012).

A *boundary object* is an object that sits at the intersection of multiple disciplines or areas of expertise and provides a shared object that everyone involved can relate to. A boundary object therefore helps diverse groups communicate effectively with each other around a shared interest. For example, a sketch of a new skyscraper is something that involves many parties because, based on this sketch, they may discuss different interests and ideas. Architects may have interests in design, while the city's traffic department may be concerned about the increase in traffic and parking, while the fire department may be concerned about safety. The sketch of the skyscraper thus facilitates the discussion between parties and provides a common object based on which the groups may generate and develop common ideas. For that reason, boundary objects tend to be stable and concrete to enable a productive interaction between diverse groups. An *epistemic object* is an object that is unfinished and lacks concreteness. An epistemic object is in flux and constantly evolving, thereby stimulating curiosity to generate knowledge. As such, it represents all of the things that people do not yet know about it and its consequences. For example, COVID-19 was originally an epistemic object that lacked concreteness and prompted efforts to explore it while knowledge about it was constantly changing. Lastly, a *technical object* is unproblematic and fixed. They are mainly tools like a computer or a manufacturing machine that people use in their practices and that needs no further development.

It is the particle–wave dynamic between these three types of objects that provides insight into their crucial role in processes of idea generation and development. Epistemic objects—as unfinished, emergent objects—drive relational idea generation and development processes, while boundary objects serve as temporary concrete objects that facilitate collaborative idea exchange and development between diverse parties. Fixed technical objects support these idea generation and development processes as tools in the process, e.g. computer programs or materials for prototyping. Scarbrough et al. (2015) provided empirical insights into these dynamic processes through an analysis of the role of objects in video game development. They highlighted the dynamic between epistemic and boundary objects and how it served the idea generation and development process. Illustrative in this context is the role of the concept book in video game development. The concept book is a document that contains the key features of the game, including a storyline, biographies of characters, budget, technologies, and so on. Their study showed that the concept book had an epistemic object status in the beginning of the project, which facilitated the relational emergence of ideas. During the project, the concept book turned into a more concrete boundary object that was used for collaboration and the sharing of knowledge between parties. Ideas were generated and linked to the concrete content of the concept book. Hence, the study illustrates how interactions in idea generation and development processes may shift between open-ended, emergent relationships involving epistemic objects and concretely structured interactions involving concretely defined boundary objects.

In sum this section has discussed important dimensions of idea generation and development regarding time and the dynamic process of relational and transactional processes in the generation and development of ideas. The discussion included a conception of agency that comprises the simultaneous influence of past, present, and future, and a closer look at how past, present, and future shape idea generation and development processes in terms of memory, motivation, attention, and imagination. The roles of others and objects were also discussed, linked to the metaphor of the particle and the wave. Wave–particle duality will resurface in the discussion of transactional and transformational evaluation practices in Chapter 4. For now, the discussion turns to more specific practices of generating and developing ideas.

Cognition and Interaction

Creativity techniques have been a popular topic which developed in parallel to the increased research efforts on creativity, as seen in the short historical overview in Chapter 1. Indeed, books containing advice on how to be more creative and generate creative ideas abound. Among the array of well-intended practical advice, some idea generation and development practices have been studied more systematically by researchers, and a selection of these will be discussed in this section. To structure the discussion, *cognitive* and *interactive* approaches are distinguished from one another. Cognitive approaches focus on individual mental processes, while interactive approaches consider relational aspects of idea generation and development by emphasizing group, but also social and cultural, contexts. The main distinction between these two approaches is that the former focuses primarily on the individual while the latter considers the collective nature of idea generation and development processes.

Cognitive Practices

Cognitive perspectives on idea generation are concerned with individuals' mental processes that facilitate the generation and development of ideas. As a matter of fact, most research on creativity has focused on cognition, which is mainly due to its roots in psychology. An added factor is that experiments or other controlled research environments are most suited to studying cognitive processes, and those research designs are generally easier to carry out than qualitative studies involving *in situ* observations or face-to-face interviews (Runco, 2014). There are numerous theories on cognition and creativity, but it is beyond the scope of this book to discuss them all. Instead, the following discussion focuses on two influential concepts involving cognition: *divergent thinking* and *generative metaphors*.

Imagine managing a department that carries out basic research for a large organization. The entire organization is struggling financially, and management is concerned and demands to cut costs. Pondering possibilities to tackle this issue, some managers conduct a thorough analysis of the department's finances. They identify the biggest cost factors and ways of lowering costs by letting people go, cutting travel expenses, restricting trips to conferences, and discarding travel allowances. This method of solving the financial problems is based on *convergent thinking*. Convergence means meeting in one point or coming together in one place. Hence, the metaphor of convergent thinking describes how individuals produce a single solution to a problem by applying conventional knowledge. Convergent thinking emphasizes a logical and analytical strategy. In the above case, the problem is solved by converging on the most rational and logical solution: cutting costs and becoming more profitable.

However, managers may also consider other options. They could think about raising money from an external source, such as funding for university–business partnerships. They may also consider contacting people from other departments and asking them to share common resources. They may arrange for people in different departments to commute together or provide bikes to cycle to work. They may even think about asking friends if they are able to build some of the equipment that is used more cheaply. Overall, in contrast to convergent thinking, this way of tackling the problem is referred to as *divergent thinking*. Divergent thinking means not focusing on solving problems by arriving at a single solution, but by producing unexpected ideas that may even be absurd or provocative. People generate a variety of ideas and ponder possibilities that open up problems rather than converging on a single solution.

Divergent thinking is about moving away from tried and tested solutions to consider alternatives. In the case of the cost cutting example, that means that rather than focusing on the most logical solutions, managers may generate ideas about how other means are available, such as raising money from research agencies, seeking substitutes for equipment, and finding cheaper travel options. Multiple tests and techniques of divergent thinking exist. Tests are used to define an individual's level of divergent thinking, while techniques of divergent thinking stimulate individuals to come up with unexpected solutions when performing a task or interacting in a group setting, such as a brainstorm. One technique, for example, is to think about alternative uses for common objects, such as a table or chair. Table 3.1 compares convergent and divergent thinking based on Cropley (2006), who has explored the two modes in more depth.

Generally, researchers have linked convergent thinking to producing uncreative ideas that do not contain transformative potential. However, in most cases, convergent and divergent thinking are complementary and continuous. That means that, in reality, people may generate divergent ideas but then tend to converge on the most appropriate one (Cropley, 2006). That means divergent thinking tends to be followed by convergent thinking to eventually find a solution to a problem. Convergent and divergent thinking processes are, thus, complementary rather than clearly separated from each other (Eysenck, 2003).

Another practice to generate and develop ideas is the use of *generative metaphors* or *analogies*. Think about a paintbrush. How do people use a brush to apply paint, and how could the process be improved? This is a question that a group of researchers pondered when they tried to develop a new paintbrush with synthetic bristles. However, they were not very successful until one of the researchers remarked that a paintbrush could be seen as a pump. At first, that was an odd metaphor for understanding paintbrushes, as a pump is considered a tool that moves liquid from one place to another. However, the researcher had observed that painters sometimes vibrate the brush to facilitate their painting. Hence, there seems to be a space between the bristles that acts like a channel through which the paint flows. Rather than designing synthetic brushes where paint would adhere to the surface of the bristles, the researcher set out to design paintbrushes that enabled the paint to flow through the channels formed by the bristles (Schön, 1979). Schön's example of the paintbrush exemplifies how metaphors can become generative in producing and developing new ideas, by relating a base domain (paintbrush) to a target domain (pumps). Used in this way, metaphors simplify the problem and enable people to grasp complex issues that may generate new ideas.

Generative metaphors are one aspect of what researchers have called *analogical reasoning*, which involves base and target domains that both comprise different objects and relationships. How objects and relationships from the two domains are linked in analogical reasoning is crucial. There are three possible links between objects and relationships in base and target domains (Gentner, 1983). First, there is the possibility of *similarity*, which means that many objects and relationships are shared—for instance, painting is

Table 3.1 Convergent and divergent thinking

	Convergent thinking	Divergent thinking
Risk	Playing it safe	Taking risks
Reasoning	Logical conclusions	Unconventional ideas
Outcomes	Producing the single best answer	Suggesting various alternatives
Perspective	Applying known perspectives	Shifting perspectives
Answers	Conventional answers	Surprising answers

like stroking. Second, there is *analogy*, which entails many relationships being shared between the domains but not objects—for instance, a paintbrush and the pump do not share any technical features, but they both channel liquids. Lastly, there is *anomaly*, where few relationships and objects are shared—for instance, painting is like drinking coffee.

To generate productive ideas, it is necessary to seek analogies rather than similarities or anomalies. Hence, the two domains must be sufficiently remote to create new insights, but not so remote as to become nonsensical or so close as to become common sense. If people are unable to establish any connection between base and target domain, they will be unable to generate and develop productive ideas. An example is bionics, which is a field of research that aims to generate productive analogies between biological principles and engineering (Dickinson, 1999). Velcro is one of the early successful ideas linked to bionics. The story goes that its inventor, George de Mestral, was taking a walk with his dog when he observed how cockleburs stuck to his dog's fur and his own clothing. Fascinated by the ability of a cocklebur to hook onto soft surfaces, he explored how the tiny hooks engaged with the softer material, which eventually led to the development of the Velcro patent and the proliferation of hook-and-loop fasteners.

Overall, cognitive approaches highlight the role of mental processes that underlie the generation and development of new ideas. Creative cognitive practices focus on challenging tried and tested solutions by generating ideas that seem far-fetched at first but may provide a potentially transformative idea. The general intention is to broaden one's perspective (diverge) rather than closing it down (converge), or to find new ways of understanding a problem or a process by relating it to another, remotely related, domain.

Spotlight on Practice: *Hövding*—an Invisible Helmet

Many urban cyclists have always regarded the bicycle helmet as a rather clumsy and unfashionable necessity. Two master's students at the University of Lund in Sweden, Anna Haupt and Terese Alstin, were among those who dreaded having to wear a regular bicycle helmet. This prospect prompted them to explore the possibilities of a different kind of helmet. After some deliberation, they came up with the idea of an invisible helmet. An invisible helmet, however, is not associated with protection, and many called the idea impossible—not least due to the strict safety regulations that it must fulfil.

But the two students were not deterred by the seemingly crazy idea and started working on it. For their master's thesis project, they suggested a design for a helmet that worked like an airbag (Rothstein, 2015). They called this the *Hövding* (chieftain in English). The *Hövding* is a collar in which an airbag is concealed. Motion sensors pick up characteristic signals that point to an accident and release an airbag that protects the head from injury. The only visible item, therefore, is the collar around the neck—the helmet as such is invisible.

The idea of the invisible helmet gained immediate attention, and the duo received various prizes and grant money to develop it further. They persisted, and seven years later they finally launched a finished product. Since then, the company has steadily grown, selling the *Hövding* worldwide. They continuously improve the product while working with the tag line that they 'thrive on the impossible'.

The story of the *Hövding* illustrates some of the cognitive practices discussed in this section. For example, it shows how the duo engaged in divergent thinking. Rather than generating ideas of how to change existing helmets, perhaps making them more fashionable, they asked themselves why they could not take the helmet away completely. Moreover, they used analogical reasoning by relating the idea of a physical helmet to the technology and process of an airbag which is released during impact. By productively combining these two concepts, they generated and developed a transformative creative idea.

Interactive Practices

While cognitive practices of idea generation are primarily focused on the individual, other practices include an explicitly interactive aspect. In most cases, this means that either other individuals are involved or the specific situation of the idea generation and development practice is taken into account. The most well-known interactive approach that focuses on interaction with others is *brainstorming*. A more comprehensive interactive approach is *effectuation*, which—apart from interactions with others—includes the consideration of a set of contextual influences when generating and developing ideas.

In 1942, a little book was published that would influence how entire organizations approach their idea generation processes. The book was called *How to Think Up*, and it was written by Alex Osborn, a co-founder of the advertising agency BBDO (Osborn, 1942). The method that Osborn proposed was 'brainstorming'. In the decades that followed, Osborn developed his ideas further and claimed that brainstorming in groups could produce double the ideas compared to an individual (Osborn, 1953). Osborn's practice of brainstorming was based on a few simple rules: produce as many ideas—however wild—as possible, do not criticize each other, and combine and develop suggested ideas.

Different versions of brainstorming have become very popular over the years. Yet, experimental research on the effectiveness of brainstorming has challenged Osborn's promise of producing more and better ideas in group brainstorming sessions. Researchers have compared individual and group brainstorming sessions and concluded that productivity actually decreases when people brainstorm in groups instead of individually. One of the reasons mentioned is *evaluation apprehension*, which refers to the fear of being negatively evaluated by other group members. Another potential reason is *blockage*, which occurs because of the rule that only one person should speak at a time, which prevents some people from articulating their ideas. A third reason is *free riding*, whereby group members rely on others to generate ideas (Diehl and Stroebe, 1987).

Other research has questioned the single focus on the effectiveness of brainstorming and productivity. Sutton and Hargadon (1996) argued that the assessment of brainstorming focused too much on productivity and effectiveness of brainstorming outcomes and, in many cases, just the sheer quantity of ideas produced. Based on their ethnographic study of brainstorming sessions at the design company IDEO, they showed that this single focus on productivity and effectiveness prevents a view on other important functions of brainstorming in organizations. They argued that it is important to consider the organizational context of practising brainstorming. Based on their findings, they illustrated that if organizations have regular brainstorming sessions, this produces positive social effects with regard to learning, values, and image. Regular brainstorming sessions also support organizational memory and individual learning, because in those sessions participants may remember previous solutions but also become acquainted with new products and ideas. In the study, regular brainstorming sessions were seen to reinforce organizational cultural values, such as humbleness and wisdom, and they were occasions for gaining reputation and status as a knowledgeable designer and impressing clients—not only with designs, but also by showcasing the creative atmosphere of brainstorming sessions.

Therefore, group brainstorming may not have the unequivocal benefits that Osborn claimed regarding its productivity, but it appears to be a multidimensional practice that can have many positive effects on idea generation and development processes by facilitating a conducive organizational context. To develop brainstorming practices further, suggestions have been made to overcome some of the limitations of traditional brainstorming techniques, such as including a facilitator to ensure fair processes, limit the amount of ideas, and increase cognitive diversity (Paulus, 2000).

Spotlight on Research: 'Creativity in Practice'

Andrew Hargadon and Beth Bechky were interested in how groups, during their regular work days, come up with ideas. To study these processes, they explored real-time practices of creative groups at the design company IDEO (Hargadon and Bechky, 2006). One of their findings was that idea generation and development happens between people in specific 'moments', which are characterized by four basic and interrelated practices: *help-seeking, help-giving, reflective reframing,* and *reinforcing.* First, individuals must seek help to develop their ideas. This may sound trivial, but in many organizations the willingness to seek help may be seen as a sign of weakness or lack of knowledge. Second, others must be willing to provide help and become involved in the idea generation and development process. Help-giving aims at tapping into the knowledge that other people have and that may complement initial ideas, and requires the willingness to share knowledge with others and be open to requests for help. During their interaction, individuals commonly reframe the initial idea and further develop it. Thus, reflective reframing means that everyone involved in the interaction pays close attention to the other person's ideas and hunches to provide additional input that enriches and reworks the idea. Thus, in contrast to just answering questions, reflective reframing requires an active effort to engage with others. Crucial in reflective reframing is the dialogue between individuals in which ideas are connected to existing products, other ideas, visions, and previous experiences. Lastly, help-giving, help-seeking, and reflective reframing processes must be reinforced by a culture that values these practices and reinforces them.

Consider the difference between doing a jigsaw puzzle and making a patchwork quilt. In the first case, a person assembles the pieces that fit together to create an image. Now, consider the making of a patchwork quilt. A patchwork quilt comprises different patches sewn together, which the maker can choose to their liking. However, the quilt must also fulfil a function: either keeping people warm, or appealing to their aesthetic sense. These two metaphors represent the differences between two theoretical perspectives of generating and developing new ventures: a causal process and an effectual process. Though these theoretical perspectives were both developed to theorize entrepreneurial practices, they also highlight important things about practices of idea generation and development in organizations.

The metaphor of a jigsaw puzzle describes a causal view of the entrepreneurial process: people clearly define goals, select a target market, and then develop strategies to achieve their set goals. Like in a jigsaw puzzle, the opportunity already exists, and the entrepreneur just needs to put together the pieces in the right way. Causal models of generating and developing ideas are based on achieving preselected goals (the final image of the jigsaw puzzle) and highlight problems of decision-making and achieving those goals. However, causal explanations of coming up with and developing an idea for a new venture do not appear to reflect actual practices of how individuals generate and develop ideas. The entrepreneurship researcher Saras Sarasvathy illustrated how, in practice, the entrepreneurial process seems to be an inversion of causal principles (Sarasvathy, 2009). She referred to this process as *effectuation*, which starts with given means and how these means may help people create certain ends. Individuals first take stock of what they know and who they know. They then reflect on what they can do and connect with others to secure commitment and input to their idea. These activities lead to new goals and new means. Like a patchwork quilt, individuals piece together the patches that they have at their disposal to create their quilt.

Based on her extensive empirical work, Sarasvathy boiled effectuation practices down to five principles. First, there is the *bird-in-hand principle*, which refers to how people use their existing means to create a new idea. Second, the *affordable loss principle* means that people commit to what they will lose rather than what they will gain. Third, people may follow the *crazy quilt principle* by taking all people who are willing to contribute somehow. Fourth, people leverage surprises for something productive by using the *lemonade principle*, which refers to the common proverb 'if life gives you lemons, make lemonade'. Lastly, the *pilot in the plane principle* suggests that people trust in their ability to complete actions rather than passively exploiting opportunities.

As is the case with most theories, in empirical reality, effectuation and causation are both part of the idea generating and developing process. In some situations people set clearly defined goals and seek ideas that help them reach that goal, while in other contexts they 'effect' their ends by taking stock of the means they have at their disposal. All in all, the principles of effectuation help people understand practices of the idea generating and development process by looking at it as a dynamic and interactive process that is characterized by various contingencies—that is, how different elements of the situation and the individuals interact to facilitate practices of generating and developing ideas.

In sum, interactive practices of idea generation and development highlight the essential input of material, social, and cultural influences on the process of idea generation and development. In the case of brainstorming, it seems that, apart from the generation of ideas, it fulfils an important role in maintaining a conducive and creative organizational culture. Effectuation, on the other hand, explicitly considers the social and material context when generating and developing ideas through a focus on how the individual draws on the immediately available resources from their environment.

Many studies have either confirmed or challenged common assumptions about practices such as divergent thinking or brainstorming. This was evident in the findings on how brainstorming works and how effective it is. As seen in the group brainstorming example, practices that may make sense and have become popular may not be as effective as previously thought. However, group brainstorming may fulfil important social and cultural functions in organizations. Another example is 'lateral thinking'—discussed in the Spotlight on Practice on Edward de Bono—which seems to be a practice that works for many organizations, though it has not been researched systematically. This begs the question of how to assess good practices of generating and developing ideas. As will be seen in the conclusion to this chapter, one way is to assess these practices with regard to the important influence of context and process.

Spotlight on Practice: Edward de Bono

Edward de Bono is one of the pioneers of applied creative thinking, and his consultancy services have been in demand all over the world. He is most famous for his concept of 'lateral thinking' and his brainstorming practices of the six thinking hats. De Bono (2014) used the metaphor of digging holes to describe lateral thinking. Lateral thinking, according to him, is not digging holes deeper, but digging different holes. In other words, people should not think within the existing frames, but try different perspectives. For de Bono, lateral thinking and new ideas depend on changing perceptions. People are too strongly trained in logical and vertical thinking, which means that they look for and apply single solutions to problems and that they rarely consider challenging those solutions or finding ideas that do not fit their preconceived notions.

De Bono related this back to Western society's philosophical heritage and what he calls the 'gang of three': Socrates, Plato, and Aristotle. These three philosophers, according to de Bono, established ways of thinking by using logic (Aristotle) to argue (Socrates) and get to the truth (Plato). This influence has led to an ingrained way of thinking that neglects thinking differently and in parallel. Importantly, thinking differently is not an innate talent that some people possess; for de Bono, everyone can be creative if they just practise the right methods and remain open to different possibilities and eager to explore alternative paths.

While his lateral thinking has become a fixed term in the discourse on creativity, his meeting practice of the six thinking hats has enjoyed equal success. Faithful to his change of perspective philosophy, this exercise instructs groups to put on different coloured hats which symbolize different perspectives, such as green for new ideas, yellow for positive thinking, white for information, and so on. In this exercise, members are then instructed to assume the perspectives that their hat is suggesting in their brainstorming session. For example, say a green hat means a sustainability perspective, then the member with a green hat needs to always assume a sustainability perspective in the generation and development of each proposed idea.

De Bono's ideas have had tremendous commercial success, as they greatly appeal to organizations. However, some scholars have remarked that his concepts and methods have never been systematically studied, and the predominantly positive assessment of their effectiveness is mainly based on anecdotal evidence of his work with organizations (Runco, 2014).

Conclusion

This chapter has discussed the context, process, and practice of generating and developing ideas. To make sense of how contexts may influence idea generation and development processes, the chapter highlighted two analytical dimensions: the strength of a situation, and the nature of the problem. Strength of situation refers to the level of clarity and guidance that a situation provides, while the nature of the problem can either be closed, because problems and solutions are known, or open, which means that either no predefined solutions exist or the problem may not be known. The strength of the situation combined with the nature of the problem renders a typology of distinct organizational contexts for idea generation and development: routine, loose coupling, weak ties, and organized anarchy, all of which link to an influential concept in organizational theory.

Routine contexts are characterized by closed problems and strong situations, which seems at first glance not to be conducive to new ideas. Nevertheless, research has suggested that routines may be performative, which means that they change from one iteration to the next, providing the seed for transformative ideas. Loose coupling combines strong situation with open problems. Regarding loose coupling, this chapter discussed the concept of mind wandering, which describes contexts where someone's main activity is only loosely coupled to their ruminations about unrelated issues. Weak ties' contexts, in contrast, combine closed problems with weak situations. Weak ties expose people to diverse networks and thus stimulate new ideas that may be needed to tackle a closed problem. Lastly, organized anarchy combines weak situations and open problems. In these contexts, there is a high degree of ambiguity concerning problems, solutions, and participants, and ideas may be generated without a defined problem and in the absence of clear rules and regulations.

The discussion then shifted its focus to temporality and relationships as key aspects of understanding the idea generation and development process. To set the scene, it was argued that rather than drawing on linear notions of time, people should understand past, present, and future as simultaneously present in their idea generation and development activities. Past, present, and future were linked to respective process aspects, such as memory and knowledge, motivation, and attention and imagination. The discussion shifted then to the role of relationships and interactions. Regarding the nature of ideas, two different conceptions that influence how people make sense of relationships and interactions when organizing creativity were discussed. A particle perspective argues that ideas can be exchanged between people, while a wave perspective postulates that idea generation and development processes are inherently processual. Drawing on the wave–particle duality as an analogy to idea generation and development processes, it appears that they are two sides of the same coin. In other words, for a holistic understanding of the idea generation and development process, it is necessary to consider that both perspectives are simultaneously relevant to a general understanding.

Lastly, the dynamic role of objects influencing the idea generation and development process was discussed. Most importantly, a distinction was drawn between boundary objects that bring diverse groups together around a common object, open-ended epistemic objects that prompt curiosity in knowledge development, and closed technical objects that support processes. In particular, the shifting emphasis on epistemic and boundary objects in idea generation and development processes was of interest here. Boundary objects serve as concretized objects that facilitate collaboration among groups, while epistemic objects may drive more open-ended relational idea generation and development processes.

The final part of the chapter discussed idea generation and development practices. Overall, there is an abundance of practical advice, though the focus was on two of the most systematically researched types of practices: cognitive practices that focus on the mental processes of individuals, and interactive processes that consider the influence of other individuals and context. Two cognitive practices, divergent thinking and analogies, were elaborated in more depth. The former seeks to generate a wide array of non-conventional ideas, while the latter seeks to find productive analogies between different domains. With regard to interactive practices, brainstorming and effectuation were discussed. The former has been one of the most popular approaches to organizing creativity—to the point that it is almost synonymous with creativity. Yet, researchers have shown that people should not only focus on the productivity of brainstorming sessions, but consider the negative effects of group dynamics and the implications for the broader context. Lastly, effectuation, a popular concept in entrepreneurship studies, was discussed. Effectuation challenges the causal model of idea generation and development practices by illustrating how people do not generate and develop ideas by first analysing the situation, setting goals, and then aiming to reach them, but by engaging in a much messier process in which they make do with the means at their disposal. With regard to the idea generation and development process, effectuation demonstrates that ideas are not generated with regard to preconceived goals, but may emerge based on the possibilities and resources at hand.

As broached in the conclusion to the last section, it is common to focus squarely on practices of idea generation and development. In the end, this appears to be the most important aspect. People should do what seems to work for them and others. Yet, to evaluate the feasibility and benefits of their practices, people must consider the triangular relationship between context, process, and practice. This means that people should not isolate single practices, but aim to understand their link to contextual and processual dimensions. People should view idea generation and development like a flow rather than a sequence of steps to be followed. In the flow of time, different contexts, process dimensions, and practices of generating and developing ideas interweave dynamically to produce various configurations (see also chapter 7 for a deeper discussion). For example, anarchic organizational structures, intrinsically motivated staff, and frequent periods of slack that allow for serendipitous encounters may favour more divergent thinking practices rather than, say, a combination of strict routines, external rewards, and no slack at all. Or, consider a context of weak ties and structured organizational memory but no slack. This may facilitate more effectual practices because people must use the resources at their disposal and draw on a wide network and knowledge resources.

Admittedly, this is a simplification of a complex reality. Generally, it is hard to predict and control the generation and development of ideas. Yet the interplay of context, process, and practice provides a much more nuanced understanding and, as such, a point of departure for possible actions. In the end, knowing where one is makes knowing where one wants to go easier. In the following chapter, this book turns its attention to the evaluation of ideas, which will add more layers to a nuanced understanding of what dimensions organizing creativity entails.

4

Evaluating Ideas

In 2018, two design students at the University of Arts, Craft and Design in Stockholm worked on an assignment for their course. Their task was to design something 'Scandinavian'. The project was carried out in cooperation with a well-known chain of design stores in Sweden. The students, who were exploring different options, shared a deep connection with and love for the forest. They believed in its ability to relieve stress. Fresh wood releases phytoncide, which the two designers believed had positive health effects and may even assist in curing cancer. Then, the two of them had a striking idea. Why not design something that would connect individuals to the forest? In particular, they thought of designing something that brings the positive health effects of phytoncides to peoples' homes. They proposed a simple idea: a fresh piece of wood that would be placed in the middle of a room. Over months, it would release its phytoncides and contribute to reduced stress levels at home. This idea was snatched up by the design store chain, and they started selling blocks of wood in their store for 199 Swedish krona (SEK). The product was called 'Skog' (Forest).

A short time after it was offered in the stores, a debate ensued. People commented on how a piece of wood could be sold for so much money. Some suggested going out in the forest instead of wasting money. Others offered their own pieces of wood for less money. Debates were mainly initiated on social media, but they were also picked up by national newspapers. Confronted with this discussion, the design store felt obliged to answer. On its homepage, it offered a further explanation of the product. They argued for the health effects of Skog. Furthermore, they claimed that wood has more value than just timber. In fact, the debates surrounding Skog were expected and intended by the students. One of them aimed to initiate reflections on what the forest means by bringing physical evidence of it to people's homes. Yet the debate around taking money for what many believed to be just a simple piece of wood eventually led to the product being withdrawn from sale.

The events that occurred around Skog illustrate many of the aspects that will be discussed in this chapter, which focuses on the what and how of evaluating ideas. Returning to Skog, it is obvious that there were different forms of value connected to it. First, there was monetary value, as the company and the people who bought Skog valued the idea by paying SEK 199. Second, there was a health value attached to it in the form of stress-relieving substances. Third, Skog was valued as an object that would ornament the home. Fourth, it was designed with sustainability aspects in mind, intending to inspire debate and reflections on the effects and functions of the forest. Hence, a piece of wood contained many contested values at once.

The case raises important questions. What values do people attach to something or someone? Are there values that people commonly invoke when evaluating ideas in organizations? If so, what are these values? How do people agree when their idea evaluations differ? What do they do when they evaluate someone else's ideas? This chapter addresses these questions by first discussing the concept of orders of worth as a reference for

Organizing Creativity. Stephan M. Schaefer, Oxford University Press. © Stephan M. Schaefer (2023).
DOI: 10.1093/oso/9780198893509.003.0004

evaluating ideas, which will be followed by proposing a process model of evaluation and insights into evaluation practices.

Worthy Ideas

Take an object that is used daily and its values—for example, the train to work. People may value that they do not have to get stuck in a traffic jam in their car or the efficiency and speed of this mode of transport. Or they may appreciate that it contributes to decreasing air pollution and may even like the companionship on the train. The context of commuting to work is full of such value judgements which influence people's actions. It also suggests that value is not only expressed in monetary or economic terms, commonly understood as price*quantity; there are apparently multiple values in play. What are these multiple values, and is it possible to extract some general, overarching values that seem to be more frequently used when evaluating ideas in organizational contexts? This is the question that guides this section, which will discuss the work of two French sociologists—Luc Boltanski and Laurent Thévenot—who have been intrigued by the question of how people challenge, discuss, and compromise, as well as what values they evoke when doing so. Agreements, they argue, are based on seven different sets of values that they refer to as *orders of worth*. This chapter section examines their work, the seven orders, and how they affect idea evaluation in organizations.

Orders of Worth

One important concept that will reappear throughout this part of the book is the influence of implicit theories. Implicit theories impact how people evaluate their and other people's ideas. Theories are abstracted statements with the aim of understanding or explaining relationships between different variables. Theories can be classified according to the degree to which people are aware of them. Based on their awareness, people can talk about explicit and implicit theories. Explicit theories are theories that people are conscious of and articulate by reflecting, talking, or writing about them. For example, if I argue that creative behaviour is based on high degrees of freedom, I articulate explicit theoretical statements about creative behaviour. Implicit theories, in contrast, are theoretical assumptions that people are not consciously aware of. They determine what people do and think without consciously reflecting on it.

The organizational learning researchers Chris Argyris and Donald Schön referred to these implicit theories as 'theories-in-use' that people draw on but seldom make explicit (Argyris and Schön, 1978). Individuals usually only become aware of their implicit theories when they break down. For example, people may have an implicit theory that inventors are confused, absent-minded, nerdy people. Yet the encounter with such a person who is not overly creative may challenge this assumption (Elsbach and Kramer, 2003). Thus, the theory breaks down.

When evaluating ideas, implicit, as well as explicit, theories play an important role—not least in how people think about creative people. At first glance, it seems that each person has their own implicit theory about what they value. For example, some think that heavy metal music is just noise, while others love its raw energy. Digging a bit deeper, however, one may realize that implicit theories are based on some more fundamental and shared assumptions of what something is believed to be worth. This general notion of worth is, on the one hand, determined by national-cultural aspects. For example, researchers have found that in a Chinese context the usefulness of an idea is more valued than in the US context, which seems to favour novelty (Loewenstein and Mueller, 2016). Such cultural influences, however, seem to be influenced and complemented by a generalized set of principles that people draw on when evaluating the worth of someone or something.

The French sociologists Luc Boltanski and Laurent Thévenot explored specific categories and values that people use to justify their actions, as well as how these categories influence efforts to achieve order in a society. Of course, other thinkers had pondered these issues before and, for example, argued that people invoke the power of a transcendent being (e.g. religious philosophers), the existence of eternal ideas (e.g. Plato), or the ability to reason rationally (e.g. Kant). Yet Boltanski and Thévenot thought that those philosophical ideas were too far removed from the realities and practicalities of how individuals and groups justify their beliefs and actions. For that reason, they intended to combine academic analysis with an exploration of practices and looked at political philosophy as well as management handbooks to extract how individuals and groups justify their actions.

Their insights into how management handbooks prescribe actions based on a specific perspective is of specific relevance to the purpose and focus of this book. What they found is that there are indeed distinct overarching arguments and values that influence practical recommendations for organizations, which they call 'orders of worth' (Boltanski and Thévenot, 2006). While there are other similar notions and terms to describe such a general set of principles, this book sticks to their evocative term. Crucially, it is important to bear in mind that orders of worth are not transcendent natural value systems, but deeply ingrained social constructs (see Chapter 2 for a discussion on social constructionism).

To get a first grip on their concept, think of a debate club. Debate clubs have long been an important institution connected to universities, with the intention of fostering critical and reflective thinking. In a debate club, individuals or groups discuss a controversial topic. The intriguing set-up of such a debate is that an individual or team is assigned a specific perspective on the topic. During the debate, they must argue for their assigned perspective, even if it does not reflect their actual opinions. The intention of debate clubs is to familiarize debaters and audiences with different justifications because arguing for a certain perspective necessitates appealing to a set of principles and evidence to justify it. Moreover, people must engage with other people's arguments and try to refute them. The principles of how a debate is organized highlight important aspects of the orders of worth. First, there must be *higher order principles* that people invoke when they justify and argue for their assigned opinion. Second, there is a *plurality* of opinions that individuals or teams deem to be justified. Third, people must justify how their position is legitimate by using *evidence*.

Generally, orders of worth highlight two key dimensions that are important in social interactions in general and the evaluation of ideas in organizations in particular. First, the concept refers to the necessity of *order*. All social interactions, including the evaluation of ideas in organizations, require a set of principles on how people should relate to one another. Orders of worth are invoked to justify and maintain a social order. That means that people appeal to an order of worth to legitimize and justify their beliefs and actions.

Though there are different degrees of order, individuals never fully sink into a state where they do not have at least a minimally structured way of interacting with each other. Second, the notion of *worth* qualifies the nature of the order. Worth refers to the assigned value of objects and subjects within a specific order. It specifies how much people deem something important and valuable within the order of relationships. This process of assigning value is referred to as evaluation. The notion of evaluation challenges the claim that things possess intrinsic value by arguing that value is the result of practices (Lamont, 2012). For example, the product Skog, discussed in the introduction to this section, illustrates how value is not inherent in a piece of wood but rather bestowed on the object in social processes of valuation and evaluation.

The coexistence of various orders of worth means that there are opposing and even contradictory evaluation criteria for ideas. The coexistence of different principles means that evaluation is pluralistic, as there is not one single, unified order of worth. This leads to debates and disputes between adherents of different orders of worth. The likelihood of debates and disputes is especially prevalent in organizations with numerous stakeholders with divergent interests (Freeman et al., 2010). For example, top management may appeal to costs and efficiency when evaluating an idea, while unions may appeal to fair working conditions and time for recuperation. Thus, to grasp the process of evaluating ideas, it is important to understand in more detail the most influential orders of worth that are invoked.

Moreover, an order implies the possibility of referring to established relationships between subjects and objects to justify one's actions. For example, in a classroom situation, the relationship between teacher and student is ordered in the way that the teacher, as a subject, has been given the role and authority to impart their knowledge and assess the student's ability to understand and recall such knowledge. Accordingly, to justify different teaching methods and regular assessments, one must refer to the value of learning to legitimize the authority of university teachers to impart their knowledge. Objects that would play an important part in justifying this role include textbooks, presentations, seminars, and assigned spaces in the university.

The need to account for actions and beliefs by appealing to an order of worth is an ongoing process referred to as 'justification work' (Boltanski and Thévenot, 2006). Justification work is necessary because a social order is continuously confronted with creative new ideas, as will be seen below. Note, however, that justification work based on orders of worth is only one way of maintaining social order. Other possibilities include violence, routine, and love. Violence means that values are forced on a social order. Love tends to eschew rational justification, while routine refers to the ingrained, mindless actions that need no ongoing justification.

In their foundational work, Boltanski and Thévenot suggested six orders of worth, which have since been complemented by a seventh (Thévenot et al., 2000). To compare the seven different orders, *four categories* will be used here. The first category encompasses the *mode of evaluation*, which refers to the dominant conceptions that people invoke when they suggest and evaluate an idea. For example, if an engineer were to present an idea for a new machine, she would tend to talk about its efficiency and how it helps improve processes. The second category is *forms of proof*, which includes all of the evidence that is used to strengthen conceptions and concepts. To prove her point, the engineer uses some statistics or other data that show how the machine will lead to more efficiency. The third category is *worthy objects*, which are significant tangible expression of value in each respective order of worth. Here, the engineer may appeal to a specific method or theory in engineering that supports her claim. The fourth category encompasses *worthy subjects* and refers to the representative types of individuals that embody the values of the order of worth. Due to her qualifications and background, the engineer is linked to the value of professional expertise in constructing and building machines and is, therefore, a worthy subject.

Table 4.1 provides an overview and comparison of the different orders of worth based on Boltanski and Thévenot (2006), Denis et al. (2007) and Patriotta et al. (2011). The table provides examples from an organizational context to illustrate how the orders of worth may influence organizational practices regarding creative ideas and the characteristics of ideas of each order. The discussion that follows covers each order of worth in more detail, complemented by examples and significant characteristics of ideas.

Inspiration

The *inspired order of worth* includes a focus on *creativity and uniqueness*. The dominant principles that guide the evaluation of worthy ideas are whether they are unique or divergent. They should, therefore, defy rational and logical perspectives and solutions. The worth of ideas cannot be exactly measured—as opposed to other orders of worth, such as the industrial one discussed later. They arise spontaneously. Furthermore, ideas are deemed valuable if they are based on inspiration and question established knowledge. Passion, emotional involvement, and the outpouring of inspiration are further signs that an idea is valuable. Subjects who show these traits include artists, poets, and children. They are commonly associated with going against the norm and not caring about established conventions. The objects that are considered significant for creating and justifying value are the emotionally invested body and creative mind. Those are the tools that assist subjects in creating value. Notably, the inspired order of worth resembles a romantic perspective on creativity, which was briefly discussed in the Introduction. In the inspired order of worth, ideas are evaluated as *divergent*, meaning that they challenge established conventions within the organization. Thus, rather than converging on a single solution, they suggest a range of unfamiliar ideas, as discussed in Chapter 3.

In 2004, a project was launched in Sweden which placed artists in residence in various organizations. The overall goal was to challenge conventional ways of making art and working in organizations by learning from each other and generating unconventional ideas. In a pharmaceutical company, AstraZeneca, the visual artist Anna Persson became the artist in residence. She initiated a project that aimed to inspire employees to reflect on the core values of the company. She invited staff to workshops and instructed them to 'embody' the core values. Thus, rather than talking about how people make sense of the core values, she wanted them to use their body to express them. To capture these moments of interpretation, she took pictures of the shadows that were projected on a brightly lit white screen so that only the silhouette was visible. These photos were then enlarged and placed around the organization. The goal was to inspire people to stop and reflect on how these silhouettes represented core values (Dombrowski et al., 2007). Such artistic interventions in organizations have become more common, and they illustrate how an inspired order of worth can help organizations shift perspectives, illuminate different values, and come up with

Table 4.1 Seven orders of worth

Orders of worth	Inspiration	Market	Domestic	Industrial	Fame	Civic	Green
Mode of evaluation	Singularity Spontaneity Irrationality	Price Costs	Esteem Tradition	Efficiency Functionality	Renown Fame	Collective welfare	Environmental friendliness
Forms of proof	Emotional involvement and expression	Monetary	Oral Exemplary Personally warranted	Measurable: criteria, statistics	Semiotic	Formal Official	Ecological ecosystem
Worthy objects	Emotionally invested body	Free circulating market in goods or services	Good manners Proper behaviour Rank and title Gifts	Technical object Method Plan	Signs Media	Rules and regulations Fundamental rights Welfare policies	Pristine wilderness Healthy environment Natural habitat
Worthy subjects	Artists Poets Children	Consumers Sellers Businessmen	Authority Leaders	Engineer Professional Expert	Celebrity Fans	Equal citizens	Environmentalists Ecologists
Examples from organizations	Artists in residence	User-driven ideas	Paternalistic leadership	R&D work	Self-branding	Works councils	Internal activists
Characteristics of ideas	Divergent	Profitable	Deferential	Functional	Image-based	Equitable	Sustainable

divergent ideas (Styhre and Eriksson, 2008). Overall, while an inspired order of worth appears to be less applicable to organizations, they may be useful to stimulate different perspectives on how organizations are run and commonly understood by their members.

Market

The most frequently heard argument when someone pitches or evaluates an idea is that it will bring in money for the organization. It must be profitable. Such arguments are based on a *market order of worth*. The main criteria for judging worth are price and cost. Hence, ideas are evaluated in monetary terms, which in most cases highlight the economic gain and costs. One of the central notions in a market order of worth is maximizing one's economic gain or profit. Worthy objects are freely available goods and services that can be sold to customers and consumers. In a market order of worth, individuals who sell and purchase goods are regarded as the most valuable. Hence, one often hears the argument that customers will like this idea and spend money on it. However, businesspeople are also regarded as important subjects who are skilled in selling products and services and maximize the organization's profits.

To evaluate the future success of an idea in monetary terms is tricky because the future is uncertain. One possibility to evaluate the market worth of an idea is to involve prospective users. This requires a shift from thinking about selling products to producing what will be sold. The researcher Erik von Hippel, who conducted extensive research on the role of the user in innovation processes, referred to this shift as 'user-driven' innovation (von Hippel, 1988). One common way to perform user-driven innovation is to involve end users more directly and extensively in the idea evaluation and development process. This could be achieved by conducting interviews with focus groups, which discuss a product or service idea. Focus groups usually consist of individuals of different ages, ethnicities, and gender to ensure that the group generates input from a diverse range of users. Generally, the aim is to find out what could be improved to make the idea a more successful product. The objective here is to understand the needs and demands from users better and evaluate the product's market worth.

Domestic

Think of the movie *The Godfather*, in which a clear family hierarchy exists with the Don at the helm of the family making the decisions about important issues. The structure of a family illustrates the central idea of a *domestic order of worth*. The domestic order of worth emphasizes respectability, honour, and tradition. Evaluations within this order of worth will invoke trusted relationships that are based on give and take, or what sociologists refer to as reciprocity. Evidence of worth includes politeness and good manners in interactions with others. Sincerity, honesty, and respect for reputable authorities are also valued. The central institution within the domestic order of worth is the family. Family ties tend to be based on dependence, trust, and tradition. Families also tend to have hierarchical structures in which the head of the family has the authority. The head of the family has the role of taking care of others, while others reciprocate by acknowledging and respecting their authority. Linked to building and maintaining these hierarchical relationships and esteem is learning proper behaviours, giving gifts, endowing ranks and titles, and showing integrity in all interactions. Undesirable behaviour includes spreading rumours, displaying insincerity, and disrespecting authority. An idea evaluated based on a domestic order of worth may thus be characterized as *deferential*. Ideas should be respectful towards the authority of the organization and not offend the invested trust.

It may be claimed that justifications and evaluations based on a domestic order of worth are outdated in today's organizations. This is partly true, as tradition and reciprocity have been on the decline in modern organizations based on the spread of a more individualistic culture (Sennett, 1998). However, some organizations still appear to practice what researchers have called 'paternalistic leadership' or 'benevolent leadership', especially in Pacific Asia, Latin America, and Middle East business contexts (Pellegrini and Scandura, 2008). Paternalistic leadership includes many of the aspects discussed with regard to the domestic order of worth. It is based on an authoritative leader taking care of their employees. Another example is a Japanese form of organization called *Shinise*, which are organizations that have been in business for more than a hundred years—often much longer—and have been family-owned the entire time. *Shinise* honour their traditional craft and community values and seek to keep traditional values and family structures alive by engaging closely with the local community and selling traditional artefacts and crafts (Sasaki et al., 2019). Ideas evaluated within a domestic order of worth thus focus on the fit with traditions and values and whether they are approved by family authority. Ideas that are evaluated positively do not violate any of the values of trust and reciprocity. A domestic order of worth seems to oppose transformative ideas as it aspires to conserve the status quo and eschew opposing ideas. Yet there may be cases where the enactment of traditional values may lead to incremental changes as we discussed with a view to performative routines in Chapter 3.

Spotlight on Practice: Succession

Popular culture does not only serve to entertain; it also reflects the current and past zeitgeist. Therefore, television series, movies, popular art and designs are useful to illustrate the application of theoretical concepts. For example, the HBO show *Succession* provides a case in point for the principles of a domestic order of worth. The backdrop of the show's narrative is an international family-owned media conglomerate called Waystar Royco, which is firmly led by the patriarch Logan Roy. The plot of the series focuses on the developments following Logan's intention to step down as CEO.

His second son, Kendall Roy, is ready to take over, but his father is not yet ready for him to seize control. What ensues is a long drama with multiple narrative strands, including the meaning of family relationships, traditions, and the role of the patriarch in the organization. Kendall continuously tries to take control of the company after his father has a stroke. Though Logan is not fully able to work, he refuses to name his son Kendall as CEO. Kendall grows more and more frustrated over this and schemes against his father. One such move is a vote on the company's board which declares Logan incapacitated and incapable of being CEO. For that purpose, Kendall plans to convince his uncle Ewan, who is a member of the board, to vote against his brother. Ewan fell out with his brother long ago because he was upset about the unethical and immoral values of the company. When he meets Logan and the rest of the family for a dinner, the two brothers enter a fierce argument and Ewan leaves the flat in anger. Kendall sees an opportunity to convince his uncle to vote against his brother and follows him into the elevator. After Kendall pitches his case, Ewan tells him that his brother is an 'ex-human being', but that 'he is still my brother' and walks away.

This short scene encapsulates how principles of a domestic order of worth dominate the relationships in the organization. Though Ewan hates his brother on a personal level, he would not question his authority as a CEO of the company because his brother is still family. Moreover, it also shows how Ewan disapproves of Kendall's scheming and dishonesty against his father. For him, family loyalty is more important than his own hatred for his brother. During the entire series, family tradition and loyalty is invoked, questioned, tested, and transformed, while Logan Roy endeavours to remain the patriarchal leader of the company.

Industrial

A common observation is that engineers are prone to automate processes to make them more efficient. These practices are justified by an *industrial order of worth*, which highlights productivity, scientific evidence, and expertise. The main overarching criteria for assessing worth are efficiency in use and functionality. Justifications typically involve evidence in the form of measurable criteria and statistical evidence. In other words, proof is usually quantitative and comparable. Objects that play a central role in an industrial order of worth are plans, scientific methods, and infrastructures, which are complexes of functional relationships. Since these objects require in-depth knowledge, engineers and other experts are the most valued individuals. They assess the worth of ideas regarding how they lead to increased efficiency and better functionalities. In an industrial order of worth, ideas are thus evaluated according to their *functionality*. Individuals and groups appeal to those values to justify how processes become more efficient and products more functional for customers.

R&D departments in organizations usually evaluate ideas with a view to an industrial order of worth. This is not surprising because the key individuals in this order of worth are experts and engineers. In a study of the car maker Volvo in Sweden, a group of researchers empirically confirmed the dominance of an industrial order of worth in an engineering-driven company (Backman et al., 2007). They studied how different concepts are evaluated when a new car is developed. They showed that most concepts that are positively evaluated in the first stages of the development process are technological concepts, which are ideas that suggest technical solutions and improvements. One reason for the dominance of technological concepts in the first stages of the new product development (NPD) process is the familiarity of engineers with metrics and quantitative measurements that facilitate the evaluation of ideas. Notably, the researchers also found that market-based evaluations were less commonly used to evaluate ideas. There were less efforts to determine which features customers may like and which ones may improve their experience due to the strong influence of an engineering culture and an industrial order of worth.

Fame

In a *fame order of worth*, image, recognition, and signs are central elements. The main criterion that defines this order of worth is how renowned and famous an individual or object is. Crucial in creating fame is public opinion. In general, the public decides whether an individual or object becomes famous. Important subjects are fans who promote the fame and reputation of a celebrity. The celebrity then projects an image that arouses positive emotions and conveys certain attributes. Signs and media are essential to creating such reputation and fame. Signs are objects which the audience link to specific meanings and emotions. Furthermore, signs are commonly used in branding—for example, the Nike Swoosh, which suggests fitness and athleticism, or the Mercedes star linked to high-quality cars. Thus the evidence for fame is semiotic. In the fame order of worth, signs are deliberately used to create positive meanings that boost reputation and fame. In the fame order of worth, since ideas are linked to *reputation* they are evaluated based on the images they evoke. This means that they may be linked to the reputation of someone within an organization or supported by efforts to brand new ideas with signs and symbols. Yet since public opinion can be volatile, fame can also be short-lived—for instance, Andy Warhol is said to have once remarked that with the invention of television, everyone will be able to get their 15 minutes of fame.

This remark was written when television was just starting to become an influential medium in society. Of course, life and work today are, to a large extent, mediated by information and communication technologies. Modern technologies have made it possible for almost everyone to produce, share, and interact with a broad audience on numerous social media platforms. One consequence of this development is that judging worth based on fame and image has proliferated in society and organizations (Alvesson, 2013a). For example, the phenomenon of the social media influencer shows how a celebrity's image and reputation may be linked to a product or an idea. Many organizations use internal social media platforms on which people can share content and build a positive image of themselves. The practice of 'self-branding'—that is, building the reputation and fame of an individual or a group in an organization—may then impact idea evaluation because ideas are not necessarily judged for 'what' they are, but 'who' has proposed them. This notion is revisited below in the discussion of pitching ideas and evaluating them based on image and reputation.

Civic

The *civic order of worth* highlights solidarity, representation, and freedom. The central principles are those linked to a civil society. Civil society features unhindered participation in collective action and the expression of a collective will in democratic processes. The ultimate goal is to achieve collective welfare. The collective—as opposed to the individual—is the most important when justifying activities because increasing the welfare of everyone is the ultimate value to strive for. Worth is hereby mainly attributed to equal citizens, who are collectively organized to express and act on behalf of the collective will. Examples include unions and other non-governmental organizations that act to ensure that the group's interests are considered. Worthy objects include regulations, equal rights, and welfare policies.

Those objects pre-empt some groups gaining too much influence over others, thus levelling the playing field for all citizens. When invoking a civic order of worth, ideas are evaluated as *equitable* and should therefore not violate basic rights and rules. The overarching principles used for evaluating ideas are therefore related to equality and fairness.

Idea evaluations based on the principles of a civic order of worth use justification that refers to the benefits for the collective and equal rights. For example, organizations in countries such as Germany are required to provide the possibility to elect works councils (*Betriebsrat*), which represent the will of the employees. These works councils have the right to evaluate certain ideas and concepts and ensure that they do not violate the collective will of the employees. Of course, not all organizations have institutions that express the collective will of the employees. However, a civic order of worth may still be influential when evaluating ideas that may exclude certain groups. Take the example of modern technology and senior citizens. The rapid development of technologies and their increasing influence on public life means that senior citizens tend to be disadvantaged since they do not adopt technologies at the same pace as the younger generations. In many cases, the motivation of the older generation to use technology is there, but the design of it has been top-down, which means that designers have not explicitly considered the needs of the older generations (Seaton, 2019). Hence, when proposing ideas, they may be justified and evaluated by drawing attention to how they may lead to equal opportunities for all age groups.

Green

In 1972, an organization called the Club of Rome published a report titled *The Limits to Growth*. The report asserted that the world economy cannot grow limitlessly without depleting and destroying the resources of the planet. The depletion of resources and the need to protect some of them has been of increasing concern ever since. Today, it is discussed almost daily in newspapers, conferences, and parliaments, as well as organizations. It is also the central concern of the *green order of worth*, which contains a focus on environmental friendliness and ecological sustainability. Judgements of value relate to how something would impact an ecosystem in a positive or negative way. High value is attached to actions that preserve an ecosystem by sustaining its flora and fauna. Hence, pristine wilderness and natural habitats are regarded as worthy objects that people should strive to maintain and—in cases where they have been destroyed—rebuild. Activists who strive to protect ecosystems from destruction hold the most worth and are regarded as valuable advocates for this cause. They care deeply for the environment and want to ensure its continued existence by all means. Ideas evaluated based on the green order of worth pay attention to the impact on the environment and how they would potentially harm ecosystems and natural habitats. Hence, ideas should be *sustainable* which, in the context of this book, refers to making decisions that satisfy present needs without compromising future needs (Berns et al., 2007).

Corporate social responsibility (CSR) has become an important issue for organizations in recent years, not least because of the public's awareness of the threats to the planet's ecosystems. Most organizations today seek to implement strategies or policies to make practices more sustainable. Yet it still appears to be difficult to convince all members of an organization of the importance of ecological and social sustainability. Many organizational members, especially managers who care about sustainability issues, still find it difficult to inspire colleagues to think about the negative ecological consequences of their actions. Wickert and de Bakker (2019) illustrated how 'internal activists' advocate and justify sustainability practices in an organization. These internal activists, mostly CSR managers, face notable internal resistance. To advocate their cause, they employ various strategies, such as building a network of allies, discussing CSR constantly, and creating internal competition for the best CSR practices. Their example shows that it is still rather uncommon to evaluate ideas and processes with regard to how they may impact the environment negatively. Yet it appears that in some organizations, managers are becoming more and more aware of environmental issues and using justifications from a green order of worth to evaluate ideas. The issue of creativity and sustainability will be revisited in more detail in Chapter 6.

Spotlight on Practice: Marina Tex

The abundance of plastic used daily has become a pressing environmental problem. Plastic is durable and degrades at a slow pace, and much of it ends up in landfills or the ocean. In particular, the pollution of the oceans with plastic trash poses a problem for its flora and fauna, and alternatives are needed to relieve this environmental pressure. Design student Lucy Hughes, from the University of Essex, was acutely aware of this problem and alarmed by statistics that claimed that, by 2050, there will be more plastic in the sea by weight than fish. She decided to tackle this problem in her thesis project. Living by the sea, she reflected on how the waste of the fish industry could be used to produce an alternative to plastic. Lucy started examining the waste produced by the fishing industry, which was mostly skeletons and fish skin. She discovered that some of the fish waste seemed to be elastic and, if bound together, could produce something akin to plastic. She conducted over 100 experiments with different substances and finally found a process that produced a plastic-like structure out of fish waste. She called this substance MarinaTex, and it can be used like common plastic but is fully biodegradable. This means that, in contrast to common plastic, it decomposes and does not emit toxic substances during decomposition. Moreover, the production of MarinaTex reuses fish waste, and since fish waste is a natural product it does not need fertilizers or other chemicals to grow—in contrast to other bio degradable plastics—which reduces its negative environmental impact further. This makes MarinaTex a viable alternative to plastic and other bioplastics.

MarinaTex is, of course, a product idea that was developed with a concern for preserving the natural habitat and ecosystems of the ocean. As such, its worth is justified and judged mainly based on principles of a green order of worth. However, a green order of worth is not the only justification used to evaluate this idea. Each year, the prestigious James Dyson Foundation awards design ideas that 'employ clever yet simple engineering principles and address clear problems' (https://www.jamesdysonaward.org/en-IE/). This statement signals that the evaluation of ideas is mainly based on an industrial order of worth: efficiency and engineering solutions. Yet the evaluation criteria for the James Dyson Award also include commercial viability (alluding to the market order of worth) and, recently, a sustainability aspect. In 2019, MarinaTex won the James Dyson Award, and James Dyson said that he picked this entry because it solved two problems: plastic pollution and the efficient recycling of fish waste. As such, MarinaTex is not only an idea justified by its sustainability, but also its efficiency and functionality. The case of MarinaTex shows that, in many cases, different orders of worth are used to evaluate an idea. In those cases where various orders of worth can be combined without friction, the outcome seems to have more purchase than ideas based on a single order of worth.

As seen in this section, multiple orders of worth are important contextual influences on the evaluation of ideas in organizations. Such pluralistic valuation means that organizing involves not only economic rationalities, but the maintenance of social relationships and networks (Granovetter, 1985). This makes each organization different in terms of what values dominate and how those values may influence the evaluation of ideas. The following sections will dig deeper into the unfolding of idea evaluation processes and concrete evaluation practices.

Interaction and Friction in Evaluation Processes

Creativity is a complex and messy process, and its evaluation dimension is no exception. Hence, to get a better grasp of the process, it is helpful to break it down analytically into different aspects. First, this discussion will look at who and what is involved in the process of evaluating an idea. To do this, the systems perspective on creativity, which marks the transition from a psychological perspective to an interactive and to some extent pluralist perspective, will be drawn on. While systems theory simplifies the process of evaluation, it illustrates some of the key process dimensions involved in the evaluation process—the influence of experts and other powerful people and existing rules, regulations, and values. Moreover, systems theory illustrates the dynamics of the structure–agency relationship applied to evaluation processes as it illustrates the interplay between an individual who proposes an idea and how it fits and is received by the evaluating structures. While systems theory flags the importance of interaction in evaluation processes, it does not elaborate in too much detail on the unfolding of evaluation processes. To conceptualize the evaluation process in more detail, a model will be presented which revolves around the central notion of friction and dissonance.

The initial evaluation of an idea takes place within an individual. This is referred to as intra-individual evaluation on a subconscious and conscious level. On a subconscious level, people constantly generate ideas, and evaluate them. At this level, individuals are not aware of how their ideas are formed until the ideas reach their conscious mind and they are able to articulate them. This is linked to what Wallas called the 'incubation' stage, at which somewhat inexplicable and sudden insights occur (Wallas, 1926). Incubation has intrigued researchers as it appears to play an important role in generating and evaluating ideas, but is notoriously difficult to systematically study because it happens subconsciously and thus escapes our and researchers' attention. Thus, subconsciously, people are hard at work, even when they are not explicitly engaged in a task or trying to solve a specific problem. Hence, their subconscious is already selecting, making connections, and evaluating the soundness of their ideas before they even reach the conscious mind (George, 2007). Accordingly, people are not even aware of the first act of evaluating an idea.

However, people also tend to withhold ideas they are consciously aware of. Here, the literature on creativity speaks of 'self-censorship', which refers to the intentional withholding of ideas (Williams Scott, 2002). Self-censorship was first observed in brainstorming groups. Researchers found that individuals are afraid of being negatively evaluated by their peers and judged as incompetent. For that reason, they refrain from articulating their ideas to the entire group. This may be connected to a fear of losing one's reputation and projecting a bad image. Individuals who expect such negative evaluation feel 'psychologically unsafe' (Edmondson, 1999). Psychological safety refers to group members' perception that their active participation, such as articulating ideas, will not be met by ridicule, punishment, or other negative reactions. The notion of psychological safety highlights a crucial aspect of group effectiveness and a prerequisite for producing creative ideas.

If it is assumed that an idea has been articulated it becomes part of an *interactive evaluation process*. The emphasis on the collective nature of idea evaluation challenges a psychological perspective on creativity, which runs the risk of assuming that creative ideas are independent of the judgements of others. The reason for this is that a psychological perspective focuses primarily on the traits and individual processes of creativity, including its evaluation. However, as discussed previously, creativity is an inherently interactive process—not only when generating and developing ideas, but also when evaluating them. In other words, an idea only becomes creative when others judge it to be creative.

Systems Theory of Creativity

This perspective has gained broad recognition based on the work of Mihaly Csikszentmihalyi. Csikszentmihalyi's influential systems theory comprises three components (Csikszentmihalyi, 1990). First, there is the *individual or group* who articulates an idea. Second, the theory includes the *field*, which comprises experts, professionals, or other influential people, as well as gatekeepers who are most influential when evaluating an idea. Third is the *domain*, which includes the knowledge, rules, and values of the field. The domain is also referred to as the grammar, which denotes its ability to establish clarity about what does and does not fit and what should or should not be included in the knowledge, rules, and values. Field and domain are closely linked to the notion of an order of worth, which charts established relationships or grammar that define the worth of ideas, while the field of worthy subjects is deemed to evaluate ideas competently.

The general logic of how these components unfold is based on the *variation-selection-retention* sequence, which is in turn inspired by an evolutionary logic. Figure 4.1 illustrates the relationships between field, domain, and individual based on Csikszentmihalyi (1990). Following an evolutionary logic, the systems theory argues that an individual or a group present a novel idea to the field inspired by existing knowledge and rules (variation), which evaluates its feasibility based on the grammar of the domain and either accepts or rejects it (selection). If the idea is accepted, it will lead to changes to the domain (retention).

An evocative example for the systems theory is the peer-review process for scientific journal publication. When an author or a team of authors come up with an idea and write a paper, they will submit it to a journal who assigns it to an editor. The editor decides whether

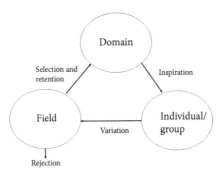

Figure 4.1 Systems theory

they will send it out for review and thus acts as a gatekeeper. If it is sent out, the field will evaluate the paper and write an assessment regarding the novelty and originality of the idea and how it will improve the understanding of a specific issue. Their review will be based on the previous knowledge of the field, the rules and regulations, and its values—what is referred to as the domain. If accepted, the paper's ideas should change the understanding of the domain.

As the systems theory of creativity is a general theory of creativity, it is important to discuss how it is applicable to an organizational context. Applied to an organizational context, it is possible to distinguish four important domains and fields at different levels of analysis (Ford, 1996). The team or group level includes the closest colleagues and management, while the organization level comprises all subunits and departments and direct members of the organization. The institutional environment includes all important stakeholders and experts linked to the organization—such as unions, shareholders, or government agencies—and the market covers existing and prospective customers and consumers of the organization, as well as suppliers. Ideas can be introduced to each of these domains, which all possess their own gatekeepers and fields that influence if and how an idea is evaluated. The fields decide on whether they retain the ideas—that is, they evaluate the idea positively or negatively. Should the idea be retained, it will introduce a variation into the domain and change it. This in turn will influence individuals' and groups' knowledge and decisions. This dynamic of how an idea may be evaluated in an organizational context is illustrated in Figure 4.2 (adapted from Ford, 1996).

The different levels interact, meaning that it is usually not only one field that evaluates an idea but several. This, of course, depends on the scope of the idea. For example, suppose someone suggests an idea at the team level to develop a new service. The idea will most likely be evaluated by colleagues and a line manager (team level). If the idea only concerns team-level processes, it will not need to be evaluated by anyone else. Yet the idea may impact the organization's strategy and other departments, which would mean that higher-level management (organization) may need to get involved. It may also be evaluated with regard to current laws (institutional domain). Lastly, the person may have to evaluate its value with customers of the organization (market).

The systems models suggest two outcomes of evaluation processes: rejection and assimilation. *Rejection* simply refers to an outcome whereby an idea is evaluated negatively by a field and not accepted. *Assimilation* is a positive evaluation which leads to the incorporation of the idea into the field. Rejection is one of the most common outcomes of articulating

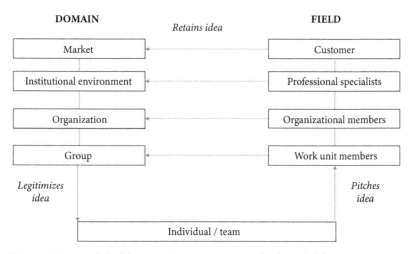

Figure 4.2 A model of the creativity process in multiple social domains

an idea. This may have some interrelated reasons linked to individual and organizational factors. First, on the most basic level, the rejection of an idea may occur if no one seriously engages with the idea. Rehn (2019) argued that, in many cases, even subtle body language may signal disinterest and dissuade people from articulating or elaborating their ideas. Second, the acceptance or rejection of an idea depends on its quality. An idea must be outstanding enough to count as a variation of the field, but not too wild to not be attainable. In other words, the idea must simultaneously be *distinct and legitimate* (Navis and Glynn, 2011). Third, if the idea is conceivable for the organization, gatekeepers may influence the field in a negative way. The gatekeeper in an organization is usually a manager who is responsible for evaluating and selecting ideas (Berg, 2016). If a gatekeeper is unwilling or unmotivated to engage with an idea, it will not be passed on or taken up by the larger field for evaluation, and it is stopped in its tracks. Fourth, many organizations have implemented idea suggestion systems that are designed to circumvent the personal influence of a superior manager. Moreover, they ensure that an idea is evaluated by a committee of experts. However, these experts may reject the idea because they adhere too closely to the grammar of the domain, which limits their perspective. Many organizations and institutions follow their ingrained traditions, rules, and routines based on their preferred domains, especially in more hierarchical structures (Hutter and Stark, 2015). This in turn means that the dominant experts and professionals may have a hard time accepting other people's ideas. In other words, their domain knowledge may hinder an unbiased evaluation of creative ideas.

Examining the rejection of ideas, researchers and consultants have found a recurring paradox: *people often talk about how they desire creative ideas in their organization yet routinely reject them* (Mueller et al., 2012). For example, teachers tend to emphasize the importance of creative ideas but are not too fond of curious and creative students (Dawson et al., 1999). How can this observation be explained? One influence on evaluation practices and a likely rejection of ideas may be the expertise and knowledge of the evaluator (Ward, 2004). Transformative ideas may require a broad knowledge base so that ideas can be evaluated from different perspectives. What has come to be known as the *knowledge–ignorance paradox* refers to how the explosion of information means that people cannot keep up with knowledge developments, and when they focus on their narrow subfields, they may not see the broader relevance of the idea (Ungar, 2000). This is also linked to what the organizational scholar Herbert Simon referred to as 'bounded rationality' (Simon, 1997). In many situations, people lack the time and skills to make a sound assessment, leading them to rely on the knowledge that they already have rather than making efforts to explore more options and listen to other people's opinions.

Another explanation is that individuals refuse to admit openly that they do not like creative ideas. Creativity is seldom questioned, as there is a strong social norm that creativity is inherently good and beneficial. For that reason, people do not want to talk about their hesitation about creativity—and may not even be aware of it. They are driven by a social desirability bias, which means that an individual wants to appear in the best possible way as judged against the prevailing social norms (Zerbe and Paulhus, 1987). Chapter 6 will deepen the discussion of the social desirability of creativity and its instrumental purpose in more detail.

Another possible explanation is that individuals want to avoid uncertain and ambiguous situations, as those make them uncomfortable. The widespread uncertainty avoidance influences idea evaluation, as people tend to reject ideas for which they cannot predict outcomes in some way and that may not fit their scenarios. Hence, when evaluating ideas, ambiguity and the tendency to avoid risk may lead people to reject more ideas than necessary.

A second outcome of articulating an idea is that it is readily *accepted by the field* and incorporated into the domain. This is usually the case for ideas that are not too distinct and are legitimate. Hence, ideas that are pitched may tweak the grammar of the domain without impacting its general structure too much. Commonly, the idea fits into the general way that the organization makes sense of its internal and external environment. For example, if an engineer in the R&D department proposes to add a functionality to a product that makes it more efficient but not more expensive, the idea will most likely not be hotly debated or rejected straightaway. Of course, evaluation processes are influenced by individual and group biases and the influence of power and politics, which may influence the evaluation negatively. However, it is generally the case that ideas that lead to incremental changes are accepted by the field and integrated into the domain as, for example, performative routines discussed in Chapter 3. Yet if an idea is readily accepted by the field, it is probable that it will not lead to transformative and disruptive changes because ideas that fundamentally challenge established structures tend to be initially resisted. Hence, transformation or disruption is more likely to occur if ideas are contested and different orders of worth influence the evaluation and further development of the idea.

Overall, the systems model provides an apt starting point to assess the interrelationship between structure and agency discussed in Chapter 2. The dynamic of the evaluation process and the dimensions involved illustrates how the domain and field restrict as well as enable individual creative agency. Such a perception challenges the prevailing notion of creative individuals, which are seen to singlehandedly introduce transformative ideas. Moreover, the systems theory highlights how value is not inherent in ideas; evaluation is a social process in which actors make sense of and evaluate an idea. As argued throughout the book, creativity emerges from the triangular relationship between context, process, and practice. In terms of the systems model, those correspond to the domain as the defining context and the unfolding of processes and interactive practices between field and individual. Yet while the systems model illustrates the interactive dynamic between structure, individuals, and field, it does not discuss in more detail how the process of evaluation may unfold in an organizational context, especially considering the plurality and friction of different orders of worth that have been discussed in the preceding section. Thus the next section elaborates a more detailed process model of idea evaluation.

Spotlight on Practice: Brekeriet

Brekeriet is a small micro-brewery in Southern Sweden and was founded by three brothers, Fredrik, Christian, and André Ek, in 2010. The name 'Brekeriet' is a wordplay combining 'Br' for brothers, 'Ek' for their last name, and 'eriet', the Swedish word for brewing company (*bryggeriet*). Brekeriet brews and sells sour beers fermented with Brett yeast, which gives the beer a distinctly dry flavour without much of the malty sweetness that people are used to in beer. Sour beers are certainly not for everyone, but Brekeriet has been very successful in producing and selling them in Sweden and other markets. Brekeriet is also popular among home brewers, who are inspired by the taste and brewing process of Brekeriet's beers. In 2019, Brekeriet decided to run a competition in which home brewers could send in their beers, which would be evaluated by Brekeriet. The winning beer would then be brewed on a larger scale and sold commercially. Brekeriet received many submissions, and in June 2019 they scheduled a tasting of the beers to identify the winning one. I participated in this event as an observer.

The panel consisted of the three brothers, the two brewers of Brekeriet, and a brewmaster from another brewery. The panel was served the beers in unmarked glasses, and they rated the beers on different qualities, such as taste and appearance. Once a set of beers had been evaluated, they compared their notes. Their comparison showed some interesting insights into the interaction between field and domain. The panel agreed on their ratings of most beers. Only seldom were they in disagreement. Their consistent agreement illustrated their common grammar of how a sour beer should taste and look. One beer, however, stood out because it was a flashy pink. It looked out of place, and the panel immediately reacted to the colour. Pink did not fit the common colour scheme of a natural sour beer, which ranges from golden to amber or adopts the colour of a natural ingredient, such as cherries or cranberries. If the colour had been based on natural ingredients, it would have been evaluated as a possible variation of the field. Yet it was obvious that the colour was artificial and added afterwards to the finished beer. This variation could not be accepted by the panel as it violated the rules of the domain of how a sour beer should look. Moreover, it would also violate the consumers' notion of a sour beer, potentially leading to its rejection. Additionally, adding colour may also violate hygienic rules and regulations and, thus, encounter negative evaluations from an institutional domain. This example of Brekeriet's panel thus illustrates the complex interplay of domain, field, and idea that governs the creative process in craft brewing.

A Frictions Model of Evaluation Processes

As previously discussed, organizing requires coordination and agreement on common goals. To reach a goal, everyone in and outside of the organization should work towards it. Therefore, organizations strive to have a common frame of reference or a strong value base to ensure coordination. In other words, people in and around organizations should have the same grammar that defines the domain and is used for evaluation. While disruptive and transformative ideas threaten the grammar of the domain, they are necessary to create new products and processes. Hence, where there is neither an immediate rejection of an idea because it does not fit into the domain nor a ready acceptance that does not disrupt the domain, evaluation processes may lead to *friction*. Friction is considered to be the basis for transformative ideas. Furthermore, friction that leads to transformative ideas may be broken down into different process dimensions, which are illustrated in Figure 4.3.

Dissonance describes the interplay of different tones in musical composition. A melody that sounds pleasant and harmonious is consonant, while a melody that is harsh and unpleasant is dissonant. This metaphor captures the effects of idea evaluation quite well. The evaluation of ideas can be pleasant and agreeable, which means it does not arouse any unpleasant feelings, or it may create dissonance, which means that it does not feel right. Dissonance is an unpleasant state that generally causes people to seek to return to a harmonious and consonant experience. Thus it is common for people to seek information that confirms their previous beliefs to reduce dissonance.

How far this can go was shown in a fascinating study of a cult that predicted the end of the world (Festinger et al., 1956). The cult believed that they were chosen to be taken away by extraterrestrials on a certain date, while the rest of the world would be destroyed. Obviously this prophecy failed. Confronted with contradictory evidence, Festinger et al. observed three ways of reducing dissonance. First, a person may accept new evidence and learn. Second, they may cling to their beliefs and actively seek evidence for their previous beliefs. Third, they may simply ignore the evidence. Accordingly, when someone experiences dissonance there is the risk that they will ease dissonance by either ignoring it or seeking evidence that confirms their previous beliefs—commonly referred to as confirmation bias. Reducing dissonance is one of the reasons that, for example, the mobile phone operator Nokia may have failed to recognize the growing trend of the smartphone and failed to develop new creative products (Vuori and Huy, 2016). However, organizations or individuals may also actively engage with dissonance and increase the chances of creating transformative ideas.

Active engagement with dissonance is linked to what may be called *productive dissonance*. The sentiment of productive dissonance was aptly expressed in an interview with the inventor of the podcast Radiolab, Jad Abumrad. When asked how he came up with and evaluated the creative idea of Radiolab, he talked about his constant unease about his ideas and how it created anxiety. In the end, he concluded that

we as a community can either run from that feeling [of dissonance], or we can run TO that feeling. We can treat that feeling as an arrow that we need to follow. Like, OK, I'm about to vomit, my stomach is about to leap out of my mouth ... but maybe that just means I'm on the right track. Maybe that just means I'm doing my job.

(Abumrad, n.d.).

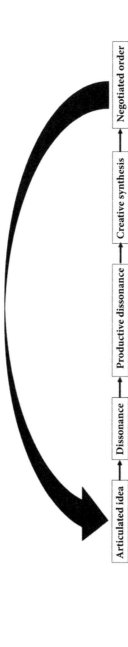

Figure 4.3 A frictions model of evaluation processes

His rather evocative description captures the essence of the productive dissonance of creativity—the ability to withstand tension when ideas are evaluated from different orders of worth. Multiple orders of worth are simultaneously debated and kept in play, and there is no immediate rejection of an idea, but there is also not a ready agreement. Rather, as discussed in the analogy of the debate club, different angles, critiques, and elaborations are discussed. Yet even if different evaluations are debated and dissonance is engaged, how do groups and organizations move on?

The process of evaluating and debating ideas may lead to *creative synthesis*, which is based on a dialectical perspective. A dialectical perspective focuses on processes of organizing by arguing that organizations are constantly rearranged and in a constant state of renewal (Benson, 1977). This renewal happens when a dominant perspective (thesis) is confronted with a challenging perspective (antithesis) to generate a novel outcome in the form of a synthesis (Harvey, 2014). This dialectical dynamic was illustrated in a study on organizational creativity regarding the development of the Boeing 777 (Drazin et al., 1999). In the Boeing 777 project, engineers and management constantly renegotiated their ideas and positions. For example, when the costs of the project increased disproportionately, management introduced ideas for cutting costs that were accepted more readily. In contrast, when there was a crisis related to technical features, engineers had a stronger bargaining position and got more ideas accepted. With their example, Drazin et al. showed that to reconcile divergent interests and ideas, groups constantly worked to find a creative synthesis to establish a *negotiated order*. A negotiated order is a temporary but stable state in which there is little to no disruptive dissonance and in which groups coordinate their work based on their agreements. However, should there be a *crisis*, which leads to dissonance, the involved groups would engage in renegotiating the order to achieve a new creative synthesis. That means the process of stimulating productive dissonance begins anew.

To further illustrate the working of the friction model consider a concrete situation: a local government proposes to build a spa resort in an area known for its ecological diversity and pristine nature, as well as its local heritage (*articulated idea*). When evaluating the idea of such a project, the stakeholders will most likely raise arguments based on a market order of worth, a green order of worth, a civic order of worth, and a domestic order of worth (*dissonance*). Local businesses will argue that the spa will draw many customers and provide profits and jobs to the community. Environmentalists will argue that a spa will destroy the sensitive ecosystem. The local government will justify its action to grant building a spa by referring to their political authority based on a democratic election process. Local historians, in contrast, will draw on a domestic order of worth to argue that the historical heritage must be preserved. One outcome of this dissonance would be that the local government ignores arguments from the historians and the environmentalists and builds the spa, which satisfies the local business (*reducing dissonance*). Alternatively, the tension between these different orders of worth may lead to a willingness to find a compromise (*productive dissonance*). The different groups may then reach a compromise to build the spa in a way that does not harm the environment and brand it as an ecological spa situated in a pristine nature reserve. The local historians could put up signs and exhibitions and lead tours around the area to important sights of local history (*creative synthesis*). Hence, initial disagreement on evaluative principles, prolonged discussions, and willingness to engage may lead to new transformative ideas on how to design the spa. This compromise will enable everyone to work together for now (*negotiated order*). Then, it is possible to imagine that the local businesses discover that building the spa with sustainable materials will exceed their costs and challenge the established order (*crisis*). This would then lead to new ideas, dissonance, and friction.

The potential pitfall of working with frictions is finding the *diversity sweet spot*. In many cases, groups will be too diverse and conflicts too strong. In other cases, team members may know each other so well that the social bonds between them may prevent people from speaking up because of the fear of impacting the group negatively. Thus the challenge with productive dissonances and creative synthesis is that they require a finely tuned group diversity. Researchers have found that one way of producing creative ideas in teams based on friction is the interplay between cognitive and social factors. A team can possess cognitive diversity, which refers to the difference in thinking styles and exposure to different knowledge domains. Socially, team members must create a space in which tensions resulting from cognitive diversity are not necessarily resolved, but at least tolerated. This could happen through members of the team who have knowledge in various domains and can thus act as mediators between team members (de Vaan et al., 2015).

For example, imagine a team that includes software engineers and game designers. The designers may demand that a feature of a game look a certain way, while the engineers may argue that it is not possible with the tools they have. Now imagine that a couple of team members have trusted expertise in software engineering *and* game design. When engaging with the friction in the team, those team members become central because they can evaluate suggestions from both perspectives, vouch for other team members' ideas, and strengthen the bond between both camps. When trying to reach a compromise, the mediation of these team members will support building a space for trying to work productively through the friction. The implication of this is that team members that have knowledge in multiple domains, and are thus able to vouch for the ideas of different team members, will increase social cohesion and trust among team members. This will impact the potential for creating productive dissonance positively.

All in all, the theoretical concepts discussed in this section provide some insights into the process of evaluation. Importantly, they illustrate how evaluation is a complex sociocultural process based on the ongoing interaction between domains, fields, and individuals. In particular, exploiting the potential of friction and dissonance in evaluation processes seems to be a promising point of departure for transformative ideas. The reality is, of course, always more complicated than the model suggests. The default option tends to be to reduce dissonances and avoid conflict (Schaefer, 2019). In many cases, this is called for, but if the objective is to facilitate creativity, avoiding dissonance may not have the desired effect. The role of friction will be expanded upon in Chapter 5 during the discussion of the modes of coordination and paradoxes, as well as in Chapter 6 during the exploration of radical transformative creativity practices. For now, attention is turned to the last aspect of evaluation: evaluation practices.

Pitching and Evaluation Practices

If an idea is not articulated and pitched, there is nothing to evaluate. Hence, as a first step, *practices of pitching* ideas are explored. Then follows a comparison of two perspectives on evaluation practices: a *transactional perspective and a transformational perspective*. Both perspectives rest on contrasting conceptions of ideas and modes of evaluation. While the former provides the foundation for systematic approaches to idea evaluation, such as idea suggestion systems, the latter claims that evaluation practices are inherently emergent and relational. The section then presents and discusses a typology of evaluation practices based on the distinction between transformational and transactional practices and micro and meso levels of analysis.

Pitching Ideas

To initiate an inter-individual evaluation process, people must make their ideas explicit to others—whether orally, in written form, or both. After all, an idea must be communicable (Hua et al., 2022). Articulating an idea is a decisive and crucial practice because people must find the right arguments to stimulate others to seriously engage with and evaluate their ideas. Articulating ideas is a constant practice in social life. However, pitching an idea in an organizational context appears to be different in many ways, as it requires a more structured and systematic argument. Much can be learned about pitching ideas from the scientific discipline of entrepreneurship. To receive financial funding, entrepreneurs must provide systematically developed and articulated ideas on how their venture is distinct and legitimate (Navis and Glynn, 2011). Analogously, in an organizational context, individuals or groups must pitch their ideas by drawing attention to what is new about them (divergent) and how they fit with the existing structure and processes of the organizations (convergent). If the idea is too convergent, it will not lead to transformative changes, and if it is too divergent, it runs the risk of being unfeasible and regarded as outlandish, which would most likely lead to its rejection. So the central question a pitch must answer is how the idea is different—but not too different—from the current norm.

In general, there is an abundance of practical advice on how to pitch ideas. Such advice focuses on certain aspects of the idea that must be highlighted. One popular method for pitching an idea is the 'needs, approach, benefits, and competition' (NABC) model. For example, if someone would like to pitch the idea of going for a walk after lunch to their manager, they may employ the following line of argument: they have been so tired and uncreative lately (need), so it may be beneficial to get some fresh air after lunch (approach) to make the group more alert and more creative (benefits), which has worked in the neighbouring department which just won an innovation prize (competition).

Notably, researchers who have studied practices of how entrepreneurs pitch their ideas have found that entrepreneurs draw extensively on such a structured line of argumentation. A recent study showed that they pitched their ideas by pointing out that customers are in need of their solution, that the product adds benefits, that there is a market for the idea, that first trials have shown that it works, that they have the skills and experiences to make the idea a success, and that funding will help them grow (van Werven et al., 2019).

By taking a closer look at the pattern of pitches it is possible to identify some *common generic argumentation strategies*. Since a pitch is fundamentally a string of arguments, it is helpful to first look at the basic structure of an argument before examining specific strategies of pitching ideas. *An argument* usually consists of a claim, grounds, and warrants, as displayed in Figure 4.4. A claim is asserted to be true, and grounds are meant to support the claim. However, a sound argument must demonstrate that the grounds support the

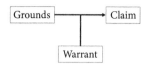

Figure 4.4 The basic structure of an argument

claim. Hence, it is necessary to have a warrant that connects the grounds to the claim. For example, suppose someone argues that the software program they developed will save the company 25 per cent of their time to produce a product (claim) because it uses a state-of-the-art algorithm for the program (grounds). Yet the link between the new algorithm and saved time is not entirely obvious. So someone may ask the person how the new algorithm saves time. The creator of the software may then need to provide more evidence linking their grounds and claim (warrants) by, for example, producing data from another company that has implemented the program or referring to studies on the efficiency of the new algorithm. If the warrant sufficiently links the grounds and claim, the argument is sound; if not, the argument will not be considered credible.

The basic structure of an argument informs multiple generic argumentation strategies used in pitching practices. First, people may pitch their idea by referring to *reasons* why their idea will work. In other words, people will try to establish a strong warrant for their claims in the form of evidence or statistics. However, for novel ideas it is very difficult to provide strong warrants that support the claim, as the effects of an idea are commonly uncertain (van Werven et al., 2015). Second, people may rely on *commonly accepted norms* or taken-for-granted background knowledge to provide the warrant for an argument. This is called an enthymeme. For example, imagine an idea pitch containing a sentence like this: 'My idea will lead to sustainable processes.' In this sentence, the audience is left to complete the meaning of sustainability. The implied premise, of course, is that sustainability is good and will succeed. However, this premise is not explicitly stated in the pitch, but left to the audience to make the connection. An enthymeme can create a strong bond between speaker and audience if the implied premise has a positive cultural connotation—note however that it may also backfire if the connotation is negative (Hartelius and Browning, 2008). Third, a pitcher may argue for an idea based on their *authority and expertise* that warrants their claim. Reputation and previous ideas that have been successful serve to establish trust in the expertise and the idea of a pitcher. So, rather than warrants, claims, and grounds, the reputations, social network, and known expertise play a key role (Baron and Markman, 2000). Fourth, a pitcher could signal that the idea is supported and endorsed by someone reputable and credible within the organization. Here, it is not necessarily the expertise of the pitcher, but the alleged support for the idea, that will generate favourable evaluations. These endorsers may be referred to as idea champions who are not the originator of an idea but have a vested interest in it and work to promote it (Chakrabarti, 1974). Fifth, the pitcher may *use analogies or metaphors* to make the idea more palatable and positive sounding. Here, the pitcher tries to warrant their claims by using evocative images that highlight the underlying benefits of the idea.

All in all, pitching an idea includes different approaches to building an argument. Naturally, those can be combined and extended. The main goal is to clearly articulate the idea and then convince the audience that the claims are warranted. Once the idea has been articulated and pitched, it is ready for evaluation by others. The next discussion examines how these evaluation practices can be conceptualized.

Transactional and Transformational Evaluation Practices

Pitching an idea always contains a value proposition. As seen earlier, evaluation practices are informed by appealing to different values, which are usually linked to orders of worth. Now, regarding evaluation practices, the way that people understand the nature of these value propositions matters. Based on two contrasting conceptions of value—value as transferable and value as co-created—and their influence on evaluation practices, it is possible to distinguish between two perspectives on evaluation practices: *transactional and transformational*. Before delving into a deeper discussion of these two perspectives, it may be helpful to think more generally about the notions of singular monetary value and pluralistic sociological values in different research traditions. Stark (2009) pointed out that there is an unofficial pact between economists and sociologists. Economists study single monetary value, while social scientists study pluralistic values. In other words, economists are concerned with a singular notion of value, usually price, while social scientists study how different values affect relationships within a society based on beliefs and norms.

Think of this distinction in terms of the value of a car. Its value from an economic perspective may be €15,000, but its sociological values comprise safety, sustainability, and mobility. The economic value of a car in the form of price is usually unambiguous. The values of safety, sustainability, and mobility, however, are contested and evoke emotions and discussions. Returning to the discussion of two perspectives on idea evaluation, it may be argued that an unambiguous value can be transmitted to an audience (transaction), and a contested notion of value is debated and emerges from group discussions (transformation). Whether one sees evaluation practices as transactions or as transformations has consequences for evaluation practices, as we shall see in the following discussion. Table 4.2 compares these two perspectives regarding their basic assumptions, the general conception of value, popular practices, evocative metaphors, and their intentions.

Table 4.2 Transactional and transformational evaluation practices

	Transactional	Transformational
Basic assumptions	Value of an idea can be exchanged and transmitted to an audience	Value of an idea is co-created interactively within a group
Conception of value	Value as a noun—that is, an essential property of the idea	Valuation as an ongoing process in a specific situation (situated evaluation)
Practice	Formalized evaluation systems	Group discussions or spontaneous interactions
Metaphor	Funnel perspective—particle	Fermentation vat—wave
Intention	Control	Amplification

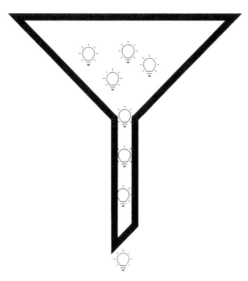

Figure 4.5 The funnel depicting transactional evaluation practices

In a transactional perspective, value is understood as something that can be exchanged from the one who pitches the idea to the one who receives the idea. Think of a market where goods and services are traded. The seller sets a price which signals its value, and if the price is right, the buyer is ready to pay its value and the good is exchanged. Similarly, in a transactional evaluation perspective, the pitcher sells an idea to a buyer who assesses its value in fixed categories (e.g. price). Depending on the context, those are most likely connected to a market, industrial, or inspired order of worth (Bobadilla and Gilbert, 2017). A transactional perspective commonly guides formalized idea evaluation systems, which are based on specific criteria used to evaluate ideas. One evocative metaphor that has been used to highlight a transactional perspective is *the funnel* (Dubinskas, 1993), which is used to channel liquid or any other substance into a tight opening, as illustrated in Figure 4.5. In this process, the substance usually stays unchanged as it is channelled into an opening. The funnel thus highlights how ideas in a transactional perspective are transmitted and evaluated based on established criteria, and then either rejected or selected. The main motivation here is to control the process of selecting the right ideas and not expose the process of evaluation to the fancies of the evaluators. Further linked to the transactional perspective is the *particle metaphor*, discussed in Chapter 3, which argues that ideas are regarded as concrete, identifiable entities that can be counted and selected for either rejection or acceptance (Hua et al., 2022). Hence, the particle metaphor would suggest that ideas can be transferred unchanged as they move through the funnel.

Spotlight on Practice: Intuition and Expertise in Architectural Competitions

Between October 2008 and March 2009 a competition occurred in Copenhagen, Denmark. Its aim was to find the best design for a state school and an adjacent library. Three firms of architects were chosen to compete. In February 2009, three proposals for the buildings were submitted by the firms. They included a physical model, posters, and a written presentation of their design proposal. The three firms also presented their models to an assessment committee, which was given the task of evaluating each of the three designs and selecting a winner. The basis for the written report and evaluation was the competition brief, which was a document containing over 500 specifications of the buildings. It not only specified how the buildings should look, it also contained specifications on sustainability aspects, political agendas, and pedagogical elements. In theory, the competition brief should be the basis for picking the winning design. However, the evaluation process turned out to be upside down. During the first meeting, the expert members of the committee gave their initial review of the three submissions. It turned out during that meeting that the experts had already picked a clear winner and made up their mind, without having consulted any of the specifics in the competition brief. Though a follow-up meeting took place with external experts in pedagogy, urban planning, and outdoor facilities (who challenged the favoured design), none of the lay members of the committee seriously challenged the experts' opinion. The proposal favoured from the beginning by the experts would be the winner. Only after the third meeting did the committee turn to the official document that would quantify and justify the choice of the winning proposal. Thus the document that should have been used to evaluate the idea was filled in *after* the decision about a winning design had been made. The experts in this case seemed to have made up their minds intuitively from the start. What they did was rationalize their decision in retrospect and convince the lay people on the committee of their choice (Kreiner, 2012). The case illustrates how ideas may be evaluated by experts. In many cases, decisions—even though they should seemingly rely on objective standards—are based on the experience and intuition of experts. Intuitive evaluation relies on tacit knowledge, and objective standards are, in many cases, not directly applied when intuitive decisions are made. In those cases, objective reports only serve to rationalize and justify intuitive choices in hindsight.

The *transformational perspective* assumes that value is created in the interaction between group members. During interaction, different values are discussed, and during the discussion ideas are transformed, extended, deselected, or accepted. A fermentation vat is an apt metaphor to capture this process, as shown in Figure 4.6 (Dubinskas, 1993). Fermentation happens when small microorganisms trigger chemical processes that change the chemical composition of other matter or organisms. For example, in beer brewing, sugars dissolved in liquid are converted into alcohol and esters during fermentation processes. Fermentation is a volatile process that depends on temperature, chemical compounds, and other situational factors. Analogously, transformational evaluation practices lead to reactions and combinations that transform and integrate previous ideas. Like in a vat, these processes are situated and contained, yet they are exposed to various contextual influences that can affect the process. Similarly, the *wave metaphor* discussed previously highlights the emergent and indeterminate nature of transformational evaluation practices because it conceived of ideas not as discrete objects but as emergent and indeterminate outcomes of a process (Hua et al., 2022). The intention of transformational practices is not

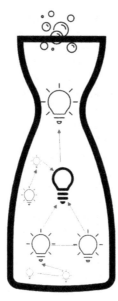

Figure 4.6 The fermentation vat depicting transformational evaluation practices

to control the outcome, but to have an amplification effect in which stakeholders develop and produce integrated ideas and solutions. The transformation of ideas does not necessarily have to involve other people, but it may occur during an interaction with an object, as is demonstrated by the case of the haute cuisine chef below.

Spotlight on Practice: A Happy Accident in French Haute Cuisine

Haute cuisine is among the most creative occupations, as haute cuisine chefs and their teams are expected to constantly produce new and inventive dishes for their customers. Especially in restaurants that have been included and rated in the Michelin Red Guide, a constant stream of creativity is necessary to maintain ratings. Since cooking is a practical, hands-on and sensual practice, the value of a new idea emerges with the chef's experiments with different cooking ingredients. Consider the sequence of creating a new version of a potato chip (taken from Bouty and Gomez, 2015: 230):

the kitchen is quiet with only Chef C, his kitchen-chef (his son) and second-chef attending. Chef C explains his thinking about potato chips: he would like to interpret them differently, but he has no specific idea. His notebook is open. First, he sketches a horizontal strip and then a rose-shaped figure while explaining that he does not know which shape to explore further. They start peeling and slicing potatoes. The kitchen-chef arranges a strip of potato slices. Chef C watches and frowns, not fully convinced: 'You need a shape and it has to be long. [pause] Yeah … [unconvinced] perhaps … We need to try.' They start aligning potato slices on a cooking tray. Chef C: 'No it doesn't work … We should slice it.' He picks up a potato and cuts thinner slices with the mandolin. They place them on a corrugated cooking tray, potato slices overlapping and forming about 10-centimetre-long strips. Then, they place the tray directly into the oven. Sometime later, the potato strips are cooked and have taken a u-curved shape; they are roasted on the edge and still bright yellow in the middle. Chef C delicately appreciates them with his fingertips: 'It's beautiful, it's soft and crunchy; I think we have everything there.' Kitchen-chef: 'But we lost the shape.' Chef C: 'Yes I think ... but it's not a problem. I find it an enhancing accident. [He calls on the second-chef while examining both sides of the potato strip] Look, Regis, look how nice it is ... And all in all, we lost it [the initial shape], but we have two textures of potato, soft and crusty, and it's beautiful ... It's the magic of creation; sometimes you start with an idea and suddenly boom ... But it doesn't mean that it denaturizes it.'

This episode of how a creative potato chip was produced is telling in how value may emerge through direct experimentation and interaction. The short episode illustrates how value was not determined from the outset (the chef had no clear idea of what kind of chip he wanted to produce), but value emerged through experimentation with the sliced potatoes. As such, it is an illustrative example of transformative evaluation practices in which the value of an idea emerges from indeterminate actions. Valuation is an ongoing process in which concrete value propositions are not passed on, but values emerge and change in the process of working on an idea.

A Typology of Evaluation Practices

To unpack idea evaluation practices in an organizational context further and link them to concrete organizing practices, a typology based on the level of organizing and the type of evaluation practices is helpful. The typology depicted in Figure 4.7 renders four distinct level-dependent evaluation practices based on two dimensions. The first dimension is the previously discussed transactional and transformational evaluation practices. The second is the micro and macro levels, which refers to the level of analysis that ranges from small-scale group interaction (micro level) to a large-scale, structural level (macro level). Both dimensions constitute important conceptions of evaluation practices that scholars have systematically studied and, as such, the typology provides a systematic overview of research on evaluation practices. The sections that follow will discuss, and give examples for, each quadrant of the typology.

Transactional macro-level evaluation practices combine large-scale organizing practices that comprise various organizational groups or departments linked to objective criteria that are used to evaluate ideas. An example is the structured NPD process. One of the most influential approaches to structure a NPD is the stage gate model (Cooper, 1990), which is designed to map and control the development of an initially fuzzy idea into a final product. For that purpose, the NPD process is broken down into different stages. For example, a stage gate process could be divided into evaluation of an initial idea, preliminary assessment, preparation of a business case, development, testing and validation and, finally,

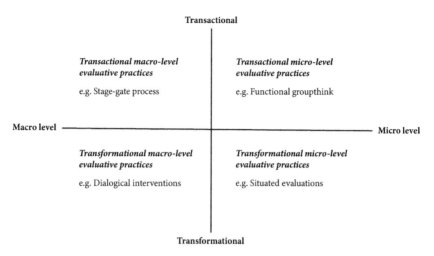

Figure 4.7 A typology of evaluation practices

market launch. Each stage of the process is completed with an assessment—also referred to as a gate. At the gate, selected gatekeepers decide whether to proceed with the project or not based on the project team's efforts to convey the positive value of their previous efforts. In the context of organizing creativity, the initial phase of a stage gate process is the most relevant. At this stage, ideas are screened and evaluated by an innovation or creativity board in which experts and other decision makers commonly use fixed criteria, such as fit with the strategy, potential adoption by consumers, or feasibility of the idea's technical realization (Cooper, 2008). With a view to such criteria, it is assumed that articulated ideas contain a fixed value proposition that can be assessed by a team of experts. In other words, value can be transmitted from sender (project initiator) to receiver (team of experts). Therefore, the stage gate process follows a transactional logic of evaluating ideas against the criteria and objectives of each stage and is designed on a larger scale involving many different process stakeholders.

In contrast, *transactional micro-level evaluation practices* shift from the macro level to the group level. They describe how groups evaluate ideas based on a set of objectively perceived criteria based on idiosyncratic group norms. Here, the concept of *groupthink* is helpful to develop this further (Janis, 1982). This concept describes the gradual development of strong group norms and criteria against which all articulated ideas are evaluated. This means that ideas that do not fit group norms are disregarded, while those that fit the group norms are accepted. Overall, a certain degree of groupthink is necessary to enable group cohesion and goal-directed actions. This may be referred to as *functional groupthink*, whereby the group has established an objectively perceived set of criteria to evaluate ideas. So, in a functional groupthink setting, the evaluation of ideas against common norms and their acceptance or rejection may provide coherence to the group's internal processes and decisions. However, in some cases group norms may lose their sense of critical appraisal of ideas and slavishly stick to previous norms. This may be called *dysfunctional group-think*, which is the concept that most researchers refer to when they speak of groupthink. Dysfunctional groupthink occurs when group members become immune to any critique or challenge of their norms and ideas. In dysfunctional groupthink, groups may never consider evaluative criteria other than their own, thereby preventing any creative ideas or critiques from emerging (Vaughan, 1996).

If groups have no strong objectively perceived group norms and idea evaluation emerges from group interaction, it is possible to speak of *transformational micro-level evaluation practices*. The concept of *situated evaluations* is helpful to shed some light on these practices. In the spirit of a transformational approach, situated evaluation refers to an ongoing and emerging valuation process that involves the continuous transformation and discussion of contributions to emerging ideas by building on each group member's input (Harvey and Kou, 2013). In their in-depth study of creative groups, Harvey and Kou presented two sequences of how situated evaluation practices may unfold. First, a 'generation-centred' sequence—in which the generation of ideas dominates—resembles a traditional set-up of a brainstorm session whereby many ideas are first generated and then subsequently evaluated. In a generation-centred sequence, the emphasis is on divergent thinking followed by the convergent selection of ideas. Second, in an 'evaluation-centred' sequence, a small number of ideas is first generated and then evaluated. This leads to an early discussion of the problem framework, which means that the group discusses the problem to be solved early on and then retains and integrates ideas that address the problem framework. According to the study, an evaluation-centred sequence appears to be more productive and effective, as the group focuses their efforts on the problem at hand early on, rather than randomly proposing ideas. This means that the group will agree on more ideas than when using a generation-centred sequence.

Finally, *transformational macro-level evaluation practices* include establishing large-scale structures within which representatives from all parts of the organization are given the ability to articulate, discuss, and transform seeds for ideas. Such system-wide evaluation practices are part of 'dialogical organizational development' (Bushe and Marshak, 2009). This means that change processes in organizations are facilitated by conversations, dialogue, and mutual learning to achieve system-wide transformative changes. For example, in 2009 the Swedish health authorities decided to improve cancer care by designing patient-focused pathways. The objective was to establish a holistic process in which all elements of the cancer care process would be seamlessly integrated. The local municipality of Gothenburg chose to collaborate with researchers and arranged a dialogue conference with 120 participants from various disciplines in healthcare. All participants were encouraged to discuss seeds for their ideas with others and transform those in the process. The key idea was that, through dialogue, ideas would emerge and jointly develop (Huzzard et al., 2014). Dialogical intervention methods thus aim to facilitate the emergence and transformation of ideas on a macro level by involving a wide array of organizational members.

All in all, the four evaluation practices highlight different dimensions of evaluation practices, to distinguish various organizational practices, and may stimulate reflections about the design of new idea evaluation initiatives. Importantly, transactional and transformational evaluation practices are not mutually exclusive practices, as the analytical distinction may suggest. Analogous to the discussion of the duality of idea generation and development in Chapter 3, evaluation practices may assess concrete value propositions as well as emerge from situated valuation processes. For example, in organizing practices there may be structured evaluation systems, such as NPD, based on fixed value propositions that are still discussed and adapted as a result of group discussions at each gate. An important issue to bear in mind is avoiding a focus on facilitating either practice. A one-sided focus on transactional evaluation practices may lead to rigidity because evaluations do not deviate much from the fixed evaluation criteria, while purely transformational evaluation practices may lead to evaluation practices without clear directions as discussions may veer off into many different disconnected directions. As usual, striking a healthy balance may be the optimal approach.

Spotlight on Research: Assessment in Hollywood Pitch Meeting

In a close-up study of screen writers' pitch meetings, the organizational researchers Kimberley Elsbach and Roderick Kramer explored the assessment of creative people (Elsbach and Kramer, 2003). They made in-depth observations during the meetings and conducted interviews with writers and directors. They found that when producers assessed individual creativity, they first attended to behavioural and physical cues, and in a second stage drew on cues stemming from the interaction itself. With regard to behavioural and physical cues, producers constructed different stereotypes. For example, producers perceived writers to be the most creative when they appeared quirky, unconventional, and unpolished. They also perceived writers to be creative when they pitched a script in a funny and 'writerly' manner by drawing on metaphorical and dramatic descriptions. If a script was pitched by someone who had a professional appearance that suggested proficiency with business affairs and efficient organization—rather than writing ground-breaking scripts—they were assessed as moderately creative. If the writer appeared to be desperate, jaded, and slick, the producers tended to assess them as not creative.

In addition to the physical appearance and behaviour of people, Elsbach and Kramer found that how the producers perceived the relationship exerted an important influence on assessment processes of whether or not the script was creative. If they perceived an interaction as enthusiastic and based on a 'we' language, it provided cues for them that the writer may be more creative. In contrast, a relationship in which the producer had more knowledge of the industry and writers did not acknowledge input from the producer led the writers to be characterized as uncreative.

Their research highlights an important practice and influence on assessment practices. It appears that, rather than the idea itself, people put too much emphasis on assessing physical appearances, behaviours, and relationships as cues for assessing creativity. Those may serve as a way for evaluators to simplify the complexity of assessing all facets of the idea. The danger is, of course, that such stereotypes and categorization methods will prevent a more thorough engagement with an idea.

Conclusion

This chapter discussed the context, process, and practices of evaluating ideas. The context provides criteria that may be used to assess the worth of ideas. These criteria are manifold, but—especially in an organizational context—there seems to be an overarching set of values that influence idea evaluation. These sets of values are referred to as orders of worth, which consist of higher order principles that justify and legitimate opinions, decisions, and practices. An order of worth influences how individuals and groups judge other people's ideas and argue for their own. Crucially, in pluralistic societies and organizations, there is not only one but several orders of worth. This chapter discussed inspiration, market, industry, domestic, fame, civic, and green orders of worth with regard to their importance for organizations, and highlighted how they influence the content and characteristics of ideas.

The chapter then moved on to evaluation processes by presenting and analysing a systems model of creativity. The systems model illustrates the interactive sociocultural processes involved in evaluation processes. According to this model, ideas possess no inherent value, but the value of an idea is established when a field of experts and other influential individuals evaluate its feasibility based on the grammar of a domain and either choose to accept or reject it. While the systems model is an important contribution, it barely touches on how evaluation processes unfold in an organizational context. Considering opposing orders of worth and potential conflicts in evaluation processes it is important to elaborate how friction and dissonance may lead to transformative ideas. To that end, this chapter explored how an articulated idea may lead to dissonance between parties. If the parties allow dissonance to fuel their discussion, they may have a productive deliberation of the value of an idea based on opposing orders of worth. This may result in a creative synthesis whereby the parties negotiate a compromise that enables them to move forward with an idea that integrates aspects of their respective value propositions. While a creative synthesis and negotiated order enables the parties to move on, it may be challenged again by a crisis which induces dissonance and leads to a renewed need for productive discussions.

Lasty, the chapter turned its attention to practices of evaluation. To evaluate an idea it must be articulated, so diverse pitching strategies were presented. The nature of the articulated idea is an important aspect when making sense of different evaluation practices. Based on different ways of conceptualizing the nature of ideas, a distinction was identified between transactional and transformational perspectives on evaluation practices. Transactional practices are based on the notion that an idea possesses an inherent value that can be judged with preset criteria based on which it is possible to evaluate ideas. Transformational practices, on the other hand, assume that ideas may be transformed in the process of situated evaluations. Hence, rather than selecting or discarding ideas, evaluation is a process that includes an ongoing interaction in which different aspects of value are discussed and ideas are transformed. Lastly, a typology of four evaluation practices and concrete examples was suggested to trigger reflections on how organizational practices facilitate idea evaluation.

The following chapter discusses in more depth how to facilitate the processes and practices of generating and evaluating ideas in an organizational context.

5
Organizing Creativity

Massive Entertainment is an internationally renowned gaming development studio based in Malmö, Sweden which has produced numerous blockbuster video games. David Polfeldt had been its CEO from 2008 to 2021, and in my interview with him about his approach to managing creativity during his time at Massive he uses an analogy to painting:

> I prepare the canvas for other people to express themselves. I am perfectly fine with that. I enjoy being the painter myself, but the worst thing you can have is a manager who wants to be the painter. So if you are the manager you need to give the brush to someone else. Even if you are making the brush, do not believe you are the painter!

The canvas metaphor David employs to capture his ideas on managing creativity hardly comes as a surprise. Among CEOs and top managers, David is the odd one out. He graduated with a master's degree from the University of Arts, Crafts and Design ('Konstfack') in Stockholm and started his professional career as an illustrator for comic books and advertisements. Yet with the advent of the new economy in Sweden in the 1990s, David became more and more involved with the IT business and, eventually, video game production.

David's love for art and his education shaped his management approach. For him, creating the best conditions for his employees to express their creativity is a

> holy obligation that I have towards my younger art school self. As a manager I will never mess up your job. I will never do that. I happen to know what it means, so I know what a bad decision of a manager looks like from a craft person's perspective.

When trying to facilitate creativity, bad decisions involve pretending to be the painter when micromanaging the creative process and not trusting the potential of one's employees. Letting go of control is, of course, easier said than done, and it may feel 'like herding cats, but that also means asking the question—what does the cat require from me?' What the cat requires, according to David, is trust. A manager must trust the willingness and resolve of creative employees to do their utmost to produce high-quality products. However, not only trusting creative potential is important, but also seriously committing to the inevitable fact that failure is a natural part of the creative process. This commitment involves not shaming or sanctioning failures, but appreciating the passion and dedication of attempting to realize high-quality ideas.

Yet, naturally, it is not simply about providing the freedom to be as creative as one wishes. For David, there must be clear boundaries to keep the creative chaos in check. For that reason, the organic creative process must be juxtaposed to a simple, traditional, hierarchical structure, which means that any idea, concept, or feature of a project can be stopped and discarded by a simple decision from a director or, even, David himself. For example, when this simple, traditional hierarchy is used, David mentions the cutting of features for games.

Organizing Creativity. Stephan M. Schaefer, Oxford University Press. © Stephan M. Schaefer (2023).
DOI: 10.1093/oso/9780198893509.003.0005

For a creative team, a specific game feature may be awesome and absolutely essential. However, over time, this feature may turn out to be rather costly and weigh negatively against the benefits. This may be the time that a director uses their decision power to discard the feature, a moment that is usually accompanied by objections from the creative team, who may hold a grudge afterwards and sometimes even work on the feature in secret. Ideally, such decisions should not be necessary. As David says, 'pulling rank in a military fashion' means that the objectives to provide the right conditions and visions for the creative process have utterly failed, and that means going back to the drawing board and assessing possible reasons for why an escalation up the hierarchy was necessary. But this is also an inherent aspect of managing creativity because 'things change all the time', and what may seem to be the right decision today may not be applicable tomorrow.

This, then, is David's overall answer to the question of how to successfully manage and organize creativity: 'it depends'. According to him, it is better to acknowledge the fact that there is no more straightforward answer than simply sticking to rigid management principles. It means that what may be learned from Massive does not translate easily into other contexts, but may simply serve as inspiration. In other words, the 'right approach' to facilitating a creative process is always fluid. A manager must situationally explore appropriate responses and important factors, such as time, quality, talent, and budget. Beyond those overarching factors, there is a complex matrix of small and large factors that could affect the result enormously. Accordingly, to identify these it is essential to explore what a team wants to accomplish in more detail and get a clearer understanding of important issues and managerial responses.

David's insights into his way of organizing creativity at Massive provide some intriguing points of departure to start reflecting on how creativity may be organized. His approach involves the creation of the right conditions for allowing the emergence of creative processes in which trust and safety play a pronounced role. During the interview, David also repeatedly mentioned the central notion of a team and how important it is to provide the right context and conditions for the creative team to work effectively. This idea of a team, however, is complemented by a traditional, hierarchical structure which makes it possible to exert unilateral power to stop creative projects. Yet organizing creativity does not seem to be simply about juxtaposing creative chaos and structure; it also requires a sensitivity to the characteristics of each situation and deciding on the most appropriate response.

To capture the diversity of different modes of organizing, which David Polfeldt alludes to, Alvesson and Blom (2019) suggested the metaphor of the Swiss Army knife, which has a set of tools that help in different situations. Sometimes the user may need a saw to make a serious cut; at other times they may need a knife to sharpen something or a corkscrew to open a bottle of wine. Similarly, different modes of coordination in organizations are useful in different situations, not least when organizing for creativity. As David's example illustrates, depending on the context, powerful visions, tight controls, or strong group cohesion may be needed to varying degrees.

This chapter aims to shed light on these different approaches to organizing creativity. Since Chapter 2 has already discussed the context of an organization in detail regarding the eight metaphors, this chapter will dive straight into the practices and processes of how creativity may be organized. To that end, *four distinct modes of coordination* and their relation to organizing creativity will be discussed, by using a running case study based on another recent empirical research project that I conducted.

Moreover, this chapter will elaborate on the limitation of the Swiss Army knife metaphor—that it may not be as simple as switching from one tool to another in different situations when striving to stimulate creativity. As seen in the case of Massive Entertainment, organizing creativity often involves a *both/and*—rather than an *either/or*—approach. To mention a few dilemmas of organizing creativity in which both actions seem appropriate: management must control and provide freedom, organizations should exploit old ideas while exploring new ones, groups should be cohesive and diverse, and an organization should maintain its structure and allow changes. Looking at these conflicting and contradictory demands, it becomes apparent that stimulating and influencing organizational creativity is *paradoxical*. For example, how can an organization provide freedom but also control its employees? Or how can groups be created that develop strong norms but remain diverse? These demands make sense in isolation, but if they are juxtaposed they seem absurd. This is the essence of a paradox, and this chapter explores the nature of paradoxes when organizing creativity and how people may deal with them. This discussion may then shed a different light on David Polfeldt's initially unusual approach to treat art and management as productive complements and not antagonists when organizing creativity.

Modes of Organizing for Creativity

Organizations are social collectives that deliberately strive to achieve a particular goal (Daft et al., 2020). So what would someone need to do to run an organization successfully and ensure that everyone in the organization strives towards the same goals? In the simplest terms, that person would need to specify their goals, determine what is needed to achieve them, find out who is doing what, and establish how people know that they have achieved those goals. All of this requires coordination and controlled efforts to ensure that everyone moves in the same direction towards the goals. This is not an easy task, and there have been different suggestions for what someone should do when they want to successfully run an organization (for a historical overview, see Barley and Kunda, 1992).

A good place to start is the work of sociologist Max Weber, whose ideas have been influential in organization theory and practice to this day. Weber suggested establishing a system in which an individual gives the most knowledgeable people the authority to tell others what to do. To make sure these knowledgeable people are acting in the interest of the organization, the individual provides them with the authority to make decisions and formulate specific rules for interacting with their subordinates and what the outcomes should be. Weber called this structure 'bureaucracy' (Weber, 1978). The concept of bureaucracy has fallen into disrepute, yet bureaucratic structures and principles are part of each organization—even seemingly unbureaucratic ones that seek to eschew routines or formalized structures (Turco, 2016).

The same Max Weber influenced yet another concept that has exerted great influence on how people wish to organize: leadership. He argued that some individuals seemed to have personalities that were extraordinary, almost superhuman, and that those individuals seemed to impact ordinary people with their mere presence and vision. He called this 'charisma' (Weber, 1978). Though Weber explicitly saw charisma as primarily spiritual and non-economic, his idea of charismatic leadership has informed most concepts of leadership in management and organization studies (see Spoelstra, 2018). The overarching theme is that leaders influence followers' actions—not by establishing firm rules, but by their sheer presence and inspiration.

Notions of coordination and organization have understandably come a long way since Weber's work, but his two ideas of bureaucracy and charisma still form the basis of distinguishing two forms of achieving *vertical coordination and control* in organizations. Vertical forms of coordination are based on asymmetrical relationships in which someone has authority or another form of influence over someone else. The bureaucratic principles based on rules and authority are linked to the concept of *management*. The central role of charisma, vision, and inspiration can be associated with the notion of *leadership*. Both concepts play a role in stimulating and influencing organizational creativity, which will be discussed in more detail below. Yet before taking a closer look at management and leadership, it is helpful to consider other possible forms of coordination that may help an organization achieve its goals.

Most organizations define a general goal—e.g. sell a service or product, educate students, help the homeless—which is usually referred to as the organization's mission. To pursue its mission, an organization may break it down into smaller goals. To work on these smaller goals, an organization may assemble groups of knowledgeable individuals that work on a specific task for the organization for a short or long period of time. This may involve the development of a feature for a product or the creation of a marketing campaign. Working independently within more or less defined boundaries towards a common goal is, therefore, another form of coordination, which can be referred to as *teamwork*. The members of teams may work on selected parts of the task and must coordinate their actions carefully to achieve the overall goals of the group. Teamwork should ideally be based neither on a predefined hierarchy of authority nor on the overriding charisma of an extraordinary person (Katzenbach and Smith, 1993). Instead, team members should interact based on equal terms, though a hierarchy and control through charisma and informal authority will emerge informally in most cases (Roy, 1959).

In contrast, individuals and groups may also direct their attention not to the members of their specific group, but towards individuals and groups that are not formally part of their immediate group or organization. By directing attention outwards, groups and individuals go beyond, or span, the formal boundaries of their group or organization to make new connections, collect information, or bring in additional resources. Spanning boundaries and establishing links with others outside the group or the organization leads to the establishment of *networks*. Teamwork and networks, in contrast to management and leadership, are both based on *horizontal forms of coordination* which means that there should be no asymmetrical, vertical form of coordination through formal rules or a leader's influence.

In what follows, these four modes of coordination and their practices will be unpacked with regard to organizing creativity. Since these issues have been treated extensively in the literature, it is only feasible to broach the most important aspects that may be used to distinguish the four modes of coordination and their link to creativity. Table 5.1 provides an overview of the main dimensions used to distinguish the four modes in this book. Each mode of coordination is based on some *key principles* which suggest what an individual or an organization *should do*. Each of these key principles contains certain *objectives* that are considered essential for the respective mode of coordination. Moreover, since organizations are social entities, *relationships* play an essential role. Thus, each mode of coordination is characterized by a specific type of relationship. The fourth

Table 5.1 Four modes of coordinating organizations

	Management	Leadership	Teams	Networks
Key principles	Planning, organizing, staffing, directing, coordinating, reporting, budgeting (POSDCORB)	Creating, maintaining, and influencing the meanings and values of organizational members	Assembling a group with complementary skills which commits to a common purpose	Establishing social ties with the anticipation of future benefits
Objectives	Maintain organizational order and control outcomes	Exert indirect control through preferred values and symbols	Reach goals connected to the team's purpose and hold each other responsible for the collective output	Internal and external 'boundary spanning'
Relationships	Hierarchical and based on authority	Leaders and followers	Horizontally shared responsibilities among team members	Weak ties
Link to organizing creativity	Set and control the boundaries of organizational creativity (passive management) Switch between loose and tight controls (active management)	Build and maintain creative organizational cultures Top-down creative leadership Bottom-up creative leadership	Diverse composition 'Psychologically safe' context	Technological and creative brokerage
Observed behaviour	Managerial work driven by responsive, fragmented planning rather than deliberate, rational planning	Breakdown of leadership based on different interpretations of what leadership involves and means	Teams evolve dynamically ('teaming')	Networking practices, such as liberating, inspiring, and maintaining
Dysfunctionalities	Stifle creativity through fear of losing control, influence, and standing in the hierarchy	Not recognizing misalignments Excessive positivity	Dysfunctional groupthink Group fragmentation	Information overload Abuse of power as a broker

dimension examines how each mode of coordination is linked to research on organizing creativity. While the first three dimensions of each mode of coordination mostly demonstrate norms and principles on what someone should do, empirical research has shown that principles, objectives, and relationships are generally difficult to apply in practice. Many close-up studies of organizational and managerial practices have shown that there is often a misalignment between aspiration—what someone should do—and reality—what they actually do. Hence, it is important to highlight research findings that have examined *observed behaviour*, what people in organizations actually do, and how much these practices are aligned with the way things should be. Lastly, *dysfunctionalities*, which refer to how actual behaviour deviates from common expectations concerning the different modes of coordination when organizing creativity, will be discussed.

Before delving into the discussion, a few caveats are necessary. First, the distinction between the four modes of coordination is analytical. This means that, in practice, the four modes of coordination are linked in a complex nexus of intentions, actions, and outcomes. For example, teams may use tight management controls, or leadership may influence network dynamics. Second, the four labels have become part of everyday language, which means that they have no clear-cut meaning. This is most evident regarding leadership and management, which are used constantly without always being clear. Similarly, researchers use these labels without always sharply defining their concepts, sometimes even using several definitions within the same study. Therefore concepts will be defined and delineated carefully to distil the most important features. Yet they do represent ideal types. Third, there is a general preference for—but also stigmatization of—concepts. This mainly applies to the distinction between management and leadership, which are considered bad and good, respectively. To come full circle, the sociologist Max Weber also proposed that scientists should be 'value neutral', which means that they should try to take a neutral stance towards their research (Weber, 1978). Though being completely free of biases is impossible, it is necessary to try to take a neutral stance towards these concepts initially and not judge them prematurely.

Management

How does one manage a team of highly creative engineers? This was the question for a freshly appointed and experienced manager put in charge of a group of engineers working on new ideas at HighTech (a pseudonym). The manager, John (also a pseudonym), noticed that the group was hostile towards being managed, making it a difficult experience for him, as group members resisted his efforts. Managing this group involved ensuring that people were on time for work, present at meetings, and meeting deadlines. Overall, John struggled to establish order within the group and integrate their outputs with the rest of the organization. Dissatisfied, some group members exited the organization because they felt unnecessarily restricted. To keep the group going, John hired other skilled engineers for his group to replace those who left and added extra ones as well.

However, up to the present day, he has struggled with the 'right' way of structuring his group of engineers. Educated as an engineer himself, he wants to be part of the technical details and discussions, but at the same time, he must represent and account for the group's output. For that reason, he must sometimes stop the development of ideas and restrict people's work, which he may have found appealing from a technical point of view. Sometimes, John is surprised about what his group expects from him. For example, when he asked the group to reflect on what they expect from him, 'the conclusion was that they actually requested more specific deadlines from me. That I should push them a bit more because they noticed that it would drive their performance. They get more motivated.' This, for

John, somewhat surprising insight, meant he had to think about ways to introduce more formal structure for the group.

John's struggle to organize the creative work of his group of engineers provides some intriguing insights into management and creativity. When John became responsible for his group, he drew inspiration from the principles of 'planning, organizing, staffing, directing, coordinating, reporting, and budgeting', often abbreviated as POSDCORB (Gulick, 1937). In fact, considering the different departments in an organization, POSDCORB mirrors some of the major functions of an organization, such as HR (staffing and organizing), accounting (reporting and budgeting), strategy (planning), or top management (directing). POSDCORB also suggests that a manager should be rational, calculating, and superior to impose order on their organizational environment based on the application of unequivocal principles. For John, the group was obviously in disorder, so he tried to structure, plan, and account for what it was doing. When some members left the group, he staffed it with other engineers. His overall objective was to be able to control the process and outcomes of the group and structure their work. To do so, he became part of a hierarchical organizational structure in which he was given the authority to make decisions—even though it was hard for him sometimes.

However, it did not seem that he was entirely sure of what he *was actually doing*. He did not appear to be the calculating, rational decision maker, but was unsure about the best way of managing his group and occasionally caught by surprise by the group's demands. Indeed, researchers who have studied what managers do have found that there is a sizable divergence between what managers should do—that is, POSCODRB—and what they actually do. These studies are now considered seminal in the development of management and organization studies because they offered insights into how managerial behaviour deviated sharply from the firmly established normative management models (e.g. Carlson, 1951; Stewart, 1967; Mintzberg, 1973; Watson, 1994). A general set of findings across these studies suggests that managers make decisions based on uncertain information and must cope with the ambiguity of many situations. Therefore, managerial work is mainly reactive rather than prospective, which means that, rather than deliberately planning and controlling, a manager reacts to emerging situations. The upshot seems to be that effective management may only be possible by being responsive to situations and people and not slavishly following abstracted management principles and systems. However, it would be misleading to argue that there is no connection at all between principles and practices. Principles are certainly influential, but there appears to be what may be called a loose relationship to actual practices (Watson, 1994). This means principles are not entirely without value but may help managers to make sense of situations and choose a general direction for their actions—whatever its outcome may be (Engwall et al., 2005).

There is a tendency to argue that management and creativity are incompatible. Indeed, John's efforts to organize his group showed that some engineers felt that they lost their autonomy, resisted his efforts, and even left the company. Yet, others welcomed his changes and even demanded more deadlines and structure. It may therefore be too simple to claim that management and creativity are mere opposites. Instead, it seems that they are related—albeit in a complicated manner. Adler and Borys (1996) argued that bureaucracy can be perceived as either *coercive or enabling*. In a coercive bureaucracy, rules stifle creativity because each deviation from a set rule is punished and each change discouraged. An enabling bureaucracy, in contrast, provides rules that support employees in their work and, rather than discouraging creativity, provides a supportive framework for employees or makes it possible to challenge established rules. Therefore, with regard to enabling bureaucracies, two types of relationships between organizational creativity and management can be distinguished: passive and active.

With regard to the former, the German philosopher Friedrich Nietzsche used the image of *dancing in chains* when he talked about the creative process, and it is a useful image for discussing passive management of creativity (Ortmann and Sydow, 2018). This image conveys how someone can express their creativity through dancing, even while restricted in some of the possible movements. Thus the chains restrict complete freedom of movement, but the dancer still has possibilities of expressing their creativity—even in restricted moves. Hence, passive management of creativity may set the basic boundaries—or sticking with the analogy chains—in the form of deadlines, resources, or objectives, but leave the process of achieving creative outcomes up to subordinates. An alternative and closely related suggestion is to accompany the creative process more actively. This means that, during the creative process, a manager loosens and tightens control depending on the demands of the situation (Bilton and Cummings, 2014). At this point, management itself turns into a creative process which means that, like an artist, a manager needs to combine structure with freedom in transformative ways (Reckhenrich et al., 2009). The notion of management as a creative process will resurface below in the discussion on how to cope with the paradoxes of organizing for creativity.

Naturally, people should be cautious with advice on how to behave when managing creativity. As seen above, there is a divergence between aspiration and reality in management in general, which extends to the management of creativity. The overarching reason is that just because someone has the role of manager, that does not automatically mean that they are a rational and calculating decision maker. People tend to downplay the fact that managers get emotionally involved, cope with their own insecurities and irrationalities, and strive to project a favourable image to their environment. On top of that, managers must navigate formal and informal relationships and hierarchies that influence their status and career paths. For that reason, managers may have difficulties letting go of controlling processes and allowing the freedom to experiment or deliberately tolerating temporary creative chaos, as this may jeopardize their reputation and career prospects within the organization. Managers are held accountable for their results and are, therefore, hesitant to take too many risks that may reflect badly on them. Jackall (1988) demonstrated such dynamics in his study of managers. In this study, managers refrained from openly endorsing ideas until they were certain that they would be successful, and then either claimed that they supported them or even that it was their own idea.

Leadership

The myth goes that the founders of HighTech, the organization John was a part of, scrawled the values that they envisioned for their new venture on a napkin during a dinner. Their scribblings allegedly formed the basis for the strong values that the company has adopted to this day. Among these values was the desire to always be open to other people's ideas and inquiries. Indeed, at one point HighTech had made the decision to discard its initial unsuccessful product, and to be open and seize the opportunity to develop and market a novel and innovative product. This strategic move was always evident in presentations about the company. People discussed how openness included an attitude of not formalizing processes or getting stuck in a specific way of doing things. Instead, openness meant to find the most effective way of working and solving problems and people offering their help if needed.

Talking about openness, an early member of the organization, Erik (a pseudonym), remembered the unconventional methods of developing and testing new products. For example, they used a hose in the founder's garden to test how different weather conditions affected their prototypes. Erik was, in fact, a part of the group of engineers that John was responsible for. He was well known by everyone in the organization for his active involvement in all kinds of projects and processes. People usually did not question his involvement, but Erik felt the strong urge to provide his opinions and ideas concerning various issues. Not surprisingly, Erik irritated many people with his interference. The founder of the company was a close friend of Erik and supported such behaviour, as he felt that the organization had lost some of its earlier spirit of openness. He missed the mavericks who would come with new ideas. Some people opposed the founder's attitude because they felt that the growth of the company did not allow for such radical openness. It was simply disturbing daily operations. They perceived Erik and the founder's actions as 'meddling' in issues that did not concern them. At the same time, HighTech was considered by employees to be an organization that awarded openness in the form of constructive critique, informal processes, and mutual aid. In internal and external surveys, employees expressed the value of openness as a key success factor for HighTech. Apparently, valuing openness and actually experiencing openness in some individual's actions seemed to contradict each other.

The activities and events connected to the value of openness at HighTech illustrate some of the key dimensions of leadership and creativity. Overall, the founder and Erik did not order people to be open, but they communicated and acted in certain ways to set an example for others to follow. This relates to the key principle of leadership, which is to influence and instil favourable meanings and values that people in an organization associate with actions, objects, and events (Smircich and Morgan, 1982). Leadership is thus considered to be *extra-ordinary*, which means that it is placed outside (extra) the order of the organization (Spoelstra, 2018). In other words, leaders should rise above the nitty-gritty of organizing and provide directions and visions for the organization as the founders did when they jotted down their preferred values on a napkin.

This understanding links leadership to a symbolic perspective on organizations, which means that leaders influence meanings and values of others. A strong overlap with culture is especially noticeable here. Indeed, leadership is closely linked to establishing and maintaining an organizational culture by aiming to instil guiding values and norms. The objectives of leadership are to create and maintain preferred interpretations of situations and guiding values, which decrease the need for direct control. Preferred interpretations and values may inspire people to neglect their own preferences and instead focus on what the organization considers important. For instance, Erik and the founder's interference had the intention of making people realize the value of being open to new ideas and not clinging to strict processes and formal rules in the interest of the organization. However, the actions of Erik and the founder also question the notion that successful leadership hinges entirely on the acts of the leader since other people in the organization considered their actions a disturbance. Consequently, leadership should not be understood as solely originating in the figure of the leader, but as emerging from an asymmetrical relationship between leaders and followers (Alvesson et al., 2016). Leadership, in other words, is only possible if it has a followership that recognizes it—leaders and followers mutually constitute leadership.

In recent years, research on the link between leadership and organizational creativity has surged. However, it seems that there are no consistent findings concerning appropriate leadership styles or practices that are positively linked to organizational creativity (Hughes et al., 2018). This may be due to the paradoxical nature of organizational creativity that defies standardization and variance-based methods of researching creativity. In other words, it may be difficult to adequately capture leadership's dynamics, influence, and reception by followers through standardized questionnaires and rigid definitions of creativity. For that reason, there is no unified scientific basis that can be drawn on when discussing leadership practices and organizational creativity. However, a recent review of the subject provides some interesting clues for reflecting on appropriate leadership practices for organizing creativity related to the 'spaces of influence' of leadership practices (Mainemelis et al., 2015).

By combining the definitions of creativity and leadership used in this book, it can be observed that leadership influences meanings and interpretations of how leaders and followers feel about and respond to generating, articulating, and evaluating transformative ideas that are in the interest of the organization. This notion alludes to two main points: the symbolic aspects of leadership, and the relationship between leaders and followers. First, symbolic actions target individuals' inclination to generate and articulate ideas. Here, leadership establishes and influences interpretations of whether ideas should be generated and articulated, what sort of ideas may be needed, how they may be evaluated, and who should generate them. Second, while symbolic actions target interpretations of situations and contexts, the link between leadership and creativity also suggests specific relationships between leaders and followers. In that regard, two types of directedness of leadership may be distinguished when organizing creativity: top-down and bottom-up.

Top-down leadership of organizational creativity is leader-driven. It is mainly based on the observation that the leader is the central generator of focal and transformative ideas. Followers are generally not encouraged to come up with their own transformative ideas, but to evaluate and implement the leader's ideas. Such top-down leadership linked to organizational creativity is evident—for example, in haute-cuisine kitchens, where chefs realize visions by designing recipes that express their creativity while their followers—usually other chefs—execute and implement those visions. Consider the example of Magnus Nilsson, a Swedish chef who ran the restaurant Fäviken located in the far north of Sweden. Nilsson, who was dissatisfied with his classical French training in cooking, found new inspiration in this environment when he started using ingredients that he sourced from his own land and places nearby. Nilsson worked to create his own unique recipes and style that he implemented together with his dedicated team of employees and chefs, who willingly worked on turning his ideas into unique dishes and menus.

In contrast, *bottom-up leadership* reverses the relationship between leaders and followers, as it becomes follower-centric. Here, followers are supposed to come up with transformative ideas that are facilitated by a leader. Bottom-up leadership of organizational creativity has been studied extensively because it appears to be the most common leader–follower relationship (Mainemelis et al., 2015). Most researchers have argued that the main role of a leader is to create a conducive context in which followers feel comfortable generating and articulating ideas and leaders have the expertise and skills to seriously engage with those ideas (e.g. Mumford et al., 2002). Consider the role of Steve Jobs during the early days of Apple. While Jobs had a technical background and interest, he mainly articulated his vision for an Apple computer for which the ideas were generated by Wozniak, his early partner. Yet Jobs did not stop at formulating a vision and making things happen; he also intensely engaged with the ideas for the Apple computer, discussing them with his engineers—and, most of the time, dismissing them rudely (Isaacson, 2011). Hence, Jobs influenced the context while engaging with his follower's ideas.

Of course, everyone has heard about successful efforts at influencing meanings and interpretations of followers and inspiring them to go the extra mile. The history of organizations is littered with stories about the practices of extraordinary leaders such as Steve Jobs. The crucial aspect to consider when it comes to these leadership practices is, however, the acknowledgment of their relational character. Again, the case of HighTech illustrates how the symbolic dimension of leadership may not be as straightforward as commonly portrayed when Erik tried to transport his vision of the value of openness to the rest of the organization.

While the founder or Erik were convinced of their leadership practices—advocating a radical openness—others deemed their interference neither constructive nor effective. Hence, there appeared to be a misalignment between their visions, intentions, and perceptions and followers' reception, agreement, and acceptance. This illustrates that leadership practices are rarely viewed as effective, necessary, or appropriate by followers. If that is the case, ideals and fantasies of one's own leadership simply break down in practice (Alvesson and Sveningsson, 2003). That means that when leaders practice leadership, it is important that these actions are understood and accepted by followers. Again, leaders *and* followers mutually constitute successful leadership; without followers, there is no leadership. Leadership may therefore be better conceived of as truly relational, involving an active dialogue about how a leader may be able to help facilitate creativity and, if necessary, even refrain from an overactive role.

Practicing leadership as part of organizing creativity appears to be appealing as people do not want to be associated with management they deem to be mundane and even boring (Alvesson et al., 2016). Yet for all of its appeal, leadership comes with some common *dysfunctionalities*. First, the problem is that leaders often do not notice the misalignment between their efforts and followers' reception, as noted above. They continue their leadership efforts and initiatives unperturbed. However, while in some cases these efforts may be simply ignored, in other situations they may be perceived as disturbing and ineffective. The upshot may be that people in the organization become cynical because a serious engagement with their needs and substantive changes through leadership is lacking (Rehn, 2019).

Second, though leadership may be intended to increase transformative ideas and is well meant in practice, it may lead to the opposite. More often than not, leaders are supposed to be cheerleaders spreading an atmosphere of positivity and motivation (Collinson, 2012). While a positive attitude is, of course, desirable, it may also prevent critical questions and reflections (Ehrenreich, 2010). The mandate to be positive all of the time may lead to unnecessary risk-taking, where leaders create a sense of invulnerability and overestimate possibilities. This could potentially create an atmosphere where dissent—that is, the willingness to critique and reflect on leadership's intentions and practices—is stifled because negative emotions are frowned upon and critique discouraged. Indeed, an overly strong emphasis on positive emotions neglects the potential of negative emotions for organizational creativity (Schaefer and Paulsson, 2013).

Consider the Finnish telecommunication company Nokia, which is well known for its leading role in the early phases of developing mobile phones, but also for reacting too late to the disruptive smartphone devices, failing to recognize the growing trend and develop new creative products. Vuori and Huy (2016) demonstrated how the failure to acknowledge and act on the external threat was due to an overconfidence in Nokia's capabilities and a pervasive 'culture of fear' in which middle management was terrified of criticizing or defying top managers. In an effort not to rouse the anger and negativity of top management, middle managers delivered optimistic analyses, even though they were aware of their untruthfulness. The pressure of delivering solely good news and creating a positive vibe prevented Nokia from taking a critical look at their operations and taking notice of threatening developments in the mobile phone market.

Teams

At HighTech, John had carefully selected the members of his team based on their expertise. For instance, Erik, the veteran of the team, was an expert in transmitter technologies, while Tom (a pseudonym), a recently hired addition to the team, was an expert in operating systems. During working days, breaks, and lunches they engaged in sometimes light-hearted, sometimes serious discussions concerning their areas of expertise, ideas, new technologies, and possibilities for HighTech's products. They frequently mentioned the work of another group which, in contrast to them, worked on completely new business ideas rather than ideas for new products. On multiple occasions, Tom suggested they try working with a specific software feature that he had worked with earlier, but Erik was resistant to his ideas and kept debating with Tom and regularly shooting his initiatives down. However, Tom kept insisting and brought it up repeatedly during discussions in various forms. He was obviously not willing to let go of his idea. For some weeks, the atmosphere was unpleasant, bordering on hostile. Tom and others would discuss and develop his ideas, while Erik tried to convince others that a specific transmitter technology had more potential. After some time, it appeared that Erik's idea really had some potential, and the group turned more and more attention to it—including Tom. In fact, Erik's idea would go on to become one of the central features of one of HighTech's products.

From bands of hunter gatherers to the division of employees into departments in formal organization, groups such as the engineers at HighTech have always played a key role in the creative development of the human species (Suzman, 2020). Groups comprise people who associate with each other to fulfil a specific purpose—for example, playing music or sports together or, in the case of HighTech, focusing on producing ideas for new products in an organization.

Formal organizations comprise various formally designated groups, including accountants, engineers, sales, and so on. Groups are also frequently referred to as *teams*. Again, analogously to the distinction between management and leadership, the terms groups and teams are used interchangeably. It is therefore important to distinguish them more sharply. A simple example illustrates the distinction. Consider how students may work on a course assignment together. In one scenario, one student takes charge of the group, decides tasks, and delegates them. Each individual student is held accountable for their individual contribution and how it fits with the goal of passing the assignment. Now consider if the students first openly discussed a shared standard for their assignment and everyone pitched in with ideas. Together they develop a common purpose, define the collective output they would like to deliver, and work towards achieving it. In the former case, it is possible to speak of a working group of students who all have individual responsibilities and work with clear directions. In the latter case, all members discuss the nature of their collective output and work towards it individually, as well as collectively, which is the characteristic of a team (Katzenbach and Smith, 1993). Here, the ideal role of the team in organizing creativity as a horizontal mode of coordination will be discussed, yet how teams may evolve into dysfunctional groups that defy the ideals of a team will also be explored.

Overall, the key principles, objectives, and relationships of teams include the collective discussion of and agreement on its purpose, shared responsibilities among members, and equal investment in fulfilling the purpose and achieving its goals. With regard to organizing creativity, three aspects of teams as a form of horizontal coordination should be highlighted: *composition*, *context*, and *process*. First, composition diversity plays an important role. Transformative ideas are based on bringing different, sometimes conflicting, perspectives together. To facilitate idea generation based on diverse perspectives, a team must include members with different perspectives, values, and ideas. Second, a team in which no one dares to voice their own ideas or challenge other team members will not be able to take advantage of its diverse composition. The feeling that the team is a space in which members can speak up and trust and respect each other is referred to as 'psychological safety' (Edmondson, 1999) which and has already been discussed in the context of evaluation processes in Chapter 4. Lastly, team processes are an important factor in generating and evaluating ideas. While research on teams and organizing creativity has focused mainly on static elements, such as team composition and how a team is influenced by context, it has not paid much attention to team dynamics and team processes—that is, what happens when a team is working together. A closer look at team processes has shown that teams are in a constant process of *teaming* (Einola and Alvesson, 2019). Teaming denotes the processes of how teams evolve dynamically over time, which involves changing patterns of how members experience working in a team and shifting interpretations of the team's purpose and output. Teaming is based on a strong process perspective, which was discussed in Chapter 2. It denotes the fluid and constantly ongoing emergence of team processes without any stable structures, and corresponds to the 'becoming' perspective on organizing (Tsoukas and Chia, 2002).

In fact, teaming plays an important role in organizing creativity. As seen in Chapter 4, transformative ideas are more likely to result from productive dissonance. This means that teams should be able to deal with tensions and conflicts by having the broader interest of the team in mind rather than individual agendas. This process involves paying attention to each other's ideas, working actively with those ideas by, for example, prototyping, and trying to see similarities rather than differences (Harvey, 2014). HighTech's team of experts is an example of how these aspects worked in practice. The team comprised individuals with different expertise who had no problem discussing and challenging each other's ideas. Yet the dynamics in the team showed how it struggled with the process of productive dissonance and combining different ideas. Over time, the team experienced an oscillation between coherence and fragmentation. This struggle is one of the most common risks associated with teams and organizing creativity, as each respective tendency may come to dominate and impede a dynamic and productive teaming process.

As a result of the struggle between coherence and fragmentation teams may end up in two extreme situations. On the one hand, they may develop what has been referred to as groupthink, which was discussed in the context of evaluation practices in Chapter 4. To recap, groupthink means that, over time, a team will develop dominant norms whereby the diversity of the group is turned into homogeneity—that is, the dominance of a single perspective. While this is necessary for developing group cohesion, it may lead to dysfunctional groupthink (Janis, 1982), which may be related to how doggedly the team pursues its goals. Research has suggested that the more a team is invested in its goals, the more it will disregard any challenges to reaching its goals. For example, a study of the deaths of people attempting to climb Mount Everest has suggested that reaching a goal at all costs—climbing the mountain—led teams of climbers to disregard even the threat to their own lives in pursuing their goal (Kayes, 2004). While this is an extreme example, it illustrates how dogged goal-orientation may render a group psychologically unsafe, as the group develops a harmful attachment to its goals. Opposed to the development of groupthink is the risk of the gridlocked fragmentation of a team. Rather than pursuing its goal, the team ends up in permanent conflict whereby its diverse perspective cannot be dealt with constructively. These two possibilities of how teams may develop create a paradoxical situation for organizing creativity. In particular, teams must be diverse enough to not develop dysfunctional groupthink, but not so diverse that team members do not discuss things with each other. This discussion will return to the central notion of paradox and how to deal with it later in the chapter.

Networks

HighTech's founders wanted to strengthen the company spirit by integrating departments and teams. One practical measure they instituted was to serve a free breakfast for everyone each morning in the cafeteria. Participation, of course, was voluntary, but John and his team were regular participants. They used to sit together chatting to each other. Other groups were dotted around the room equally engaged in their conversation. Sometimes, someone would walk past the table and stop for a quick chat. Sometimes Erik, the veteran, would arrange to meet someone over breakfast or walk over to a group and join their conversation. They would discuss the latest products, requirements, and ideas. In some cases, John, the manager, invited people he met at breakfast to visit the team's office space and learn about their latest ideas, which many did. The daily company breakfast was a manifestation of the last mode of coordination that will be discussed: networks.

As with all of the other modes of coordination discussed so far, scholars have defined and examined the concept of a network in different ways. The network perspective taken in this book emphasizes the establishment and maintenance of weak social ties, including the anticipation of future benefits (Perry-Smith and Shalley, 2003). This idea of a network is commonly contrasted with hierarchical relationships, such as management or leadership, which involve dependent and asymmetrical relationships. In contrast, networks are assumed to be based on mutual benefits, interdependent relationships, and reciprocity (Powell et al., 1990). A network perspective on organizing creativity has gained influence in recent years. Generally, researchers have argued that networks have a positive effect on idea generation, evaluation, and integration (e.g. Hargadon and Sutton, 1997). Networks expose people to various domains as well as different ways of working, which possibly change people's perspectives and may stimulate new ideas.

One of the most common objectives of establishing and maintaining a network, especially with regard to creativity, is to share and gather information across departmental and organizational boundaries. These objectives are referred to as external (Aldrich and Herker, 1977) and internal boundary spanning (Tushman and Scanlan, 1981). For example, in the case of HighTech's breakfast, the expectation was that participants would be able to exchange and receive information within the organization by spanning the boundaries between their and another department or team. In the case of establishing ties to actors and organizations outside the boundaries of the entire organization, it is possible to speak of external boundary spanning.

Relationships across networks that seek to span boundaries internally and externally usually consist of *weak social ties*, which were already discussed in Chapter 3. To briefly recap, social ties can be classified by how often actors interact (frequency), what kind of emotion they entail (intensity), and how much the actors benefit from giving and taking from each other (reciprocity). In a network, social ties tend to be on the weaker end of the spectrum, which means that an individual has less emotional investment, infrequent interactions, and less reciprocity (Granovetter, 1973). In particular, weak ties have less inhibition to challenge opinions than strong ties and, therefore, provide new stimuli (Perry-Smith and Shalley, 2003). Herein lies the contrast to a team which would more likely develop strong social ties over time working on a specific task and thus increasing the frequency of interaction and deepening emotional investments.

One of the central concepts that has been extensively discussed in the literature on the role of networks when organizing creativity is *creativity brokerage* (see, for example, Lingo and O'Mahony, 2010). A broker can be defined as someone who 'occupies the sole intermediate position between others, such that others can interact only through the broker' (Fleming et al., 2007: 443). A broker therefore has a central network position that enables them to connect individuals, networks, or ideas. There are four ways of how brokers and brokerage may be supporting organizational creativity. First, brokers may make groups become aware of each other's existence. Second, they may transfer practices from one group to the other. Third, they may draw analogies from another group that are beneficial for their own group. Lastly, they could synthesize and integrate knowledge, ideas, and processes to generate transformative ideas (Burt, 2004). The influential ethnographic study by Hargadon and Sutton (1997) on technology brokering at the award-winning design company IDEO showed how the company uses its network position as a broker to learn about solutions in different industries and then integrate those to generate creative design ideas. Hence IDEO's role as a broker is mainly to synthesize knowledge from different domains to generate novel solutions.

Stemming from an increased scholarly and public interest in networks, the call for networking has become frequent today. Scholars have distilled three important generic network practices that are relevant when organizing creativity and establishing possibilities for brokerage: *liberating, inspiring, and maintaining* (see Perry-Smith and Shalley, 2003, Anderson et al., 2010). Liberating refers to the practice of breaking away from the day-to-day demands in organizations with the aim of seeking other contacts than the regular ones. For example, the company breakfast at HighTech was instituted to allow people to get to know others outside their immediate teams or departments. Other examples of liberating practices may include visiting conferences or joining professional groups. Inspiring refers to the process of being open-minded and learning from others about, for example, new tools, knowledge, or processes, but also being open to sharing insights, knowledge, and processes with others. Lastly, maintaining refers to selecting a set of contacts one wishes to establish and maintain ties with in the future.

Naturally, the network mode of coordination is not without possible dysfunctionalities. One problem may be a disproportionate quantity of social ties. As Perry-Smith and Shalley (2003) argued, weak ties require maintenance and regular attention. Establishing too many weak ties may lead to a high degree of distraction and, at a certain point, may even constrain creativity as one struggles to cope with potential information overload. People are bounded in their ability to take in and process information, which limits the constructive use of network ties (Simon, 1997). The 'information deluge' on social media networks, for example, potentially increases the inability to take in relevant information (Leonardi and Vaast, 2017). The consequence is that information serves the purpose of projecting an image of being knowledgeable and well connected, rather than being used for rational decision-making (Feldman and March, 1981). Network ties, then, become a symbolic resource rather than a substantial means for generating and developing new ideas.

Another risk related to the notion of brokerage is the power to control the flow of information. Scholars have debated two perspectives on brokerage, which are inspired by the German sociologist Georg Simmel: *tertius iungens* and *tertius gaudens* (Obstfeld, 2005). *Tertius iungens* refers to how brokers unite and integrate people and knowledge from disconnected networks, which was discussed above. In contrast, *tertius gaudens* roughly translates as 'the third enjoys'. This phrase alludes to how a broker may be able to manipulate a network position for their individual advantage. For example, if an engineer receives information about a specific technology that may be efficient for his company but would threaten his own job, he may decide to withhold this information if possible. Hence, brokers may use their advantageous network position to prevent the flow of ideas. It appears that, in practice, a combination of both brokerage practices are necessary for 'creative brokerage', which refers to how diverse perspectives are integrated into a creative whole (Lingo and O'Mahony (2010). Based on their study of the brokerage practices of Nashville music producers, Lingo and O'Mahony showed how they alternated between integrating ideas (tertius iugens) and withholding information (tertius gaudens) in their projects. On some occasions their work called for integrating ideas and connecting people, while at other stages it was more beneficial to withhold information. Such practice of shifting between alternate modes of organizing creativity will be discussed in more depth below.

All in all, research on processes and practices of organizing creativity provides a great source for inspiration on how to approach this complex endeavour. As should have been made clear in this section, there is no universal approach to organizing creativity as modes blend and overlap with each other in the unfolding process of organizing creativity, making the ability to respond appropriately to various situations paramount. This is somewhat obvious considering the nature of creativity, which should be based on transformative ideas that are divergent and challenge the status quo. The process of coming up with such ideas is, as has been discussed throughout the book, crucial. Yet how could a standardized process of organizing creativity facilitate deviant processes? It seems to be a contradiction that a non-standardized creative process could be standardized and theorized (see also Rehn and

De Cock, 2008). This was one of the reasons why the Romantic approach discussed in Chapter 1 assumed that creativity was inexplicable and the gift of a few selected individuals.

However, our thinking and research methods have evolved over the years, and the Romantic notion has largely been dispelled—though it lingers in popular discourse. However, this should not pave the way for an overly rational or orderly approach to organizing creativity that seeks to propose various norms and steps to achieve creative outcomes. Organizing creativity is situational and processual (Schüßler et al., 2021), which means that the question of how to organize creativity should always be accompanied by David Polfeldt's resounding 'It depends!' What works for his gaming studio may not work for an equipment manufacturer, and what works for the equipment manufacturer may not work for the dairy producer. The observation that there is not one best mode of coordination adds to the complexity of organizing creativity and creates noticeable tensions for managers. It is to these tensions or paradoxes that the discussion now turns.

Spotlight on Research: Internal Social Media Networks and Idea Generation

In the face of increased pressure to adopt digital tools, many organizations have begun to implement enterprise social media networks (ESN) with the aim of facilitating knowledge exchange, interaction, and participation of employees. One of the perceived benefits of ESNs is the affordance of visibility of communication between people (the term affordance describes the potential for action new technologies provide to users). Rather than having private conversations, communication is visible to the entire digital network—or, at least, more parties than the two (Treem and Leonardi, 2013). This suggests that ESNs, in contrast to analogue networks, may have positive implications for organizing creativity. In this vein, the researcher Paul Leonardi explored how communication visibility affects the sharing of knowledge and the generation and development of new ideas (Leonardi, 2014). He found that ESN increased *meta-knowledge*, which refers to knowledge about who knows what and who knows whom in an organization. With regard to generating and developing ideas, enhanced meta-knowledge through communication visibility appeared to enable some employees to recombine existing knowledge in a creative way by accidentally taking part in other people's communication and being able to link other people's knowledge to their own idea. Yet while enhanced meta-knowledge may increase the chances of idea generation, visibility appears to be a double-edged sword. Visibility also means public exposure, which may limit people's inclination to share their knowledge or opinions if they do not know who will participate (Graaf and Gründler, 2019). Moreover, ESNs may contain a 'deluge of information' (Leonardi and Vaast, 2017), meaning that employees feel overwhelmed and even stressed and choose not to participate at all. Overall, ESNs appear to change how networks impact the creative process, but it seems that they must be actively curated and even managed to work effectively by, for example, restricting the content of posts or narrowing down specific target groups for posts.

The Paradoxical Process of Facilitating Creativity

The previous discussion on the modes of coordination has illustrated that organizing creativity is full of tensions and dilemmas. One has the option of managing through enabling structures, leading by creating inspiring visions, composing diverse teams, or facilitating weak tie networks. All of these modes of organizing creativity potentially help generate and develop transformative ideas. Hence, for a manager, which in the following refers to a person with influence and decision power in an organization, there is no straightforward choice, such as do A and then B will follow—though some creativity models propose such an approach. Organizing creativity is ripe with contradictions that managers must learn to navigate. To get a better understanding of the role of contradictions, dilemmas, and tensions when organizing management and organization, scholars have turned to the concept of *paradox* (Miron-Spektor and Erez, 2017). Using a paradox lens is not only an essential step in making better sense of the dilemmas and tensions when organizing creativity, but also a productive perspective in day-to-day practices of organizing creativity. A paradox perspective eschews simplifying the process of organizing creativity and refrains from proposing easy remedies, as we shall see in the following.

This book uses the definition from the organization and management scholars Marianne Lewis and Wendy Smith, whose contributions played a central role in diffusing and developing the notion of paradox in management and organizations studies. Smith and Lewis (2011: 382) defined and elaborated 'paradox as contradictory yet interrelated elements that exist simultaneously and persist over time'. They continued that the 'definition highlights two components of paradox: (1) underlying tensions—that is, elements that seem logical individually but inconsistent and even absurd when juxtaposed and (2) responses that embrace tensions simultaneously'. For example, organizing creativity requires providing freedom but also setting and controlling boundaries (Andriopoulos and Lewis, 2010). In an organization, people cannot be allowed to do whatever they want if there are certain goals, but it is necessary to provide the freedom to think divergently without constraints if the aspiration is to be more creative. This is paradoxical, as, when juxtaposed, these two aspects contradict each other. However, this and other paradoxes can, as Lewis pointed out, be 'embraced'. The model illustrated in Figure 5.1 is inspired by Smith and Lewis (2011) and outlines important aspects and processual dynamics of engaging with paradoxes productively when organizing creativity. The following discussion will go through the model in more detail.

From Latent to Salient Paradoxes

As seen throughout the book, organizing creativity entails many challenges for managers. In essence, they must make decisions on how to create appropriate organizational structures, implement their design, stimulate creative practices, encourage learning and divergent thinking, facilitate employees' identification with the organization, and instil guiding values. In all of these challenges, paradoxes are *latent*. Latent paradoxes become *salient* once managers recognize and experience a situation as paradoxical (Hahn and Knight, 2021). Four categories of latent and salient paradoxes can be distinguished. These four paradoxes relate to the essential functions and activities of organizing, such as establishing structures

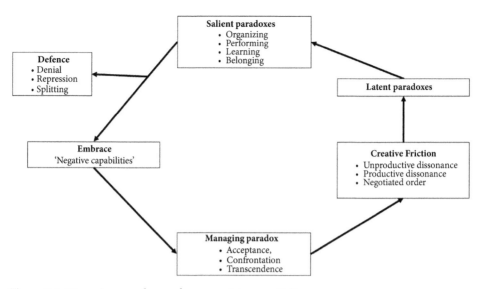

Figure 5.1 Managing paradoxes when organizing creativity

and processes to achieve goals (*organizing*), working towards the goals of the organization (*performing*), gaining new knowledge (*learning*), and feeling attached to and identifying with the organization (*belonging*) (Lewis, 2000, Smith and Lewis, 2011).

Paradoxes of organizing emerge from competing internal structures. An organizational structure is a set of repeated behaviours that persists over time and is instituted to achieve an organizational goal. For example, consider a bureaucracy in which there are formal rules on how to do things complemented by a hierarchy of authority. This creates a rather rigid organizational structure based on routines. In contrast, an organization with less rules and regulation will have a more flexible structure because people do not have to follow regulations and hierarchies. Both structures have their advantages, so—in many cases—organizational designs strive to be flexible and bureaucratic simultaneously by, for example, working on routine and nonroutine tasks sequentially, or creating different units for routine and nonroutine tasks (Adler et al., 1999). With regard to organizing creativity, this means that managers in organizations encounter the need to reconcile structures that control outcomes while at the same time allowing for the necessary flexibility to generate transformative ideas, which were discussed as 'enabling bureaucracies' (Adler and Borys, 1996) in relation to the management aspect of organizing creativity above.

While organizational designs are the 'social architecture of work' (Bolman and Deal, 2013), *paradoxes of performing* emerge when stakeholders involved in the process of organizing pursue divergent goals which leads to contradictions. The divergence of goals originates in the plurality of orders of worth that were discussed in Chapter 4. To recap, orders of worth refer to a system of signs, objects, and subjects that people use to justify their actions. In the case of the performing paradox, different orders of worth clash in the pursuit of organizational goals. Consider the example of Massive Entertainment again. David Polfeldt talked about how cutting features during game development may lead to difficult decisions. Creative teams tend to become so attached to the development of their specific game feature, but over time it may turn out that its development is very costly. Yet their creative feature may make playing the game more alluring and fun. In this case, the goal of a market order of worth—reducing costs—clashes with the goal of an inspirational order of worth which seeks to include novel and creative features that make the game more innovative. Paradoxes of performing thus emerge when conflicting goals are pursued in an organization.

The *learning paradox* refers to the simultaneous use of existing knowledge and the generation of new knowledge or convergent and divergent thinking processes. James March popularized the learning paradox in an organizational context through his work on organizational learning and elaborating the tension between exploitation and exploration (March, 1991). March argued that organizations must constantly make decisions on how and when to allocate resources and establish priorities for either developing and exploring new ideas or exploiting existing products. Yet even when individuals have been given the explicit mandate to explore new ideas, tensions between existing knowledge and opportunities for creating new knowledge exist.

A simple experiment illustrates this. Suppose someone is given the task of drawing an animal that lives on another planet. What would that animal look like? Ward (1994) found that the person would most likely draw inspiration from animals living on Earth, and that the alien animals would look very similar. Hence, people tend to draw inspiration from familiar knowledge categories to generate new ideas. In other words, they exploit past knowledge to generate future ideas. This exacerbates paradoxical tensions because previous knowledge is necessary for generating ideas, yet it also obstructs the exploration of new ideas. The implication of the learning paradox is that efforts to organize creativity need to address how to use existing knowledge to create new ideas that seek to replace existing knowledge (Ortmann and Sydow, 2018).

Organizations provide a strong reference point for identification as they provide 'the perception of oneness with or belongingness to a group' (Ashforth and Mael, 1989: 34). The struggle between identifying with a group while maintaining one's self-identity and identifying with another group creates *paradoxes of belonging* to either an organization or a group within the organization. For example, consider the role of a manager for a team of creatives assigned to come up with new ideas. The manager may also be a creative mind who likes to debate and come up with ideas and feels a belonging to his team. At the same time, the manager has authority and may identify with the role as a decision maker for the team and the management group. These conflicting group identifications lead to tensions of belonging. Essentially, the paradox of belonging goes to the heart of the tension between an individual seeking to be different from others while at the same time feeling the need to belong to a group where individual identity is absorbed by the group identity.

Defence or Embrace

Once paradoxes have become salient, managers and groups must deal with them. As Barbara Czarniawska (2001: 13) wrote:

> paradoxes are the logic's flies: although undoubtedly a part of the world, the prescription for dealing with them is clear. The paradoxes must be resolved. People refusing to do so may do it under one of two special licences: either they are mad, or else they are artists.

Czarniawska raised two possibilities of dealing with salient paradoxes. An individual can either try to resolve the dilemma stemming from the paradox or try to embrace it like an artist would. It seems, according to her, that not resolving the paradox is the uncommon option because people would be considered 'mad' as not resolving paradoxes appears to go against common prescriptions of organizing. Departing from Czarniawska's claim, it is therefore intriguing to examine more closely what resolving and not resolving paradoxes may entail for organizing creativity.

Resolving paradoxes entails a defensive reaction to tensions. Among the outright negative defences are repression and denial, which refer to reactions that ignore tensions by denying or blocking them. Schaefer (2019), for example, found that managers may talk about their good intentions of organizing creativity in a certain way but, when facing tensions, tended to do the opposite and resolve the experienced tensions. He referred to this behaviour as 'wilful managerial ignorance'. Another common defensive reaction is *splitting*, which means that managers separate tensions temporally or spatially. For example, they may focus on controlling their team in one phase while providing more flexibility and freedom in another. Such a notion is related to the popular concept of ambidexterity, which describes how organizations may be specifically structured to deal with exploration and exploitation at the same time (O'Reilly and Tushman, 2013). While splitting may lead to productive outcomes and is certainly not counterproductive to the creative process, there may be more productive ways of dealing with paradoxes, such as embracing tensions simultaneously, which leads to the approach of not resolving paradoxes.

Rather than making an *either/or* choice, people could aim to make a *both/and* choice. For example, instead of deciding on either control or freedom, people may ask how to stimulate both freedom and control simultaneously. *Both/and* decisions are the hallmark of embracing paradoxes, which requires, as Czarniawska alluded to above, a refusal to resolve them. An antecedent for embracing rather than resolving paradoxes is an individual or group's *negative capability*. The concept of negative capability can be traced back to the poet John Keats. In a letter, Keats reflected on what distinguishes a 'Man of Achievement', writing: 'Negative Capability that is when a man [*sic*] is capable of being in uncertainties, Mysteries, doubts, without any irritable reaching after fact and reason' (Rollins, 1958: 193). Keats here raised the possibility of not trying to find a quick fix or solution for situations, but rather being capable of embracing uncertainty and ambiguity.

One way of interpreting his notion is that it may be better to explore and assess situations more carefully and being able to withstand the urge to quickly find a solution. For that reason, negative capability is an intriguing concept, not least when translated into its relevance for organizing creativity. It relates to the ability of managers to cope with ambiguities and uncertainties when organizing creativity. While positive capabilities emphasize resolve and decisive actions, negative capabilities emphasize what Simpson et al. (2002: 1210) called 'reflective inaction', which means to 'resist the tendency to disperse into actions that are defensive rather than relevant for the task'. Reflective inaction suggests that a thorough assessment and evaluation of how to deal with situations, rather than jumping to conclusions on what to do, is an important aspect of organizing creativity. Relating back to David Polfeldt's experiences it means that the heuristic of 'it depends'—that he uses to assess his future course of action—should be based on a patient and thorough reflection on what may be required in any given situation. At first glance, being capable of using one's negative capabilities seems not to be a constructive recommendation because managerial work demands quick and decisive actions. Moreover, employees may perceive managers as inconsistent when they continuously change their points of views or revise their decisions depending on the demands of the emerging situation. However, negative capabilities do not mean that managers are inactive or cowardly; rather, they mean that managers prepare and make informed decisions that acknowledge ambiguity and ambivalence to productively manage paradoxes.

Managing Paradox

To embrace and manage paradox, three responses may be distinguished: *acceptance, confrontation, and transcendence* (Lewis, 2000). Acceptance in the context of paradox does not mean a passive surrender or submission, but an acknowledgement of the existence of tensions and paradoxes. Acceptance provides a sense of relief knowing about paradoxes since people realize that there is no single best solution. Regarding common defences, such as denial and repressions, *acceptance* is a first step of resisting such tendencies (Lüscher and Lewis, 2008). *Confrontation* refers to how tensions are explicitly addressed by either an individual or a group. It is the first step of externalizing and articulating tensions and making them available for discussion. *Transcendence* means that managers venture beyond tensions and engage in convergent and divergent thinking simultaneously with the aim of synthesizing seemingly antithetical requirements.

Accepting, confronting, and transcending paradoxes of organizing creativity enables managers to respond adequately to emerging situations in the process of organizing creativity. Simply knowing about the paradoxical nature of the process may provide relief and dispel the misguided perception that there is a single best solution to organizing creativity. Confronting and talking about struggles to deal with paradoxical situations offers opportunities to share experiences, but also prompts seeking help for possible strategies to deal with paradoxes. Transcendence puts one's reflections into action by aiming to cater to the needs of the situation and choosing a productive way forward. Those actions will differ from situation to situation.

While the ability to transcend paradoxes has been linked to highly creative people like Mozart, Einstein, and Beethoven (Lewis, 2000), its application when organizing creativity may be less spectacular. In that vein, scholars have compared managing and transcending paradoxes to the process of *improvisation*. Weick (1998: 551) introduced the notion of improvisation when he discussed how people may transcend *either/or* choices. Weick wrote that people tend to be compelled to choose 'between things like control and innovation, exploitation and exploration, routine and non- routine, and automatic and controlled, when the issue in most organizations is one of proportion and simultaneity rather than choice'. Weick then suggested that people address simultaneity by 'improvisation [which] is a mixture of the precomposed and the spontaneous, just as organizational action mixes together some proportion of control with innovation, exploitation with exploration, routine with nonroutine, automatic with controlled' (Weick, 1998: 551). Indeed, jazz improvisation has become an influential metaphor of how to organize more effectively (Hatch, 1999). Jazz improvisation differs from other forms of music in that there is no prescription of what to play, but 'involves exploring, continual experimenting, tinkering with possibilities without knowing where one's queries will lead or how action will unfold' (Barrett, 1998: 606). This leads back to the practice of managing paradoxes by accepting tensions and aiming to transcend paradoxes by seeking the most productive course of action in each emerging situation.

The practice of improvisation also harks back to Barbara Czarniawska's reference to mad people and artists. When organizing creativity, a one-sided conception of management as a rational and deliberate activity that involves planning and controlling must be complemented with an artistic, spontaneous, and explorative dimension. Managers, it may be argued, become more like improvising artists when organizing creativity. Reckhenrich et al. (2009) used the German artist Joseph Beuys as an inspiration for their conception of the *manager as artist*. Beuys suggested that the creative process consists of two poles: a chaotic, inspirational pole, and an organized, structured, and rational pole. The artist continuously shifts between these poles to impose order and movement in their artistic process. Similarly, a manager may shift between order and movement when actively organizing creative processes. Akin to the process of improvisation that is based on simultaneous structure and chaos, the manager as artist deals with the paradoxes of organizing creativity not by ultimately resolving the situation, but by shifting between different demands of a situation and choosing the most adequate action.

To pick up the example of the video game developers at Massive Entertainment again: paradoxes of performing may here be transcended by synthesizing diverging goals between management and the team by cutting the development of *some features* to move to a more organized pole, but at the same time allowing the team to work with some elements of the feature. Alternatively, a feature may be cut completely for a project shifting completely to the rational pole, but over time the team may be handed new requirements to develop another feature which means the team again moves to the chaotic, inspirational pole.

The attempts to manage paradoxes by drawing on negative capability and improvisation, however, do not guarantee success, and outcomes vary in every situation. If managers aim to transcend a paradox, they may inject dissonance and heightened ambiguity into situations. As David Polfeldt of Massive Entertainment mentions, when he reflects on the outcomes of his attempts to organize creativity, his actions may leave some developers angry and disillusioned. Indeed, Chapter 4 has already discussed how dissonance may lead to rejection or an unproductive discussion of ideas. However, transcending paradoxes may also lead to *productive* dissonances that inspire new ideas and creative outcomes. For example, aiming to reconcile a market and an inspirational order of worth when developing a video game feature may lead to the emergence of a creative synthesis and a temporary, negotiated order in which polarities are reconciled.

However, following Smith and Lewis (2011), a creative synthesis is merely a latent paradox if it is assumed that underlying paradoxes persist and cannot be dissolved. The example of building a spa in a nature reserve, discussed in Chapter 4, may illustrate the link between creative synthesis and latent paradox. If the parties agreed on building a spa that included sustainable architecture and the possibility of preserving the environment, they would have established a creative synthesis. Yet while the creative synthesis allows the parties to move on, the underlying contradictions between these orders of worth are not solved. In other words, paradoxes are still latent. Then consider the possibility that the spa owners realize that they must provide more parking, which means building on more protected land. In that case, latent paradoxes will become salient again, and the parties will have to deal them with anew. In other words, the example shows that paradoxes will never be ultimately resolved. There will always only be *temporary solutions* to paradoxical situations. Paradoxes will not vanish, but need to be constantly addressed whenever they impinge on efforts to organize in general and organize creativity in particular.

Spotlight on Practice: Working Through Paradox at LEGO

LEGO is perhaps one of the most recognized and iconic toy companies in the world. In fact its name comes from the Danish *leg godt*, which means 'play well'. The Danish company was founded in 1932 and over the years became one of the leading toy manufacturers in the world. From the late 1970s until 1993, LEGO doubled in size every five years and expanded to North America and other countries. It was one of the most prosperous periods in the company's history. Then, however, came a sharp decline as LEGO introduced more and more products which did not sell well enough to compensate for the increasing costs. In 1998, the company made its first loss since its foundation, and it was time for a new CEO to step in and attempt a turnaround (Robertson, 2013). During that period, the researcher and consultant Lotte S. Lüscher conducted an action research project at LEGO to study the organizational change processes taking place during the crisis and change of leadership (see, for example, Lüscher and Lewis, 2008, Lüscher, 2018). Walking around LEGO she noticed posters on the walls that described eleven leadership paradoxes. It turned out that those paradoxes were authored by former HR director Per Sørensen. The paradoxes emerged back in 1985 from the struggle to explicate consistent demands on managers. As it turned out, it was impossible to formulate such consistent demands since managers were supposed to be able to do everything simultaneously. Managerial work was clearly paradoxical, which eventually led to the formulation of the eleven leadership paradoxes at LEGO.

- To be able to build a close relationship with one's staff, and to keep a suitable distance.
- To be able to lead, and to hold oneself in the background.
- To trust one's staff, and to keep an eye on what is happening.
- To be tolerant, and to know how you want things to function.
- To keep the goals of one's department in mind, and at the same time to be loyal to the whole firm.
- To do a good job of planning your own time, and to be flexible with your schedule.
- To freely express your view, and to be diplomatic.
- To be a visionary, and to keep one's feet on the ground.
- To try to win consensus, and to be able to cut through.
- To be dynamic, and to be reflective.
- To be sure of yourself, and to be humble.

In a later interview, Sørensen used a plumbing metaphor to explain how managers should juggle the paradoxes according to the demands of the situation. He explained that a plumber either allows cold or hot water into the house, but not lukewarm water. So, like a plumber, a manager must know which tap to turn on to deal accordingly with a situation (Lüscher, 2018).

Yet as Lüscher and Lewis (2008) found during their action research project at LEGO, working through paradoxes was very challenging for managers. They organized 'sparring sessions' in which managers raised concerns about some of the contradictory demands placed on them. This led to a 'paradoxical inquiry' during which the researchers and managers aimed to increase understanding of paradoxes, but not with the goal of eliminating them. Paradoxes, they established, are always present, and there is no way of getting rid of them forever. According to their findings, the way to deal with paradoxes productively is to become aware of them and navigate them flexibly when making decisions. Working through a paradox, however, takes courage, as organizations traditionally aim to solve problems, and subordinates expect managers to be consistent and predictable. Linear problem solving and predictability, though, are impossible when working through paradox, as they *do not* 'encourage exploration of new modes of thinking, alternative perspectives, and varied means of framing reality that may facilitate action' Lüscher and Lewis (2008: 238). Just like the concept of improvisation, working through paradox requires the ability to withstand uncertainty and deal productively with the ambiguity of organizing creativity. In that vein, organizations benefit from highlighting the paradoxes of organizing creativity to make managers aware of them and possibly encourage improvisation in their efforts to facilitate creativity.

Conclusion

This chapter discussed how people may go about organizing for creativity. Since Chapter 2 elaborated on the notion of organizational contexts regarding the eight metaphors, this chapter focused mainly on the practices and processes of organizing creativity. To highlight the diversity of choices when organizing creativity, four modes of coordination were identified: management and leadership as vertical modes, and teams and networks as horizontal modes. Management entails the objective of maintaining an organizational order and ensuring that organizational goals are reached. In that sense, management is 'ordinary', which means that it aims to keep order. In contrast to 'ordinary' management, leadership is considered to be 'extra-ordinary' (Spoelstra, 2018). As such, leadership seeks to rise above the organizational order to provide long-term visions and imbue symbols with preferred meanings to guide organizational members in the right direction without exerting direct control. As a horizontal mode of coordination, teams generally work on common tasks and generate, develop, and evaluate creative ideas facilitated by diverse group compositions and the feeling of being protected from negative comments and shame ('psychological safety'). While teams direct their attention inward, networks seek to establish weak ties across departmental and organizational boundaries. Spanning various networks enables the flow of ideas and facilitates creative brokerage by integrating diverse ideas and technologies which increase the potential for creative ideas.

Overall, it was seen that while these modes of coordination propose various principles and normative ideals on how they should work in organizational practice, practical implementation is challenging and often deviates from these ideals. This may even lead to dysfunctionalities whereby creativity is impeded. This chapter discussed how management may care more about power and politics than creative ideas. Leaders may prevent critical thinking through an unhealthy degree of positivity. In addition, teams may either develop overly strong group norms that discourage new ideas or become so fragmented that they do not find any common ground. Brokers in networks may use their power to prevent the flow of information, which means that the potential of linking domains to generate new ideas is diminished.

The variety of appropriate modes of coordination when organizing creativity makes it a complex undertaking full of paradoxes and contradictions, as discussed in the second part of the chapter. A paradox was conceptualized as involving a fundamental tension between two aspects that seem straightforward individually but absurd when juxtaposed, such as providing freedom and control at the same time. It was further argued that responses to paradoxes involve embracing them simultaneously. Drawing on a model of how paradoxes may influence processes and practices of organizing creativity, this chapter first elaborated different paradoxes and then argued that managers may choose to deny that these paradoxes exist and thus refrain from embracing them. In contrast, embracing paradoxes requires negative capabilities, which refer to the ability to withstand ambiguity and reflective inaction to gauge the best possible way forward. Negative capabilities, as further discussed, enable the acceptance, confrontation, and transcendence of paradoxes. Embracing paradoxes in this way means that management becomes improvisational, which means refraining from predetermined responses and experimenting with creative solutions to management problems. This also means that outcomes become indeterminate. Embracing paradoxes may enable creative synthesis, but could also end up in undesired and unproductive outcomes.

Overall, embracing paradoxes rather than denying them when organizing creativity resembles an artistic process which challenges the predominant notion of a rational and deliberate management process and a tendency to deny paradoxes. More often than not, people are seduced into the denial of paradoxes and wilful ignorance and the allure of quick fixes and solutions—not least when it comes to the promises of generating the next creative blockbuster idea. This does not mean, of course, that people should disregard all practical advice. In contrast, they should learn as much as possible about organizing creativity, but when it comes to practice, remember the notion of reflective inaction that allows them to ponder how to proceed in the best possible way. These reflections do not only pertain to *how* people should organize and facilitate creativity, but also *why* and *to what end* they seek to generate and develop creative ideas. This crucial aspect will be discussed in the next chapter.

6

Reflecting Creativity

In 2002, Douglas Evans developed a small cold-pressed juice delivery service into a chain of stores that sold raw organic food and cold-pressed juices. The chain, Organic Avenue, hit the nerve of a clientele that sought a healthy lifestyle based on organic foods and health juices. Organic Avenue grew, but the competition became stronger as new competitors emerged and juicing technology improved the shelf life of juices so that they could be sold in supermarkets as well. Moreover, nutritionists started a critical discussion of the health risks of juice cleanses and strict dietary guidelines. These combined factors eventually contributed to the bankruptcy and closure of Organic Avenue. Evans, however, was not deterred and wondered how he could continue selling juices to promote a healthy lifestyle. He then had the idea of creating a personal juice machine that could be used by everyone at home. The important issue for him was that the machine would be able to produce cold-pressed juice. This was different from a blender, which would generate heat and chop the fruit and vegetables too much. To produce his cold-pressing juice machine, Evans raised $118.5 million from various investment firms and went to work.

Together with a team of engineers, he worked for three years in secret on his juice machine. Finally, in 2016, they revealed the fruits of their labour to the world: the Juicero. The Juicero was an elegant machine with a white glossy finish that was used to press fruit packs and produce cold-pressed juice. The fruit packs contained preprepared chopped and diced fruits and vegetables that were sold by Juicero. The selling pitch of the Juicero was that these bags made the process simple and contained fresh produce that was treated in a special way to reap all of their health benefits. Moreover, the Juicero was connected to the Internet so that customers could learn where the fruits and vegetables they were about to consume came from and whether their fruit packs were still fresh enough. In terms of its power to press packs, the Juicero was capable of exerting a pressure of four tons—enough force to lift two Tesla cars (Vargas, 2020). Naturally, this extraordinary piece of engineering had its price. The Juicero initially sold at $699 for just the machine, while the bags of fruit ranged between $5 and $8 each. The price was eventually reduced to $399.

In 2017, two curious reporters from Bloomberg carried out a test on the Juicero. They wanted to see whether a human could press the fruit bags and how much fruit juice that would produce in comparison. Alas, it turned out that the Juicero was not needed to produce a fresh glass of juice. Simply squeezing the bag with one's bare hands was enough and it produced almost the same amount of juice as the machine (Huet and Zaleski, 2017). Naturally, this discovery spread like wildfire throughout the concerned communities and to the wider public. People took a closer look at what had happened. On the technical side, a reverse engineering of the Juicero revealed that it was an 'incredibly complicated piece of engineering' that had not spared any costs. It contained so many complex technical features suggesting the engineers may have 'gone wild' (Einstein, 2017). An analysis of the decisions to fund such a venture raised the question of how ideas could receive so much funding to address 'non-issues' and catered primarily to health trends as well as the health-conscious

Organizing Creativity. Stephan M. Schaefer, Oxford University Press. © Stephan M. Schaefer (2023).
DOI: 10.1093/oso/9780198893509.003.0006

tech elite (Levin, 2017). The Juicero turned out to be an overly complex, overengineered product that attracted many investments but turned out to be worthless.

The case of Juicero raises critical questions: How is a product fiasco like the Juicero possible? What purposes did it serve? Why did it receive so much investment? How is it possible that people have no clean water in other parts of the world while other people are ready to pay $699 for a juice machine? Answers to these questions naturally differ and have no simple answer. What the case of Juicero indicates is a puzzling observation. Since the 1950s, creativity has become a key part of the economic and public discourse without leading to more substantial progressive and transformative changes—at both the individual and societal level. Instead, it seems to have led to a general *creativity fatigue* in organizations and beyond, which refers to the overuse of creativity as a buzzword that seems to no longer have any substantive meaning at all (Rehn, 2019). Thus it seems that the promises of creativity have somehow not been fulfilled. Could it be that the purposes of creativity have been somewhat misguided?

As I will argue in this chapter, the Juicero is a manifestation of an instrumental perspective on organizing creativity. An instrumental perspective views creativity as essential for economic growth, which in turn is argued to raise prosperity. The link between economic growth and prosperity, however, is not unproblematic, and an instrumental perspective on organizing creativity may exacerbate the grand challenges of today, such as inequality, climate change, and alienated labour (Jackson, 2009; Rosa et al., 2017). Perhaps other purposes of organizing creativity may guide efforts to facilitate creativity in different and more individually and societally rewarding directions. In this vein, I will discuss two other possible purposes of organizing creativity: *humanist* and *radical transformative*. Humanist conceptions of organizing creativity seek not to primarily capitalize and monetize creative ideas, but to foreground meaningful and fulfilling tasks. However, humanist conceptions of creativity are prone to be co-opted and assimilated by capitalist corporations, as witnessed during the rise of the New Economy at the end of the 1990s, when anticapitalist software coders established and eventually joined the big-tech companies (Ross, 2004). Hence, I will propose and elaborate an alternative conception of creativity: *radical transformative creativity*, which encompasses a fundamental consideration of the ends and needs of creative processes as well as its potential consequences.

Overall, the purpose of this chapter is to critically assess established arguments, theories, and knowledge on organizing creativity by unpacking the aims of organizing creativity. In the case of 'malevolent creativity', there is a clear intention to hurt individuals or society—for example, terrorist attacks (Cropley et al., 2008). The focus of this chapter however is not on such clearly intentional harmful attacks, but the generally accepted and seldom reflected ideological ends of creativity. As the historian Jill Lepore (2004, emphasis added) stated,

> in its modern usage, innovation is the idea of progress jammed into a *criticism-proof jack-in-the-box* ... Replacing 'progress' with 'innovation' skirts the question of whether a novelty is an improvement: the world may not be getting better and better but our devices are getting newer and newer.

Similarly, in her comprehensive review of creativity research, George (2007) argued that the majority of creativity research in organizations tends to treat it as the dependent variable, meaning that researchers strive to understand influences *on* creative outcomes and not consequences *of* creativity. Or, as Cropley et al. (2008: 105, emphasis in original) observed, scholars tend to conceptualize creativity 'even as somehow above social constructs such as *good* or *bad*'. Overall, research seems to treat creativity as an end in itself and not as a means to an end, and seldom critically discusses the value and ends of creativity. One may therefore argue that creativity has become an 'ideograph' (McGee, 1980), which is a frequently used expression with an unclear meaning that reinforces an *ideology of creativity*.

Eagleton (1991), in his broad overview of the ideology concept, proposes that it can be defined along a continuum from a rather value-free interpretation akin to culture to a concept which stresses ideology as false beliefs stemming from the material societal conditions such as Marxism. According to him we find in between a variety of ideologies which, in one way or another, emphasize the dominance of a power and false beliefs. Ideology thus varies in the degree of including power as a variable, the dominance of this power, and the source from which this power stems (group, society, structure). Eagleton reiterates the practice and behavioural aspect of ideology and adds strategies of universalization, naturalization, rationalization, and legitimization. For the purposes of this chapter I understand ideology similarly as a *set of beliefs which correlates to the execution of power to obfuscate other alternative ways of conceiving the state of things.*

To challenge the ideology of creativity, this chapter draws on Ian Hacking's suggestion to reflect on and unpack taken-for-granted notions (see Chapter 2). To recap, he urged readers to consider current situations and beliefs and asked them to consider whether something should really be the way it is. If it does not have to be the way it is, they should consider whether the situation is bad or good for them and whether they could transform the situation (Hacking, 1999). His inquisitive mindset underpins this chapter.

To unpack the ideological ends of creativity and propose alternatives, this chapter first discusses the broader socio-economic context in which efforts of organizing creativity are embedded—a predominantly capitalist world economy based on dynamic stabilization. Then follows a discussion of how organizing creativity is central to the growth paradigm in a capitalist system and a general overview of different ends of creativity—instrumental, humanist, and radical transformative. These three conceptions will be unpacked and discussed.

Economic Context for Organizing Creativity

What defines an age? What has led humanity here? What will life be like in 100 years? It is not an easy feat to answer these questions, and multiple insights, commentaries, and stories exist. Yet in recent decades, some stable ideologies have influenced how people live, work, and think. This includes the rise and continuous spread of capitalism as the dominant framework for organizing economic activity and the central imperative of economic growth. For both ideologies, capitalism and economic growth, organizing creativity and innovation play a central role and merit a deeper discussion to prepare the unfolding argument in this chapter. *Ex ante*, it is important to point out that both ideologies have led to positive transformations. They allowed humanity to raise levels of prosperity by combating diseases, poverty, and hunger in absolute terms, yet there are still many who have not benefited from such developments. While these positive effects must be acknowledged, it is essential to take a more critical look at the consequences of a capitalist logic and economic growth and the role that organizing creativity plays.

The Triumph of Capitalism

The year 1989 was a watershed moment in recent history when the communist systems of the East collapsed. It sent a strong signal that liberal democracies and capitalist economic systems had prevailed over the competing planned economic systems of the East. The historian Francis Fukuyama indeed declared 'the end of history' by arguing that the world had reached the point where no further progress would happen, as Western liberal democracy was accepted as the universal system and the 'final form of human government' (Fukuyama, 1989). While Fukuyama's prediction of the end of history and struggle over ideology has been seriously challenged by the flaring up of global military conflicts and the increasing political influence of extreme factions, it does highlight that at least the Western economic system in the form of a capitalist logic had become normalized and widely accepted. In his essay, however, he also concluded that humanity is entering a 'very sad time' since 'the worldwide ideological struggle that called forth daring, courage, imagination, and idealism, will be replaced by economic calculation, the endless solving of technical problems, environmental concerns, and the satisfaction of sophisticated consumer demands' (Fukuyama, 1989: 18). This, as will be seen below, was an apt prediction. Yet before delving deeper into the impact of capitalism and economic growth on organizing creativity, it is necessary to take a differentiated look at both ideologies.

In its most essential features, capitalism comprises free markets, the right to own and sell property, and unregulated price settings according to supply and demand. Yet not all capitalist systems are created equal, according to Baumol et al. (2007). They distinguished four types of capitalist systems: (i) a form of capitalism in which governments guide the market and finance those industries that they perceive as having the most potential (*state-guided capitalism*); (ii) capitalist systems in which a small group of people own most of the wealth (*oligarchic capitalism*); (iii) a capitalist system in which large enterprises carry out most of the economic activity (*big-firm capitalism*); (iv) a capitalist system in which small innovative businesses play the most significant role in economic activities (*entrepreneurial capitalism*). Furthermore, they argued that the most desirable type of capitalism is a combination of entrepreneurial and big-firm capitalism, as this would allow a degree of new inventions and ideas by small companies and the ability to mass produce and distribute these by big firms. In these capitalist systems, creativity and marketable ideas play an essential role because entrepreneurs must compete to make profits on their invested capital.

Other authors have more broadly distinguished between liberal market economies, which are part of more deregulated societies (e.g. the US, UK, and Australia), and coordinated market societies, which are more regulated and have more restricted competition (e.g. Sweden and Germany) (Hall and Soskice, 2001). Overall, different versions of capitalism are distinguished by the intervention of government and the role of firms in the society. The upshot is that it is difficult to speak of a uniform capitalist system. Yet a central tenet across all varieties of capitalism is the imperative of economic growth (Jackson, 2009).

In a capitalist system, economic growth relates to the increase of the value of all of the goods and services produced in a country or region. Economic growth indicates rising profits of companies or entrepreneurs, more employment, the possibilities of reinvesting excess capital, and the ability of consumers to raise their material affluence or standards of living. Before the rise of capitalism, growth was mostly related to the plundering and conquest of new territories and resources by force—for example, when Spain conquered much of Latin America and plundered its gold reserves. While such forceful practices are sadly still much too common, a major part of economic growth is based on entrepreneurial ingenuity and creativity.

Economic growth in capitalist systems, however, is ambivalent. While economists advocate its potential for raising the prosperity and well-being of everyone, others are more sceptical. Sceptics challenge the 'taken-for-granted assumptions that underlie traditional notions of growth—that economic growth can be endless and without limits, that resource extraction can proceed without regard for resource depletion or ecological damage, and that economic growth enhances the social wellbeing of all' (Banerjee et al., 2021: 340). Banerjee et al. highlight the need to reflect critically on the dominant principles of economic growth and its consequences. Following their call, the notion of economic growth and its sociological and individual dynamics and implications, as well as the role that organizing creativity plays, will be illuminated in the following.

Dynamic Stabilization

An intriguing analysis of modern capitalism has been proposed by the German sociologist Hartmut Rosa and his colleagues (Rosa et al., 2017). They delineated the characteristics of modernity, and central to their discussion is the notion of 'dynamic stabilization'. They put this notion metaphorically: 'Capitalist systems in all varieties resemble a bicycle that gains in stability with the speed of its forward motion, while it easily tips when slowing down or coming to a halt' (Rosa et al., 2017: 56). This metaphor highlights how capitalist systems are based on continuous acceleration, speed, and forward movement. If the system slows down—that is, decreases its pace and rates of growth—it will tumble and lose momentum.

In more formal terms, Rosa et al. (2017: 54, emphasis removed) argued that a modern society stabilizes dynamically when it 'needs (material) growth, (technological) augmentation and high rates of (cultural) innovation in order to reproduce its structure and to preserve the socioeconomic and political status quo'. Jackson (2009: 14) similarly argued that 'modern society is structurally reliant on economic growth for its stability'. Notable in both conceptions is that economic growth is not needed to achieve progressive transformations that lead to increased prosperity, but it is needed to maintain existing structures and reproduce them. An image may help to illustrate their argument. Imagine someone walks on an escalator in the wrong direction. To keep up with it and remain level, they must move constantly. Likewise, a modern society must keep growing to remain level, i.e. functional.

For Rosa et al. (2017), three imperatives—or what they call motors of dynamic stabilization—can be identified: appropriation, acceleration, and activation. *Appropriation* refers to how the market logic of capitalist systems continuously expands. Such expansion of a market logic is most obvious when it comes to resources—that are continuously mined across the world; new markets—such as the release of new products or services; and territories—such as the scramble for exploiting oil in Antarctica or other previously unexploited territories. Yet the continuous expansion also covers traditionally non-economic spheres of life. For example, in her seminal study Hochschild (1983) illustrated that work increasingly encompasses what she called 'emotional labour'. Emotional labour refers to how employees must regulate their emotions to project a positive mood to the customer so that the organization can sell more products. Hence, the imperative to sell services and products and to grow appropriates and commodifies individuals' emotions. Similarly, the rise of New Public Management, which comprises the spread of market principles to governmental administration, illustrates how public services are turned into products to be sold to customers, rather than provided to citizens. For example, universities are increasingly governed based on market logics and performance measures. Output criteria—such as the number of publications, ranking systems, and customer orientation—influence how universities are structured and ultimately managed (Enders et al., 2015). Such quantification stands in contrast to fulfilling the more ambiguous and qualitative need for educating students and meaningful scientific contributions (see, for a discussion, Alvesson et al., 2017).

Acceleration refers to the increasing speed and pace of modern societies. Acceleration is aptly captured in the observation that the quantity of activities and events has increased per unit of time (Rosa, 2013). For example, it may have taken someone an hour to write a letter by hand to one person some thirty years ago. Today, people can often write twenty emails to various people in an hour. Similarly, from my own experience as a student and researcher, I remember walking to the library, searching for articles that were shelved in physical books, locating the right article, and then copying it on a machine. Needless to say, it took a significant amount of time, while today, entire volumes are there at the click of a mouse. The paradox here, however, is that while people have more time, they use it to increase their activities. Someone could indeed write one email to the person they would have written the letter to and then take a walk. Instead, they now write twenty emails in that hour. Judy Wajcman calls this the 'time-pressure paradox', by which she means that though people should have more free or idle time since technology has made life more efficient, they seem to have even less time than before. For example, cars made travelling to work quicker and more efficient, but rather than freeing up time for other things, people moved far outside the city and now spend their time in morning traffic on their way to work, feeling stressed and engaging in bouts of road rage. Somehow, freeing up time has made people feel more pressured than before, and it seems that they have lost control over their time (Wajcman, 2014).

What are possible reasons for this paradox? Wajcman identified technological innovation, digitalization, and cultural changes as possible reasons for the time-pressure paradox. For example, writing twenty emails is now not only technically possible, but has become an intrinsic element of a culture in which work 'bleeds' into personal lives (Gregg, 2011). The upshot of the observed acceleration of life and the time-pressure paradox is that while modern technologies have made it possible to save time and perhaps even slow down life, people have become more stressed than before and the perceived and real speed of life is continuously increasing.

Finally, *activation* refers to how social responsibilities are shifted from civic institutions and communities to individuals. In fact, individuality has been a central concern of what the sociologist Richard Sennet called the 'culture of the new capitalism' (Sennett, 2007). Sennett argued that this new culture instils beliefs about the advantages of flexibility and individual freedom that lead to a loss of community and solidarity. This new culture, he maintained, forces individuals to think more short term while constantly working on their marketability or what is now called employability. For example, Andre Spicer and Carl Cederström argued that wellness is not merely a way of achieving and maintaining a healthy lifestyle; it also serves as a way of activating individuals to maintain their level of fitness and health to contribute to economic growth. Health becomes a productivity factor, and individuals are encouraged to constantly improve and work on themselves. All the while, civic and social institutions—such as unions and communities that used to ensure healthy work environments or social support—disappear (Cederström and Spicer, 2015). Hence, collective responsibility for maintaining a healthy and just working life shifts from civic institutions to single individuals. This naturally places a heavy burden on individuals and leads to a loss of sense of community and solidarity (Putnam, 2000).

In the context of the discussion of organizing creativity, it is the link between dynamic stabilization, its three motors, and the purposes of organizing creativity that is of particular interest. Central to dynamic stabilization are creativity processes that fuel economic growth and dynamic stabilization. Yet while dynamic stabilization may have started out as a promise of prosperity, individual and social growth, and positive transformations, its escalatory logic—based on appropriation, acceleration, and activation—'entails a social, psychological and ecological price' (Rosa et al., 2017: 56). As Jackson (2009: 88) argued, 'the idea of running faster and faster to escape the damage we're already causing is itself a strategy that smacks of panic. So before we settle for it, a little reflection may be in order.' Such reflections leads to the question of what characterizes processes of organizing creativity in the context of dynamic stabilization and possible alternative conceptions and purposes of organizing creativity. It is to a discussion of the dominant ends of creativity and possible alternatives that this chapter now turns.

Instrumentalist and Humanist Conceptions

This discussion will draw on the distinction between instrumentalist and humanist conceptions of creativity that were discussed and historically situated in Chapter 1 (Bycroft, 2014). To recap, instrumentalist conceptions of creativity arose as the need to compete economically and militarily increased after the Second World War. Instrumentalist research therefore studied creativity *as a means to an end*. At the same time, humanist researchers regarded creativity as an end *in itself* and aspired to explore its potential to address social and psychological problems. Instrumentalist and humanist conceptions are useful to distinguish means and ends of creativity with regard to organizing creativity and, especially, their implications for dynamic stabilization and economic growth.

The main argument that I will suggest in the following section is that instrumentalist and humanist conceptions may contribute to some of the negative social, psychological, and ecological consequences of economic growth discussed above. Both conceptions in an organizational context seem at first glance to focus on very different outcomes, yet they do complement each other, especially regarding dynamic stabilization and the imperative for growth. While this seems intuitive for instrumentalist conceptions, since they focus on creativity as an instrument for economic purposes, it requires some more elaboration for humanist conceptions which after all focus on the well-being of individuals. As a potential alternative conception, I will introduce the notion of radical transformative creativity. Radical transformative conceptions, I argue, should conceptualize creativity as a means to create sustainable ends. This requires a pluralistic approach as well as a focus on *sufficiency*

Table 6.1 Instrumental and humanist conceptions of creativity

	Instrumentalist	Humanist
Definition	Organizational creativity serves instrumentalist purposes	Organizational creativity serves self-actualization
Perspective on the individual	Homo oeconomicus	Homo creativus
Perspective on growth	Economic growth and profit maximization	Individual growth and self-actualization
Justification (order of worth)	Market, industrial, and fame	Inspiration
Intended purpose	Economic prosperity and dynamic stabilization	Self-actualization of individual, authenticity
Observed outcomes	Exploitation of limited natural resources, social inequalities and rising levels of alienation, and rebound effect	Increased individualism; exit, voice, or loyalty reactions of individuals in an organizational context

rather than efficiency. Sufficiency eschews a strict focus on maximizing gains by exhausting resources and instead emphasizes restraint and moderation in individual and collective consumption (Princen, 2005).

Before delving into the discussion, a note on the overarching connotation is in order. All three categories contain a descriptive, as well as a normative, component, which means that all three labels describe a quality (descriptive) and a desired outcome (normative). Instrumentalist conceptions connote a tool-like quality that should lead to economic growth (e.g. Florida, 2012). Humanist approaches focus on individual freedom and agency and ascribe the norm of self-fulfilment to human development (Maslow, 1962). Radical transformative approaches connote the quality of a degree of change that seeks to create sustainable solutions (Göpel, 2016). Table 6.1 provides an overview and comparisons of instrumentalist and humanist conceptions of creativity and their implications, which will be reflected and unpacked later.

Instrumentalist Perspective

In 1970, the psychologist Razik reflected on the need for the demystification of creativity and the demand for systematically extracting more creativity from people. He mused that

> 'creativity' could no longer be left to the chance occurrence of genius; neither could it be left in the realm of the wholly mysterious and the untouchable. Men [sic] had to be able to do something about it; creativity had to be a property in many men [sic]; it had to be something identifiable; it had to be subject to efforts to gain more of it.
>
> (Razik, 1970: 156).

Razik's words reflect the sentiment of the time and aptly summarize the overarching goal of creativity research after 1950. Creativity should not be regarded any longer as a trait or quality of a genius that was uncontrollable, but as something that could be systematically harnessed and used for specific ends. Note how Razik emphasized that people should *gain* more of it, which directly addresses the notion of growth. Indeed, as I suggest in the following, an instrumentalist perspective on organizing creativity in capitalist systems mainly serves the purpose of economic growth and dynamic stabilization.

The urban geographer Richard Florida has become one of the key figures advocating creativity as a motor for economic growth (Florida, 2012). He argued that humanity has witnessed a shift from agricultural to industrial economies and then to creative economies in which creativity is the central production factor. Responsible for creative ideas and economic growth is what he called the 'creative class'. Florida argued that the creative class is a workforce concerned with producing useful and new products, designs, and services that serve regional economic growth. He divided the creative class into the super-creative core—such as scientists, engineers, artists, and poets—and creative professionals who engage in complex problem solving. In essence, his distinction is akin to a divergently thinking super-creative core and a convergently thinking group of creative professionals. which is responsible for regional economic growth.

To Florida, these occupations are not based on a few selected creative talents; he argues 'that human beings have limitless potential, and that the key to economic growth is to enable and unleash that potential' (Florida, 2005: 5). To unleash that creative potential, regional decision makers must design urban spaces for the needs of the creative class and potential creatives. To do so, Florida proposed a simple theory that three factors are essential for attracting the creative class: technology, talent, and tolerance. Technology refers to the existing technological potential of a region that will assist the creative class in the development of their ideas, such as universities and research labs. Talent is the aggregation of knowledgeable individuals and creatives in a region. Tolerance refers to the diversity in a region—that is, the aggregation of different nationalities, occupations, and people with alternative lifestyles. According to Florida, regions must consider the three *T*s if they aspire to build a creative hub that will stimulate regional economic growth. Nation states, then, should design policies and strategies to support the establishment of regional creative hubs.

An instrumentalist perspective on creativity, such as Florida's, mainly focuses on market and industrial orders of worth as dominant forms of justification and evaluation of creative ideas. That is, of course, not surprising, as economic growth is measured as the value of products and services produced. This is also evident in the assumptions concerning the creative individual. Peck (2005: 746, emphasis in original), in his critique of Florida's ideas, argued that Florida depicts the '[h]omo creativus [as an] an atomized subject, apparently, with a preference for intense but shallow and noncommittal relationships, mostly played out in the sphere of consumption and on the street'. Noteworthy in this description is the emphasis on individualization and weak tie relations. This stands in contrast to, for example, a civic or domestic order of worth, which emphasizes community and long-term relationships or strong ties. Worthy subjects are, therefore, creatives who manage to sell their ideas to consumers with the main purpose of increasing the overall value of products—that is, profit-maximizing economic growth. Moreover, an instrumentalist perspective is also justified by an industrial order of worth manifested in Florida's technology dimension. Hence, overall, Florida's theory on the creative economy serves as an illustration of how he makes creativity the central linchpin of economic growth and the generation of efficient and profitable ideas.

Overall, the intended purpose of an instrumental perspective on organizing creativity is economic growth and, ultimately, societal prosperity. This line of reasoning stems from the assumption that material affluence will lead to individual and societal well-being. While economists and policymakers have emphasized this link to advocate for economic growth, other scholars have been more sceptical (e.g. Jackson, 2009; Alvesson, 2013a). Uncontested is that economic growth is essential for less developed regions and countries where basic human needs, such as food and shelter, are not met. However, the imperative of economic growth can be critically discussed with regard to more developed economies—especially the link between material affluence and prosperity. It appears that material well-being has a diminishing return—that is, more economic growth will not necessarily lead to more well-being (Myers and Diener, 2018). The discussion will return to this later. What is quite apparent, however, is that continuing economic growth seems to have some negative ecological and social consequences fuelled by the motors of dynamic stabilization discussed previously.

As already mentioned in Chapter 4, in 1972 a group of researchers published a report entitled *The Limits of Growth* that was commissioned by the Club of Rome, a group of influential business leaders, former politicians, and scientists. The report discussed the grand challenges at the time: 'accelerating industrialization, rapid population growth, widespread malnutrition, depletion of nonrenewable resources, and a deteriorating environment' (Meadows et al., 1972: 21). What the researchers concluded forty years ago has been eerily prescient. They argued that if rates of growth continued as they did, the planet would reach its limits of growth in the next hundred years—that is, around 2070. This means a rapid decline of the planet's resources and ability to sustain industry and the rapidly growing world population. The report stimulated a debate on the planet's finite resources and various suggestions on how to tackle the limits to growth. These debates included the threat of exhausting resources, but also the negative effects associated with emissions and the pollution of the natural environment through industrial activity and mass consumption. These threats have not abated—quite the contrary. Recently, a report by the Intergovernmental Panel on Climate Change (IPCC), a group of researchers commissioned by the UN to study climate change, argued that it is likely that, if humanity continues their current rate of emissions, the planet will reach a global warming of 1.5°C between 2030 and 2052. Such a temperature increase due to emissions cause what the IPCC has defined as 'reasons for concerns' that include negative impacts for ecosystems and cultures—for example, extreme weather conditions or the extinction of species (IPCC, 2022).

As the concerted attempts by the UN, IPCC, and various civic movements highlight, the limits and impact of growth have gained public and governmental recognition and have prompted a search for solutions. These solutions see instrumental creativity as pivotal. The main argument is that instrumental creativity linked to economic growth would help create efficient and energy-saving solutions that will eventually lead to less use of resources. Indeed, it was another Club of Rome report in 1997 that proposed this simple remedy:

[t]he cure is using resources efficiently, doing more with less. It is not a question of going backwards or 'returning' to prior means. It is the beginning of a new industrial revolution in which we shall achieve dramatic increases in resource productivity.

(von Weizsäcker et al., 1998: xxi).

This statement underscores the positive belief in creative engineering of solutions that would lead to a more efficient use of resources and continuing economic growth. The implication is that the development of new technologies will eventually lead to less resource consumption and ultimately a sustainable future.

Yet this seemingly straightforward solution seems to be more complicated. In 1865, an economist by the name of William Jevons studied the English coal industry and penned a treatise called *The Coal Question: An Inquiry Concerning the Progress of the Nation, and the Probable Exhaustion of Our Coal Mines*. During his study, he made a startling observation, that

[i]t is wholly a confusion of ideas to suppose that the economical use of fuel is equivalent to a diminished consumption. The very contrary is the truth ... Every improvement of the engine, when effected, does but accelerate anew the consumption of coal.

(Jevons, 1865: 140).

In other words, Jevons observed that the efficient use of resources will not lead to diminished consumption, but to an increase of those resources. His observation would come to be known as the *Jevons Paradox* and seems to be applicable not only to coal mining. Take the example of driving. Over the years, cars have become much more fuel-efficient. Now this would seem to be a great way of reducing resources. But as driving becomes more efficient and thus cheaper, people may drive more. In the long run, this will lead to the same or even more use of fuel. Alternatively, people may use the money they save on fuel to buy other products that are energy-intensive to produce, which will, overall, not lead to the desired effects of reduced resource consumption.

Based on such observations, researchers in resource economics have been sceptical about the potential of more efficient solutions and '[i]n a disturbing assault on intuition and conventional wisdom, [the economists] Khazzoom and Brookes have asserted that energy efficiency improvements might increase, rather than decrease energy consumption' (Saunders, 1992: 131). Researchers have called such adverse effects the *rebound effect*. Generally, the rebound effect occurs when 'increased consumption offsets the energy savings that may otherwise be achieved' (Sorrell, 2009: 636). The rebound effect may be directly or indirectly related to the initial energy-efficient solution. For example, driving more with an energy-efficient car is a direct effect, while buying another product is an indirect effect.

Researchers have discussed the rebound effect controversially. Generally there is a consensus that the rebound effect exists, while its absolute negative impact is debated. Some research has gone so far as to argue that the rebound effect may even lead to 'backfire effects', which means that resource consumption is even higher with more efficient technology (Saunders, 1992), while other research has argued that the magnitude of the rebound effect is too small to be considered in energy policy (Gillingham et al., 2013). The upshot of the debate, however, is that while instrumental creativity may contribute to reduced resource consumption, it may require more than creative, efficient solutions.

Moreover, an instrumentalist perspective on organizing creativity may lead to rising levels of individual and social anxiety and what Mats Alvesson referred to as the *triumph of emptiness* (Alvesson, 2013a). One perplexing question is why individuals and societies keep consuming products, even though their basic human needs are met. One convincing explanation was given by Belk (1988), who argued that material goods are not only satisfying people's basic needs but are extensions of their identities. Thus, how people define themselves is largely also a matter of what they possess and how they consume. Buying the latest mobile phone does not serve to provide more features. Indeed, providing more and more features has led to widespread feature fatigue, which means a general weariness of ever more functionalities and features that are hardly used. Possessing a product therefore mainly serves to distinguish an individual from others around them.

Doubtless, capitalism has produced some useful products, so it is important to be clear about different types of products. What may be termed positional goods are goods that follow a social rather than material logic. A social logic means that products are used to provide individuals with a way of distinguishing themselves from others, while a material logic means that products are used to satisfy material needs. As scholars have recognized, a capitalist system serves to create anxiety about needs that are subsequently met by buying products (Alvesson, 2013a). Hence, instrumentalist creativity that serves to fuel consumption practices geared towards positioning and status may leave individuals perpetually anxious in competing for status, which may negatively impact individual and social well-being. Such competitions for status appear to thwart the development of an individual sense of worth, which, as will be explored in the next section, a humanist perspective on creativity aimed to promote.

Humanist Perspective

An alternative to an instrumentalist end of creativity is to allow individuals to engage in creative acts not connected to a specific instrumental outcome. This type of creativity has already been referred to as humanist. Humanist creativity contributes to what Abraham Maslow called 'self-actualization', which describes the need of an individual to recognize their fullest potential and strive to realize it—as Maslow expressed it, 'what a man [sic] *can* be, he [sic] *must* be' (1943: 382, emphasis in original). Self-actualizing individuals work to free themselves from constraints, restrictions, and societal expectations and engage in activities with a curious, childlike attitude. They are, according to Maslow (1962: 144), less afraid of other people's opinions and, importantly, their own 'emotions, impulses and thoughts'. Creativity is pivotal in self-actualization, as it is, according to Maslow (1962: 145), the '*sine qua non*' of 'essential humanness' by which he supposedly means the essential means for developing our very own individuality.

Importantly, creativity in the context of self-actualization is not concerned with directed 'problem-solving or product-making', but can comprise any activity. As such, humanist creativity has the 'aim of investigating the power of creativity to enrich, enliven and liberate individuals' (Bycroft, 2014: 209). In contrast to an economically and instrumentally focused homo oeconomicus, the view on humankind is expressed in the notion of homo creativus, relating to the inherently creative nature of humans and their need and possibility to express it. The emphasis on emotions, inspiration, and childlike dispositions links it to what was discussed as the inspiration order of worth in Chapter 4.

A deeper analysis of societal and economic developments after the Second World War suggests the proliferation of an increased focus on self-actualization (Lasch, 1991). Notably it extended to work and organizations as well, with a steeply rising interest during the internet boom in the 1990s when commercial organizations embraced and absorbed the bohemian counterculture, most dominantly the emerging tech elite (Ross, 2004). Prior to that, organizations had mostly been regarded as uniform collective entities in which individuality and deviation were seen as detrimental to the efficiency and effectiveness of businesses—though there was, as seen in Chapter 2, the recognition of the importance of considering the needs of the individual. The trend that emerged in organizational theory and practices during the 1990s, however, was different from simply recognizing that individuals have needs that should be considered. Many organizations actively encouraged individuals not to be corporate clones, but to express their creativity and 'be themselves' at work (Fleming, 2009). Note how this development of fusing work and authenticity echoes Maslow's observation of self-actualization where '[d]uty became pleasure, and pleasure merged with duty. The distinction between work and play became shadowy' (Fleming, 2009: 139). It is precisely the blurring of work and play which organizations sought to influence by stimulating playfulness, humour, and 'being oneself'. Symbolic for this development are carefully designed quirky workspaces, game tables, nap pods, and the deliberate use of humour and fun by executives, such as Google's CEO Eric Schmidt. The goal was, and still is, to increase levels of creativity by encouraging differences rather than uniformity and expression rather than restraint.

Yet, self-actualization and its creative outcomes must contribute to corporate goals. An employee who works on their high score in foosball will not contribute much to the success of the organization. To ensure that individuals use their individual creativity in the interest of the organizations, control mechanisms must be in place. Hence, though individuals may be free *to* express themselves, they are not free *from* corporate control. Considering this dual focus on freedom and the possibility of 'being yourself', control mechanisms cannot be intrusive or direct. Instead, they pertain to favourable values and norms as well as influencing how people make sense of who they are. This was discussed in Chapter 2 with regard to corporate cultures. This form of control has been broadly labelled *normative control*, which means that an organization seeks to align personal interests and organizational goals through values, symbols, and an emotional attachment as a source for identification (Kunda, 1992). The aim is ultimately 'to win the "hearts and minds" of employees: to define their purposes by managing what they think and feel, and not just how they behave' (Willmott, 1993: 516). Normative control, in the ideal case, ensures that when individuals pursue their self-actualization projects and creativity, they will think and feel in alignment with the organization's values and goals.

In many cases, individual creative expressions may coincide with the organization's objectives. Yet there appears to be a fundamental tension or even incompatibility between the humanist expression of fun, creativity, and play, and the rational and calculative logic of an organization (Fleming, 2005). Popular ideas on culture management tend to downplay such incompatibility. Instead, the general message is that employees welcome the fusion of work and play and that it will contribute to organizational success and individual well-being (Allen, 2020). However, Willmott (1993: 536, emphasis added) pointed out that '[a]n unintended consequence of this kind of management theory is to *raise expectations about self-determination* without necessarily aligning its fulfilment to the realization of corporate objectives'. Indeed, scholars have observed various forms of resistance when corporate goals do not match expectations of being able to live out one's creativity at work (see Fleming and Spicer, 2014). To discuss possible reactions to mismatches, three strategies proposed by Hirschman (1970) will be drawn upon: *exit*, *voice* and *loyalty*.

In his original work, Hirschman discussed consumers' reactions when faced with poor-quality products. He argued that consumers principally have two options when they are not satisfied: they stop buying the product (exit), or they communicate their discontent with the poor quality (voice). A third alternative is, of course, that consumers keep purchasing a product if they are satisfied or feel that change is too costly (loyalty). Due to their simplicity, the notions of exit, voice, and loyalty have broad application to other fields—especially for this book's discussion of reacting to a misalignment of corporate objectives and individual self-actualization. Exit simply means that an individual leaves the organization and seeks a better fit between their need for self-expression and corporate objectives elsewhere. Voice, in contrast, refers to the articulation of discontent about disappointed expectations. This could take various forms involving, for example, through unions or other organized groups. Voice usually requires a space in which it is articulated. Today, digital technologies—such as social media platforms, blogs, or other digital spaces—provide individuals and groups with the ability to make their voices heard.

When individuals feel that the organization allows them the possibility of self-actualization, they have no reason to be discontent, which leads to loyalty and satisfaction. Yet loyalty includes a 'silent component' (Birch, 1975). As opposed to exit and voice, which are obvious articulations of discontent, a silent component means that individuals and groups may experience tension or misalignment between the possibility of creative expression and the fulfilment of corporate goals, but do not make it explicit through voice. As one of the quiet expressions of discontent, scholars have identified *cynicism* as a common response.

Cynicism includes a lack of belief in the integrity of the organization, which is accompanied by negative emotions and—possibly—acts of resistance (Dean et al., 1998). With a view to innovation and creativity, Rehn (2019) argued that the inflationary use of the word innovation and a constant stream of new consultants and initiatives to stimulate innovation and creativity drain the concept of any substantial meaning. This leads to what he called 'innovation fatigue', which describes how people become tired of hearing about yet another initiative to increase innovation. Spicer (2017) calls such empty rhetoric 'Business Bullshit' (BBS), which refers to phrases, slogans, and statements that sound good but, when explored more closely, have little to no substance.

When confronted permanently with empty talk or BBS, it is hard not to become cynical about real change or substantial attempts to facilitate individual self-expression and creativity. Essentially, as Blank (2019) argued, organizations create an 'innovation theatre' that puts on a performance with no real consequences for the organization, which decreases the disillusionment among employees concerning substantive efforts to facilitate creativity. Similarly, Schaefer (2019) observed that managers who intended to 'manage creativity' talked about various practices, such as allowing freedom for creative expression but then doing the exact opposite in practice. Managers thus wilfully ignored their own talk about creativity as part of what he called 'symbolic work' that explains how people project a favourable image of themselves rather than engaging with substantial problems. All these studies point to the empirical observation that talk about creativity is widespread but in many cases not coupled to substantive actions. This gap paves the way for cynicism among employees.

All in all, while humanist creativity is a desirable end in itself, it seems that its application to organizations is problematic. The objectives of self-actualization and the pursuit of corporate objectives are in many instances not aligned and, therefore, lead to empty talk about managing creativity without any substantial actions to support employees to be more creative and possibly self-actualize. Yet some organizations do manage to align individual self-expression, substantive actions to facilitate creativity, and achieving a fulfilment of corporate objectives. And I now go on to discuss the possibilities of such transformative creativity as a desirable practice.

Towards a Radical Transformative Conception of Creativity

Economic growth and the possibility to self-actualize are no doubt important organizational goals, yet they seem to lead to some undesirable outcomes. Thus the ambition in the following section is to stimulate reflections on how the ends of creativity can be reconsidered. The overarching goal is to sketch an approach to organizing creativity which combines sustainable growth with a humanist focus. Accordingly, such an approach must discuss conditions and possibilities of generating, developing, evaluating, and implementing ideas that support the sustainable growth of individuals, organization, and society while avoiding empty talk of creativity and innovation. The following section outlines such an alternative conception, which I refer to as *radical transformative creativity*. Radical transformative creativity means the generation and development of transformative ideas that encompasses a fundamental, transformational evaluation of the ends and consequences of these ideas. Radical in its original sense comes from the Latin *radix*, meaning 'root'. The metaphor of a root is generative as it highlights that creativity should not only consider the visible branches and leaves that spring up from a tree. Rather, people should also consider its stem and roots, which determine where leaves and branches come from. What, it may be asked, is the basis of an idea, and is it possible to unearth its roots?

Before embarking on this discussion, some clarifications are necessary. First, like the concept of creativity, sustainability has become a buzzword. In essence, sustainability simply describes the nature of intertemporal choices, which are 'decisions with consequences that play out over time' (Berns et al., 2007: 482). Sustainable intertemporal choices are, therefore, those choices that satisfy present needs without compromising future needs. For example, extracting all of the resources from an ecosystem in the present will compromise the extraction of resources for future generations. Sustainability, as understood here, seeks to balance short-term and long-term orientation with a view to economic, social, and environmental dimensions (Slawinski and Bansal, 2015).

Second, a critique of the growth paradigm and instrumentalist creativity does not mean to advocate an economy that refuses on principle to grow, expand or innovate (which would be sheer madness in the face of the scarcity that still persists in many parts of the Global South, or in face of the desirability of medical advances or innovations in the field of sustainable technologies, etc.)

(Rosa et al., 2017: 64).

The question is what *kind of growth* is desired, and how to acknowledge society's need for positive progress. Growth should be critically reflected when it does not contribute to societal progress in a substantial and sustainable manner. This is not at all straightforward, but—as will be discussed below—the inclusion of multiple orders of worth and participatory organizational designs will at least ensure that multiple interests are considered when defining the ends of organizing creativity and the kind of growth that creative ideas will contribute to.

Third, radical transformative creativity may seem to be an idealization and, even, a pipe dream. People may feel powerless or question the ability of single organizations to contribute to fundamental transformations. However, a first step is the recognition of and reflection on possibilities of changing processes and practices when organizing creativity to address contemporary challenges. Harking back to the notion of exit, voice, and loyalty (Hirschman, 1970), voice is a decisive and essential factor for articulating problems and initiating change. It should never be assumed that there are no alternative ways of organizing economic activity. Instead of resignation in the form of exit or underlying cynicism that may accompany feigned loyalty, people should voice what they are against, but also what they are *for* (Parker et al., 2014). When it comes to transformations, small incisive changes can indeed make a difference in organizations (Wickert and Schaefer, 2015).

As Göpel (2016: 155) argued, rather than dismissing radical transformation as unrealistic, people should recognize the potential of how choices and reflections make a difference, as it 'offers alternative meaning, delegitimizes the notion that there are no alternative claims, and offers ideas about other ways of acting or doing things'. Göpel referred to such incremental dismantling of ingrained and taken-for-granted notions as 'radical, incremental transformation'. In what follows, this stance of *radically* evaluating the transformative nature of each idea informs the discussion of how all conscious choices, when organizing creativity and evaluating ideas, may incrementally work towards the needed fundamental economic and social transformations emerging from organizations.

Spotlight on Practice: Omnipollo

In 2017, a beer was released that was wrapped in white paper on which two piercing black eyes were staring blankly at the potential buyer. The beer was called Yellow Belly and brewed by the Swedish craft brewery Omnipollo in collaboration with the British craft brewery Buxton. The description of the beer read:

> Yellow Belly—a person who is without courage, fortitude, or nerve; a coward. To us, one of the most cowardly deeds is to act anonymously, hiding behind a group.

A signifying trait of institutionalized racism. This beer is brewed to celebrate all things new, open minded and progressive.

Obviously, this beer had a message, not only from its descriptive title but encapsulated in its design as well. According to Karl Grandin, one of the two founders of Omnipollo I interviewed, Yellow Belly sparked mixed responses. Some applauded the efforts while others thought that craft beer should not be political. Yet rather than being disconcerted by these debates, Omnipollo aspired from its beginnings to transcend the notion and experience of beer. Such transcendence included not hesitating to address controversial issues—with their beer.

The seed for Omnipollo was laid in 2010 when Karl Grandin, a designer by profession, met Henok Fentie, a dedicated homebrewer. Together they conceived the idea of establishing a brewery which would create 'something that wasn't there'. What was 'not there' in 2010 was the notion of a beer being anything else but an unexceptional beverage—at least in Sweden. Karl and Henok missed a more widespread mindset that consuming craft beer was not just the weird pastime of a small dedicated fan base. They envisioned that beer could *be* and *do* so much more than just being a product. 'We wanted', says Karl, to 'render a different awareness of what a beverage could be.' To transcend the common run-of-the-mill beer drinking experience, they combined Karl's art with Henok's beers to create beers as a 'means of expression'. A craft beer became a symbol for something other than just being a thirst quencher. Something, according to them, needed to happen in the space between product and consumer which is not merely aesthetic but which transforms and pushes the boundaries of the experience. Thus for them it meant that a thorough and deep engagement with Omnipollo's beers could potentially lead to a transformative experience. 'It's like music', explains Karl: 'music potentially transforms your perspective and experience. It is the music itself, the content of the lyrics and the way the music is published. These three aspects can have a profound effect on the listener.' Similarly, Omnipollo aimed to transform the beer-drinking experience, adding aesthetic, political, and informational layers to the sensory experience. Beers as such became a communicative and even political medium as well as a more enriching way of engaging with the perceived functionality of a beverage.

Naturally, Omnipollo's beers will not solve all the world's problems. But their case illustrates how radical transformative creativity may work to problematize and transcend a commonly accepted state of things. It sets an example of how creative processes may push boundaries, question established categories, and stimulate consumers to reflect on pressing issues. In Omnipollo's case, beer may not be simply another tasty beverage but a social and political medium that may challenge and even transform people's perspectives and experiences.

Dimensions of Radical Transformational Creativity

For the following discussion of radical transformative creativity, it is necessary to hark back to themes and concepts discussed throughout the book and thread them together. More specifically, the guiding principle of critical reflection will be connected with the process

Table 6.2 Dimensions of radical transformational creativity

Dimensions	Radical transformational creativity
Objective	To generate and develop ideas that address fundamental problems and lead to sustainable growth of individuals, organizations, and society
Guiding principle	Engagement, critical reflection, and problematization metanorms
Process	Inclusion of multiple orders of worth with the aim of productive dissonance
Modes of organizing	Alternative forms of organization in terms of purpose, participation, and ownership
Examples	Creative craft
Potential problems	Idealization Greenwashing Unproductive dissonance Missing supportive context

of productive dissonance, and they will be linked to alternative participatory modes of organizational coordination. Table 6.2 provides an overview of the important dimensions of radical transformational creativity.

Consider an experience reported by Rehn (2019). He was hired to advise an organization on its creative practices when he decided to run an experiment. He gave a speech which solely contained empty phrases and meaningless, even illogical, statements. To his amazement the crowd did not protest or seem at all bothered by his nonsense. It appeared that they were used to *not* asking critical questions or seeking substantial meanings in change projects. As he concluded:

[Innovation] used to mean something but today even the smartest among us can become caught up in the sloganeering, the empty posturing, the verbiage. It wasn't that the executives were stupid. Rather they like so many of us had become so used to superficial innovation talk that they no longer knew how to tell the parody from the reality.

(Rehn, 2019: 10–11).

His anecdote highlights how people refrain from asking critical questions and a disinclination to reflect more thoroughly on substantive content when permanently confronted with what we have referred to as BBS above.

Now consider the case of Novo Nordisk. Novo Nordisk is a leading global Danish pharmaceutical company which develops and produces insulin for diabetes treatment. Apart from its success in business, it is known for its corporate responsibility activities and willingness to engage and cooperate with stakeholders to become more responsible. Within its organization, Novo Nordisk has established a group responsible for global stakeholder engagement which comprises teams that report on the company's activities in various countries. An empirical study of how one team developed new knowledge and conceptions of the company's responsibilities in various local contexts illustrates the importance of a close engagement with stakeholders to fathom some of the fundamental issues that need to be addressed (Girschik, 2020). Girschik showed how the team first produced 'traditional PR talk', which referred to generalized statements with little substantial content. Yet as the team engaged more closely with local contexts—for example, in Bangladesh and Indonesia—they 'observed alternative ways of doing business that would challenge their understanding of the company's responsibilities' (Girschik, 2020: 45). Guided by their local engagement as well as an open mind for critical reflection and problematization, the team eventually developed a new way of framing problems and possibilities to help in local contexts, which they consistently spread in the organization. Hence, rather than merely talking about ideas and engaging in BBS, the team made a substantive effort to seriously engage with fundamental problems and issues.

Both examples illustrate contrasting approaches to organizing creativity. The former illustrates what Alvesson and Spicer (2012: 1196) referred to as 'functional stupidity', which—according to them—captures how organizations support a 'lack of reflexivity, substantive reasoning and justification'. As Rehn claimed, the executives were not stupid, yet they refrained from questioning empty innovation phrases and slogans. Such a lack of questioning was functional because it did not question existing organizational norms and structures. It instilled a sense of certainty that enabled the managers and the organization to continue their practices. Yet, of course, a lack of reflexivity and questioning also means that transformative changes are thwarted and that organizations do not develop capacities for transformational ideas.

The example of the team at Novo Nordisk illustrates, in contrast, that the condition for radical transformation lies not in producing empty PR talk, but in a willingness to engage substantively with alternative ideas, contexts, and groups. Radical transformational creativity should thus facilitate engagement with alternative ideas and trigger reflections and problematizations of one's own beliefs and assumptions. This involves the possibility of questioning and experimenting with norms, processes, and structures of the organization. Rather than cementing and perpetuating the status quo, a serious engagement with fundamental issues may unsettle previous knowledge and processes. This means that organizations should strive to not only instil and reproduce norms that strengthen the efficiency and effectiveness of the existing organizational order, but to also foster norms that allow the questioning of existing norms. Chapter 2 referred to these norms as *metanorms*, which encourage individuals to question and challenge existing norms and values.

Yet being open-minded, questioning assumptions, and promoting metanorms is only a first step in generating, developing, and evaluating radically different ideas. The case of Novo Nordisk shows that substantial changes were only achieved with prolonged engagement, conversations, and dialogue with individuals and groups and, ultimately, the co-construction of guidelines and reports that included the voices and practices of a variety of different local stakeholders. Intentions must be followed by actions, and this is not an easy task. In his discussion of different perspectives on growth, Jackson (2009: 14) wrote that 'the idea of a non-growing economy may be anathema to an economist. But the idea of a continually growing economy is an anathema to an ecologist.' Jackson put his finger on the sometimes seemingly irreconcilable differences between perspectives. As mentioned previously, the dominant form of justification in an organizational context is market- and profit-based (Ferraro et al., 2005).

Yet to allow radical transformative creativity to flourish a more pluralistic approach is necessary. This includes multiple orders of worth—especially civic and sustainable which tend to be marginalized—with the goal of '"re-embedding" the economy within the cultural and political world' (Rosa et al., 2017: 65). Such re-embedding processes mean using friction productively. In this context, productive dissonance, creative synthesis, and negotiated orders were discussed as central concepts. To recap, productive dissonance relates to how groups do not reject ideas immediately if they advocate different positions based on divergent orders of worth. Instead, individuals and groups withstand tensions when problem frameworks are critically discussed and ideas are evaluated. Ultimately, the involved parties seek to achieve a creative synthesis which reconciles their different perspectives and establishes a temporary negotiated order in which the collective moves forward with no disruptions until a new challenge emerges.

Notably, facilitating radical transformational creativity requires forms and purposes of organizing business activities that differ from the ideal of a profit-maximizing corporation. A corporation has been the dominant legal form of organizing over the last century (Davis, 2009). It separates its status as a legal entity from its owners, has limited liability, and is able to act as if it were a single person. After the Second World War, corporations were part of a nexus and community of stakeholders whose interests it considered. For example, large corporations in a small town supported local sports clubs, engaged in community projects, and cooperated with local government. Such stakeholder orientation changed during the 1980s, when conservative politicians and theorists argued that the only goal of a corporation should be to maximize shareholder interest.

The often-cited essay by Milton Friedman captures this change of focus aptly (Friedman, 1970). Friedman argued forcefully that the sole purpose of running a corporation was to maximize profits for the owners, and nothing else. His famous dictum that 'there is one and only one social responsibility of business—to use its resources and engage in activities designed to increase its profits so long as it stays within the rules of the game' diffused into public discourse. It justified the drastic efforts of privatization and curtailing of trade unions by neoliberal governments in the US and the UK. Creating shareholder value without explicit consideration of negative social and ecological externalities—if they were not fraudulent—was, thus, the sole mission of a profit-maximizing corporation (Roberts, 2014). Profit maximization, however, is a problem when seeking to facilitate radical transformational creativity. If the mission of an organization is to facilitate sustainable forms of creativity, then alternative forms of the profit-maximizing corporation are needed.

Indeed, scholars have discussed alternative forms of organizations that are not merely profit maximizing, but the notion of an alternative is tricky. The question of an alternative immediately raises the question about what the alternative is an alternative to (Just et al., 2021). To answer this question, Parker et al. (2014) provided a point of departure by delineating what an alternative form of organizing should aim for. They urged readers to seek 'forms of organizing which respect *personal autonomy*, but within a *framework of cooperation*, and which are *attentive* to the sorts of *futures they will produce*' (Parker et al., 2014: 32, emphasis added). They drew attention to the delicate balance between ensuring individual freedom while at the same time being mindful of an organization's sustainable collective responsibility. Obviously, these criteria can be met through very different organizational designs—that is, the way an organization is structured and what purpose it pursues. For example, worker cooperatives are based on the right of all employees to participate in decision making as well as individual payment of dividends from shared equity (for a broader discussion of cooperatives, see Cheney et al., 2014).

In a recent contribution to the debate on how alternative organizations could be designed, Luyckx et al. (2022) developed a framework which builds on the most common critiques of the currently dominant profit-maximizing corporation. A first critique relates to the purpose of corporations, which tend to focus on the maximization of profit on behalf of shareholders. Luyckx et al. argued that people should think about how social and ecological objectives could be considered in organizational designs. The overarching issue becomes which goals and objectives organizations pursue—not only with regard to satisfying shareholders, but to society, individuals, and the natural environment.

A second critique focuses on participation: profit-maximizing corporations exclude the majority of their stakeholders from organizational decision-making processes. While in many European countries, such as Germany or Sweden, employees and trade unions have more influence on decision-making processes through co-determination practices than in Anglo-Saxon countries, the general trend is that shareholders have the most influence on important business decisions. Hence, the second overarching issue regarding alternative forms of organizing is how much influence stakeholders have on the strategic decisions, as well as the goals and set-up, of production processes.

A third critique scrutinizes current ownership models of corporations. More specifically, there are three critical aspects of ownership. First, ownership in corporations tends to be limited to shareholders, which implies that they have the exclusive right to influence business decisions. Second, shareholders are only liable for the value of their investment and not personally. This means that shareholders may reap the rewards of their investment, but due to limited liability they do not bear potential costs—only in the form of their loss of investment. Yet if risky business decisions have negative consequences, they do not disappear but tend to be borne by external parties such as governments or other local authorities. Third, concentration of ownership into the hands a few powerful shareholders implies an unbalanced distribution of profits, which eventually results in growing economic inequality. Accordingly, the third overarching issue to consider in alternative organizational designs is how ownership structures may be redesigned to break up shareholder concentration and power and establish a more equally distributed ownership. The recent resurge of craft-based organizations may illustrate how these aspects of alternative forms of organization and radical transformational creativity play out in practice.

Creative Craft

Lately there has been a renewed interest and re-emergence of craft and craft organizations. For example, craft breweries and brewpubs have popped up all over the world, small manufacturers have started producing and selling hand-crafted products ranging from chocolate to ceramics, and there have been trends to restore and repair products instead of buying and replacing them. Craft is a combining element in all these trends and can be described as 'a timeless approach to work that prioritizes human engagement over machine control' (Kroezen et al., 2021: 2). The motivation that drives craft as a productive activity is 'to do a good job for its own sake' (Sennett, 2008: 9). Furthermore, craft involves a deep engagement and continuous refinement of techniques, practices, and processes, as well as striving for a holistic understanding of the entire production process. Craft skills are developed through hands-on engagement with the entire production process and in interaction with a community that seeks to share knowledge and collaborate, rather than protect assets and compete (Crawford, 2009). As such, craft has been a counterforce to industrialization, mass production, and the increased mechanization and automatization of work processes. The revival of craft indicates a desire for a different kind of work, so—as noted by Bell et al. (2021: 2)—craft 'can contribute to the formation and transformation of alternative ways of organizing'. As such, craft provides an example of how radical transformative creativity may be organized.

At first glance, however, craft evokes an image of archaic and traditional work processes that result in small quantities of handmade products. Based on these preconceived notions, craft seems to be unsuited for today's uncertain and fast-paced world—especially considering the need to produce and sell products in large quantities. Yet while craft may draw inspiration from past traditions and processes, it is practiced in the present. This means that craft adapts to the circumstances of today's society and economy (Adamson, 2013). Notably, Kroezen et al. (2021) distinguished *three current configurations of craft*, by which they mean different ways of how craft is linked to mechanization and organizational contexts. They referred to the three configurations as technical, pure, and creative craft. In this discussion, I will briefly outline all three before engaging in more depth with the concept of creative craft that I find most relevant for the discussion of radical transformational creativity.

Technical craft refers to how the human element in craft is constructively combined with mechanical and technological support. The aim is to achieve technical perfection in the outcomes of craft processes. An illustrative example here is the use of 3D printing technology when producing material objects. Rather than producing parts by hand, the machine will render perfectly produced objects based on the design of the craftsperson. *Pure craft* is diametrically opposed to technical craft. Pure implies that craft relies on heritage and traditions and that adherents are sceptical towards polluting the craft with modern technology. An example here is the German *Reinheitsgebot*, or 'purity law', in beer brewing. The purity law prescribes that beer should only contain water, malt, hops, and yeast, and that no additives should be added when brewing beer. Lastly, *creative craft* contrasts with technical craft in the sense that it does not strive for technical perfection. It is also different from pure craft with regards to the ability to express one's individuality in the crafting process rather than strictly adhering to traditions. Craft brewing is an excellent example of creative craft whereby the above-mentioned purity law is challenged by adding non-traditional ingredients to beer, ranging from sugar to more exotic flavours, such as spruce or marshmallows. Moreover, while craft breweries strive for quality and perfectly flavoured beers, the goal is not achieving technical perfection but expressing their individuality.

The creative craft configuration is a good point of departure to unpack possible current and future practices of radical transformational creativity. Creative craft foregrounds the intrinsic joy of engaging with a task and emphasizes curiosity as a general attitude and the drive to explore problems and opportunities. Harking back to the previous discussion, creative craft overlaps to a great extent with the conception of a humanist perspective on creativity, as craft is not motivated by external rewards or instrumental motives, but by an intrinsic desire to express one's creativity. Moreover, the exploratory stance in creative craft relates to the notion of negative capabilities discussed in Chapter 5. To recap, the concept of negative capabilities refers to the ability to withstand tensions and ambiguities without seeking a quick fix. Hence, in creative craft people do not seek to reduce uncertainties, but to thrive and make use of them in the creative process. Moreover, creative craft organizations tend to be structured differently than the profit-maximizing corporations, as the latter—through a focus on short-term profits and a focus on economies of scale—may tend to stifle the development of craft (see, for example, Sasaki et al., 2019). In both cases, creativity is not merely instrumentalist or humanist; it serves to question and problematize previous assumptions underlying institutionalized ways of organizing economic activity.

A current example of how creative craft may be organized is the craft brewing industry. Recent research on the US context suggests that craft breweries aim to strike a balance between people, planet, and profit (Reid and Gatrell, 2017). This suggests the inclusion of multiple orders of worth in their creative process. With regard to social sustainability, craft breweries aim to develop the humanist potential of creativity through promoting the craft of its employees and seeking to engage with the broader community. This fosters conversation and critical reflections about creative processes and products. Moreover, craft breweries are active in seeking ecologically sustainable solutions and, thus, spend their creative energy on reducing their ecological impact. Lastly, while craft breweries are commercial enterprises, there appears to be a focus on profit *making* rather than profit maximizing. There is competition between breweries, but there is also cooperation—a combination referred to as coopetition (Mathias et al., 2018). All of this translates into the distinct purpose of facilitating quality and sustainability, the engagement and support of participation of employees, and diverse ownership structures.

Overall, configurations of creative craft, as evidenced by the craft brewing industry, seem to facilitate the notion of radical transformative creativity discussed previously by striking a balance between a humanist and instrumentalist intent of creativity. Craft organizations strive to earn money, but not at all costs. In this sense, ideas are generated that are potentially profitable. Yet the generation and development of ideas are also linked to the self-actualization and meaningfulness inherent in craft, which align with a humanist focus on creativity. Indeed, craft tends to be referred to as the 'labour of love' (Ranganathan, 2018), which indicates the intrinsic joy people derive from it. Moreover, the continuous development and honing of craft skills suggests that employees are an essential factor for the continuous development of the organization, which provides a source of appreciation for their work and grants influence on decisions.

The productive combination of instrumental and humanist ends of creativity may result in alternative forms of organizing with regard to purpose, ownership, and participation. The purpose is, as mentioned, to make profits while at the same time considering social and ecological implications. Thus ideas are not only generated with a profit-maximizing intent, but tend to consider broader implications for community and environment as well. Since the aim is not to maximize return on investment, ownership structures of craft organization disincentive short-term investment and concentration of power and provide more participation possibilities for employees.

However, there is always a risk of idealizing and oversimplifying the practical implications of conceptions such as radical transformative creativity. To put some of the ideas of this section in perspective, a few critical reflections of the conception of radical trans-formational creativity are in order. First, it is necessary to be mindful not to idealize certain ideas, concepts, and practices for sustainable transformational changes, such as craft. The proof of their worth is always in their concrete realization and implementation. Second, the risk of idealization is closely linked to the common practice of *greenwashing* (or *craftwashing* for that matter), which means that corporations merely project an image of their sustainability rather than implementing substantive changes (see Wickert and Risi, 2019). In this vein, the danger of cynicism and BBS discussed in the context of humanist creativity are also pertinent for radical transformative creativity. Third, real-izing productive dissonance is a considerable challenge for organizations. The influence of internal politics and power struggles, as well as fragmented organizational cultures, may counteract any efforts for establishing dialogue and creating a readiness for sub-stantive change in the form of unproductive dissonance. However, as seen in the case of Novo Nordisk, it is possible to implement a broader perspective on the implications of ideas and their effect on stakeholders. One of the essential elements here was the close engagement with concerned parties. Creating opportunities for engagement seems to be an essential component for raising awareness and a basis for mutual understanding and transformative changes (Wickert and Schaefer, 2015). Lastly, radical transformative cre-ativity must be embedded in a supportive legal and political context which supports alternative forms of organizing and the diffusion of transformation on a social and eco-nomic level. While organizing creativity is an essential dimension for addressing the existence-threatening ecological and social problems, concerted systemic actions that involve a multitude of actors (e.g. government, NGOs, social movements) are a necessary complement.

Spotlight on Practice: Craft and Vintage Motorcycle Repair

A great illustration of the practices and attitudes of creative craft is the account by Crawford (2009) based on his experiences of owning a vintage motorcycle repair shop. Crawford is a trained philosopher who owns a workshop for repairing motorbikes. In his reflections, he recounted in detail how he got involved in an initially uninteresting but progressively tricky repair of a motorbike that had been standing and out of use for some time. While it would have been economically more sensible to get rid of the bike because it was, according to Crawford, 'screwed every which way [...] [t]houghts of the bike's economic value receded as I wheeled it onto the lift' (Crawford, 2009: 118). The repair of the bike gripped him, and he spent countless hours in an ice-cold workshop trying to fix it. In the process, Crawford discovered an oil seal that seemed to be not quite correctly adjusted, but he could not figure out how and why. Yet the seal did not pose a particular problem for the owner of the bike, and Crawford mused that 'if it is likely not to be his problem [the owner's], I shouldn't make it my problem'. However, he could not let go of the seal and went on to explore and try to understand the problem. He struggled to understand this urge to explore and concluded that '[t]here is something perverse at work here, and I would like to understand it. The oil seal was the opening to Pandora's box: I felt compelled to get to the bottom of things, to gape them open and clean them out' (Crawford, 2009: 123). Obviously, his exploration was economically unviable and at odds with an economic mindset of minimizing input and maximizing output. Solving the problem was not in the owner's interest—it was only his own—and in the end, '[t]his pleasure [of solving the problem] brought a surge of bad conscience in its wake. In the end I knocked the labor bill from $2,200 down to $1,500' (Crawford, 2009: 125).

Crawford's experience is telling regarding the curiosity and exploratory mindset of creative craft. In addition, it suggests that maximizing profits may not be the overarching purpose of creative craft. This links creative craft and radical transformative creativity to alternative forms of organizing with regard to purpose, participation, and ownership.

Conclusion

Creativity tends to be regarded as inherently beneficial and positive. This chapter challenged and unpacked this claim and critically reflected on the function and purpose of creativity in today's economic and social context. It was determined that two primary functions of creativity can be discerned: instrumentalist and humanist. The former conceives of creativity as a means to an end, while the latter regards creativity as an end in itself. With a view to organizing creativity, the function of creativity is predominantly instrumentalist, as it serves continuous economic growth and dynamic stabilization. The concept of dynamic stabilization discussed at length in this chapter draws attention to how the current capitalist economic systems *must grow* to remain stable. This means that profit-maximizing ideas become indispensable. While economic growth is needed for social progress and welfare, the acceleration and appropriation caused by unrestrained economic growth has led to serious social, ecological, and individual problems. These developments demand a reconsideration of the functions of creativity. Therefore, a humanist conception was discussed as an alternative to an instrumentalist perspective on creativity. A humanist motivation for creativity serves the self-actualization of individuals, and expressing one's creativity is viewed as an essential human need. With regard to humanist creativity and its importance, it was demonstrated how organizations since the 1980s have recognized the need for self-actualization and aimed to implement self-actualizing practices. However, the goals of individual self-actualization and corporate profit maximization are potentially conflicting, which may lead in many cases to cynicism and the use of empty words and slogans that have no substantive content.

As an alternative to an instrumental and humanist objective of organizing creativity, the concept of radical transformative creativity was elaborated on. Radical transformative creativity means that efforts of organizing creativity should be mindful of the possible implications of the ideas that people generate and critically reflect on the assumptions and norms underlying their evaluation processes. This, it was argued, necessitates the ability to question existing organizational norms and a pluralistic approach and productive dissonance as guiding principles to structure idea generation, development, and evaluation processes. In addition, this chapter discussed alternative forms of organizing, as the profit-maximizing corporation seems to be less suited for radical transformative creativity. The re-emergence of craft and craft organizations in the beer industry served as an example to illustrate how radical transformative creativity may work in practice. Craft appears to combine a humanist focus with sustainable profit goals and alternative forms of organizing. Yet it is important to be mindful of the practical manifestations of radical transformative creativity and to retain a sense of critical distance in the assessment of supposedly more socially and ecologically sustainable ways of organizing creativity.

7

Conclusion

This book emerged from my personal experience and frustration in finding a suitable text for students to gain an overview of creativity in organizations. I found that some of the longer texts reduce the complexity of organizational creativity too much, while others treat it simply as a by-product of organizational change or innovation. I firmly believe that creativity requires its own treatment, as ideas—large or small—are the lifeblood of an organization and essential to their functioning.

The aim of this book is to contribute to the discussion of recent research on organizing creativity by framing it with regard to three constitutive dimensions: context, process, and practice. These dimensions are related to key aspects of organizational creativity, such as generating ideas, evaluating ideas, modes of organizing, and the ends of creativity. The dimensions of context, process, and practice—or what researchers have referred to as processual and situational perspectives on organizing creativity (Schüßler et al., 2021)—have gained traction among creativity researchers over recent years, but this is still the exception rather than the norm in a field dominated by variance research (discussed in Chapter 1).

Obviously, the book's purpose is not to declare a final truth pertaining to organizational creativity in organization. Rather, the intention is to build, enrich, and extend an *interpretive repertoire* of how to make sense of key dimensions, research findings, critiques, and open questions concerning organizing creativity. According to Alvesson and Kärreman (2007: 1273), an 'interpretive repertoire is made up of theories, basic assumptions, commitments, metaphors, vocabularies, and knowledge', and as such provides the basis for a deeper comprehension of encounters, observations, and experiences related to creativity. However, while an interpretive repertoire is not a passive reservoir of ideas and concepts, it is necessary to actively use it when trying to make sense of organizing creativity. Thus it is necessary to pay close attention to what is happening in the world, as discussed in Chapter 3 with regard to the agency of serendipity. This final chapter will recap the contents of the book without rehashing all the details, and suggest some of their theoretical and practical implications.

Context, Process, and Practice

To recap the broader argument of the book, this section will use the overall framing of context, process, and practice to make sense of their overall implications and usefulness to understanding efforts to organize creativity.

Context

The notion of context in this book relates to the enabling and constraining factors when organizing creativity. In fact, as discussed in Chapter 2, context was one of the first themes

Organizing Creativity. Stephan M. Schaefer, Oxford University Press. © Stephan M. Schaefer (2023).
DOI: 10.1093/oso/9780198893509.003.0007

to emerge in interactionist approaches on organizational creativity, spearheaded by Teresa Amabile (Amabile, 1988). Interactionist approaches highlighted the importance of considering the environment in which organizations operate and how it influences organizational creativity, which marked the beginning of a departure from cognitive conceptions to a social-psychological focus. In continuing work, the notion of context was further refined. At an aggregate level, it is possible to distinguish *cultural*, *organizational*, and *institutional* contexts, while acknowledging that the distinction between these contexts has been controversially discussed, especially the differences between institutional and cultural context (Alvesson and Spicer, 2019). Chapter 2 discussed cultural contexts, referring to them when describing socially constructed meanings, values, symbols that influence interpretations, and actions that affect efforts to organize creativity. Culturally driven behaviours may be so automatic that people are unaware of them. In this sense, organizations *are* cultures, as all interactions tend to be influenced to a certain degree by people's meanings and values. Yet it is easy to denote all actions as cultural, which would mean that the concept becomes devoid of meaning. Hence it is possible to further distinguish organizational and institutional contexts from cultural contexts that have an impact on organizing creativity (Ford, 1996). Organizational and institutional contexts are structural rather than cultural, which means that they aim to create rules and desirable relationships and activities between and by organizational and social actors (Barley and Tolbert, 1997). Organizational and institutional contexts do not have to be based on ingrained values and meanings, though culture, organizational, and institutional contexts strongly overlap. Overall, context is a complex mosaic of cultural and structural aspects that enable and constrain efforts to organize creativity.

How does context influence efforts to organize creativity? To provide an answer to this question, this book considers the degree to which context directs behaviours, which can range from a strong to a weak influence, as seen in Chapters 2 and 3. The strength of context is a central and ambiguous element in organizing creativity. Overly strong contexts may provide clear direction, but they stifle creative processes by suppressing other ideas. Overly weak contexts, on the other hand, may lead to fragmentation and directionless idea generation processes. It seems that there is a sweet spot between overly strong and overly weak contexts for organizing creativity. In this vein, an essential element discussed is the notion of a metanorm, which means being given the opportunity to question existing norms, as this keeps contexts from becoming too rigid and controlling. However, it is necessary to keep in mind that metanorms may lead to an illusion of autonomy, as—in the end—people are still always acting in the interest of the organization (Robertson and Swan, 2003). The implication is that metanorms may lead people to believe they have the freedom to question all issues, which increases their identification with the organization, but when push comes to shove the fundamental values of the organization will not be challenged.

In addition to how contexts influence efforts to organize creativity, it is also important to pay attention to the specific values, norms, and structures that a context provides. This is especially important with regard to evaluating articulated ideas. The notion of orders of worth discussed in Chapter 4 provides a useful systematic overview of the justifications people employ when evaluating an idea. It is important to bear in mind, however, that orders of worth are not universal, but are dependent on the context of a pluralistic society and an economy that does not restrict people's voices. Even in a pluralistic society, single organizations may curb the influence of other orders of worth—an example would be the suppression of union activities, which represent a civic order of worth. Relatedly, Chapter 6 discussed in a more critical vein the broader economic and societal contexts in which people organize creativity. This discussion touched on how, in capitalist economic systems, the function of creativity for economic growth is seldom fundamentally questioned. It is simply accepted that ideas are instrumental to unrestrained economic growth that has evident negative consequences for individuals, environments, and society. It is therefore essential to think about what values should underlie future economic growth, and how they influence individual and collective efforts to organize creativity. To that end, the concept of radical transformative creativity is outlined as an alternative to the instrumentalist view on creativity.

Another overarching aspect discussed throughout the different chapters was the function of contexts when organizing creativity. For instance, the function of context is an important concern in different modes of coordination discussed in Chapter 5. The general question for managers seeking to stimulate transformative creative ideas is how to create a conducive context for generating and developing those transformative ideas. The four different modes of coordination aim to impact context both culturally and structurally. For example, a formally structured bureaucratic context is not uncreative by default, as is commonly assumed. As discussed extensively in Chapter 3, routines are performative and contain seeds for creativity. Yet it is necessary to distinguish between a coercive bureaucracy with rigid routines that stifle new ideas and an enabling bureaucracy that allows spaces for creative deviance. In contrast, leadership does not seek to create rules and structures but to establish what was called a progressive organizational culture in Chapter 2.

Managerial and organizational influence on context is, however, not as straightforward as it is usually depicted in neat management models. Contexts are not purely structural or cultural; they are also political. The political dimension of context highlights how efforts to organize creativity are first and foremost political manoeuvres from managers or groups of managers to gain power in the organization to realize their own agendas. As such, organizing creativity is subordinated to political ends and thus decisions on whether and how to organize creativity are based on how they impact people's political agenda (for a detailed study of the dynamics of organizational politics see Jackall, 1988). The political context of organizing creativity has only been broached in this book but certainly merits more scholarly attention (see for example Frost and Egri, 1990).

Process

Process theory draws attention to the importance of the temporal nature of organizing creativity. Time plays a significant role when trying to make sense of how organizational creativity unfolds. So, rather than depicting static relationships, this book shifts its perspective to how organizing creativity happens over time. Surprisingly, as discussed throughout the book, a process perspective on organizational creativity has been the exception rather than the norm, though—in recent years—some significant contributions that draw on process theorizing have emerged.

The notion of process has been conceptualized in different ways. Analogously to the discussion regarding the strength of context, moderate and strong process approaches are distinguished and elaborated on in Chapter 2. The former argues that essentially every-thing changes all the time, while the latter concedes the stability of structures, which are amenable to inert changes over time. Overall, process perspectives on organizational cre-ativity have in common the fact that they are critical towards theories that build on static models of organizational creativity and those that depict changes in distinct shifting phases.

Considering time means drawing attention to past, present, and future. While it is common to think of time as linear, Chapter 3 discussed past, present, and future as simul-taneous influences on organizing creativity. A student of mine initially struggled to grasp this notion, as a linear conception is deeply rooted in the modern understanding of time. Yet she eventually made sense of it by evoking a chess metaphor. In chess, she explained, a player must make their move in the present while simultaneously envisioning future pos-sibilities and consequences of their moves, as well as drawing on their knowledge and past experiences. This is the essence of the chordal triad of temporality which means that indi-vidual knowledge and organizational memory (past), motivation and attention (present), and the ability to imagine various future scenarios (future) are important simultaneous influences when generating and developing ideas.

Idea generating and developing processes are nearly always collective, contrary to the stubborn myth of the lone creative genius who comes up with all the brilliant ideas. Some scholars have even argued that an idea cannot be ascribed to a single individual, as it always changes in all interactions between parties. To make further sense of the nature of ideas, the metaphorical distinction between an idea as a particle and a wave is introduced. The former conceptualizes ideas as concrete entities that can be passed on unchanged, while the latter highlights the emerging and distributed nature of ideas.

The book also describes and discusses thoroughly how organizational creativity pro-cesses may unfold. In many cases, ideas are rejected immediately or are never fully developed to a state in which they become transformational. In other cases, ideas may change organizational routines or become part of practice without much discussion. In some instances, however, ideas may affect different groups and stakeholders linked to an organization and therefore initiate debate and even conflict. Chapter 4 sheds light on these conflict-laden processes. If an idea prompts conflicts due to opposing orders of worth, it is essential that the groups involved are ready to have a productive conversation about their differences and aim to find a compromise. This general readiness to have a conversa-tion is referred to as productive dissonance, which means that the parties involved seek to establish a creative synthesis that temporarily reconciles opposing orders of worth. Such a negotiated order is temporary, as crises and other challenges will trigger renewed discus-sions and dissonance which must be dealt with in the future. As such, transformative ideas tend to be based on a more or less stable negotiated order, which is prone to changes over time. The negotiated order could provide stability over a period of time, as theorized by a moderate process approach, but it is possible that negotiated orders may also be constantly in flux, as postulated by a strong process approach.

The notion of productive dissonance has another important function—to provide a basis for a pluralistic creativity process. As discussed in Chapter 6, the ends of creativity tend to be dominated by market and engineering considerations. These are, of course, essential dimensions that should influence the creative process. Yet the existential threats and grand challenges of today necessitate the consideration of other values that influence the creative process. Transformative ideas may have a wider reach and drastic consequences beyond generating profits and increasing efficiency. Hence organizations may seek to design creative processes so that all stakeholders can ponder the potential implications of ideas and address possible negative effects.

Naturally, this is not possible or even necessary for all creative processes, so managers must actively assess situations and what is needed. Hence the complexity of the creative process poses unique management challenges that mainly stem from paradoxes emerging from conflicting demands when organizing creativity. As discussed in Chapter 5, a paradox arises when two aspects of a phenomenon are simultaneously valid and persist over time. The simultaneous existence of two aspects means that tensions emerge when both seem to be valid, and should be taken into consideration when organizing creativity. Yet people's natural inclination is to try and resolve the paradox by either denying it or ignoring the tensions. However, they may also embrace paradoxes by seeking to transcend them. In contrast to the perceived need for order and control, this requires the ability to thrive in ambiguity and uncertainty—what are called 'negative capabilities', to which the discussion of practices returns.

Practice

Last, but certainly not least, practices are an inherent part of organizing creativity. Practices are the concrete activities involved in generating, developing, and evaluating ideas and managerial and organizational efforts to organize creativity. As such, practices refer to the 'doing' of creativity, which means the ongoing activities of actors. Practices, therefore, emphasize agency instead of structures. Put simply, a practice approach asks 'What *do* people do?' Meanwhile, a structural approach poses the question: 'What *should* people do?' These seemingly basic questions are a useful guide when assessing postulates, theories, and claims on organizational creativity. As discussed in Chapter 5, asking what managers do fundamentally challenged the normative assumptions and claims of existing management theories. So, in conclusion to the discussion of practices in this book, it may be asked what individuals and groups *do* when they engage in creative acts. Answers to this question throughout the book give some theoretical and empirical answers.

Chapter 2 discusses two theoretical conceptions and related philosophies which seek to explain a practice perspective on creativity. First, pragmatism and design thinking are elaborated. In a nutshell, pragmatism argues that people may search for metaphysical and philosophical explanations of their actions and—ultimately—existence, but in the end, their concrete actions are what matters. This means that designers tend to act and experiment with their ideas rather than spending time analysing a large chunk of data before decisions are made. This notion of simply doing something resurfaces in the conception of effectuation in Chapter 3. Effectuation challenges the analytical approach to developing and implementing one's ideas based on a thorough analysis of opportunities, the assessment of causalities, and the setting of predefined goals. In particular, it explains idea generation and development processes by arguing that individuals and groups make use of their available resources as they go along.

Second, the theoretical concept of performative routines, which challenge the common perspective that routines are repetitive patterns of activity that do not change from one iteration to the next, is examined at length. This book discusses how creativity and routines are interwoven because actively performing a routine means that outcomes are indeterminate—each routine has an inherent creative potential. Sonenshein (2016) called this the 'personalization of routines' which invites creative amendments through individual agency. A similar dynamic is at play in the moderate process approach discussed in Chapter 2, which argues that structures have no deterministic influence on agency, as they are *media and outcomes* of actions. In other words, structures may direct creative process, but their performance may also lead to changes in directive structures. Indeed, the theatrical analogies of directing and performing serve as a fruitful metaphor for grasping the core of a moderate process approach because it highlights how structures direct performance but performing also includes a personal touch and interpretation. So perhaps the neologism 'organizing creativity'[1] would be more accurate in describing efforts to facilitate creativity, as it denotes the simultaneous influence of stability and fluidity by combining in a word the stability of the *organiza*tion with the process of organiz*ing*.

Since a practice approach focuses squarely on people's activities, it has a distinct empirical focus. For that reason, various individual and group activities related to creativity are discussed throughout the book. These include individual cognitive practices when generating and developing ideas, as well as collective idea generation practices like brainstorming or effectuation. With regard to evaluating ideas, transactional and transformational practices are distinguished. The former refers to evaluation practices that treat ideas as distinct, identifiable entities, while the latter refers to valuation activities that emerge from interactions within groups. Overall, many of these creativity practices seem to be very popular—for example, the ubiquitous brainstorming method or stage gate models for new product development. Yet, while it is tempting to propose generic best practices for organizing creativity, this book has shown that they are not simply transferable. It is at this specific level of creativity practices that the overarching argument of the book comes together—that context, process, and practice are inherently linked and must be considered as a triad of influential dimensions. So when evaluating the feasibility and benefits of creativity practices it is necessary to contextualize them and consider their indeterminate processual implications.

The situatedness and indeterminate outcomes of organizing creativity is one of the central themes in the discussion of practices of organizing creativity in Chapter 5. In general, managerial work when organizing creativity does not seem to be able to follow preconceived normative templates or best practices. In contrast, managerial work is messy, complex, and riddled with paradoxes. This means that managers tend not to be able to control their activities; instead, practices must be adapted to emerging situations and changing contexts. Thus managers must be attuned to the specific demands of each situation when they attempt to facilitate and organize creativity. To capture these management challenges, the metaphor of improvisation is introduced. Just like musical improvisation, it highlights the importance of knowledge and skills (being able to play one's instrument), the existence of minimal structures (tuning, harmonies, scales, and so on), and the ability to respond to emerging situations flexibly (shifting solos, adapting to feel and rhythm). Hence improvisation draws attention to the active 'reading' of a situation and responding adequately to it. It is concluded that, in essence, organizing the creativity of others is itself a creative process. So perhaps a more apt title of the book would have been *Organizating Creativity Creatively*.

---

[1] I am indebted to Jörg Sydow who suggested 'organiz*ating* creativity' as an alternative title for the book.

Theoretical and Practical Implications

Imagine several blind men or women who have never seen an elephant. Now, walking through the steppe or the jungle, they come across one. They want to know what it is and use their remaining senses to describe what they experience. When each man and woman explores one part of the elephant, they would of course describe the part that they sense—perhaps the thickness of the legs, the movements of the trunk, or the thinness of the flapping ears. Every individual would have their own account to tell when describing what an elephant is like. The well-known parable of the elephant and the blind people is helpful when reflecting on the theoretical implications of the book (see also Styhre and Sundgren, 2005). The obvious message of the fable is that no one theory can claim the truth about organizational creativity; different theories are added to our interpretive repertoire that must be used to understand certain aspects linked to creativity and organizations. The fable thus highlights the importance *of considering multiple theories and perspectives to understand and explain organizational creativity.*

Apart from this overall message, the fable also conveys that if all men and women work together and communicate with each other, they can establish an outline of what the elephant in question looks like based on some of the shapes of its individual features. They may establish that an elephant is tall and has small ears, a long trunk, and short tusks. Analogously, the theoretical framing of this book provides a basis for establishing specific *configurations of organizational creativity.* A configuration is a distinct form or shape based on a specific arrangement of elements (like each single elephant). Hence, departing from the triad of context, process, and practice, it is possible to use the theoretical framing to establish varying configurations that link creativity to organizing and organization.

The theoretical framing of the book is an explicit theory that can be used to guide systematic empirical research. As discussed in Chapter 4, implicit theories, in contrast, are theories that people are not aware of, and they play an important role for managing and organizing creativity. However, many implicit theories tend to break down when things do not work out the way they were intended. The practical aim of the book is to provide practitioners with multiple interpretations to make better sense of these situations when attempting to organize creativity. The aspiration is that the contents of the book serve as an inspiration to reassess ingrained understandings of organizational creativity and learn about alternative explanations, actions, and potential dysfunctionalities. Equipped with such knowledge, it may make it more likely to attempt to *organizate creativity creatively* by questioning oversimplified models and instructions on how to organize creativity, and draw inspiration from the notion of manager as artist discussed in Chapter 5.

This is a never-ending, formative learning process, however. The psychologist MacKinnon (1978: xvi) wrote, '[T]he very essence of creativity will, I believe, always elude us. That, however, is no reason for giving up on our research; rather, it is all the more reason for continuing our research.' In this spirit, the aim of this book is not to provide a definite answer to all questions of creativity, but to serve as a sensitizing guide to making sense of creativity's complexity and developing the capability for critical reflection and action. Ideas are the lifeblood of an organization. Understanding where they come from, how to evaluate and facilitate them, and what ends they should serve is one of the most important qualities that decision makers in organizations should have to deal with the wicked problems of this age.

Bibliography

Abumrad, J. n.d. *Jad Abumrad* [Online]. Available: https://transom.org/2012/jad-abumrad-gut-wrench [Accessed 13 July 2022].

Adams, G. S., Converse, B. A., Hales, A. H., and Klotz, L. E. 2021. People Systematically Overlook Subtractive Changes. *Nature*, 592, 258–261.

Adamson, G. 2013. *The Invention of Craft*. London, Bloomsbury.

Adler, P. S. and Borys, B. 1996. Two Types of Bureaucracy: Enabling and Coercive. *Administrative Science Quarterly*, 41, 61–89.

Adler, P. S., Goldoftas, B., and Levine, D. I. 1999. Flexibility Versus Efficiency? A Case Study of Model Changeovers in the Toyota Production System. *Organization Science*, 10, 43–68.

Aldrich, H. and Herker, D. 1977. Boundary Spanning Roles and Organization Structure. *Academy of Management Review*, 2, 217–230.

Allen, D. 2020. *Why Every Company Needs a Chief Fun Officer* [Online]. The Conversation. Available: https://theconversation.com/why-every-company-needs-a-chief-fun-officer-128330 [Accessed 13 July 2022].

Alvesson, M. 2013a. *The Triumph of Emptiness*. Oxford, Oxford University Press.

Alvesson, M. 2013b. *Understanding Organizational Culture*. London, Sage.

Alvesson, M. and Blom, M. 2019. Beyond Leadership and Followership: Working with a Variety of Modes of Organizing. *Organizational Dynamics*, 48, 28–37.

Alvesson, M., Blom, M., and Sveningsson, S. 2016. *Reflexive Leadership: Organising in an Imperfect World*. London, Sage.

Alvesson, M., Gabriel Y., and Paulsen, R. 2017. *Return to Meaning: A Social Science with Something to Say*. Oxford, Oxford University Press.

Alvesson, M. and Kärreman, D. 2007. Constructing Mystery: Empirical Matters in Theory Development. *Academy of Management Review*, 32, 1265–1281.

Alvesson, M. and Spicer, A. 2012. A Stupidity-Based Theory of Organizations. *Journal of Management Studies*, 49, 1194–1220.

Alvesson, M. and Spicer, A. 2019. Neo-Institutional Theory and Organization Studies: A Mid-Life Crisis? *Organization Studies*, 40, 199–218.

Alvesson, M. and Sveningsson, S. 2003. The Great Disappearing Act: Difficulties in Doing 'Leadership'. *The Leadership Quarterly*, 14, 359–381.

Alvesson, M. and Willmott, H. 1992. On the Idea of Emancipation in Management and Organization Studies. *Academy of Management Review*, 17, 432–464.

Amabile, T. M. 1988. A Model of Creativity and Innovation in Organizations. *In*: B. M. Staw and L. L. Cummings (eds) *Research in Organizational Behavior*. Greenwich, JAI Press, 123–167

Amabile, T. M. 1997a. Entrepreneurial Creativity Through Motivational Synergy. *Journal of Creative Behavior*, 31, 18–26.

Amabile, T. M. 1997b. Motivating Creativity in Organizations: On Doing What You Love and Loving What You Do. *California Management Review*, 40, 39–58.

Amabile, T. M. 2011. *Componential Theory of Creativity*. Boston, MA, Harvard Business School.

Amabile, T. M. and Pratt, M. G. 2016. The Dynamic Componential Model of Creativity and Innovation in Organizations: Making Progress, Making Meaning. *Research in Organizational Behavior*, 36, 157–183.

Anderson, A. R., Dodd, S. D., and Jack, S. 2010. Network Practices and Entrepreneurial Growth. *Scandinavian Journal of Management*, 26, 121–133.

Andriopoulos, C. and Lewis, M. W. 2010. Managing Innovation Paradoxes: Ambidexterity Lessons from Leading Product Design Companies. *Long Range Planning*, 43, 104–122.

Argyris, C. and Schön, D. 1978. *Organizational Learning: A Theory of Action Perspective.* Reading, Addison–Wesley.

Ashforth, B. E. and Mael, F. 1989. Social Identity Theory and the Organization. *Academy of Management Review*, 14, 20–39.

Atchley, R. A., Strayer, D. L., and Atchley, P. 2012. Creativity in the Wild: Improving Creative Reasoning through Immersion in Natural Settings. *PLOS ONE*, 7, e51474.

Backman, M., Börjesson, S., and Setterberg, S. 2007. Working with Concepts in the Fuzzy Front End: Exploring the Context for Innovation for Different Types of Concepts at Volvo Cars. *R&D Management*, 37, 17–28.

Baer, M., Dane, E., and Madrid, M. 2020. Zoning Out or Breaking Through? Linking Daydreaming to Creativity in the Workplace. *Academy of Management Journal*, 64, 1553–1577.

Bakhtin, M. M. 1984. *Problems of Dostoevsky's Poetics.* Minneapolis, Minnesota University Press.

Banerjee, S. B., Jermier, J. M., Peredo, A. M., Perey, R., and Reichel, A. 2021. Theoretical Perspectives on Organizations and Organizing in a Post-Growth Era. *Organization*, 28, 337–357.

Barley, S. R. and Kunda, G. 1992. Design and Devotion: Surges of Rational and Normative Ideologies of Control in Managerial Discourse. *Administrative Science Quarterly*, 37, 363–399.

Barley, S. R. and Tolbert, P. S. 1997. Institutionalization and Structuration: Studying the Links between Action and Institution. *Organization Studies*, 18, 93–117.

Baron, R. A. and Markman, G. D. 2000. Beyond Social Capital: How Social Skills can Enhance Entrepreneurs' Success. *Academy of Management Perspectives*, 14, 106–116.

Barrett, F. J. 1998. Coda—Creativity and Improvisation in Jazz and Organizations: Implications for Organizational Learning. *Organization Science*, 9, 605–622.

Barron, F. 1958. The Psychology of Imagination. *Scientific American*, 199, 150–169.

Baumol, W. J., Litan, R. E., and Schramm, C. J. 2007. *Good Capitalism, Bad Capitalism, and the Economics of Growth and Prosperity.* New Haven, CT, Yale University Press.

Belk, R. W. 1988. Possessions and the Extended Self. *Journal of Consumer Research*, 15, 139–168.

Bell, E., Dacin, M. T., and Toraldo, M. L. 2021. Craft Imaginaries—Past, Present and Future. Organization Theory. Published online 23 February.

Benson, J. K. 1977. Organizations: A Dialectical View. *Administrative Science Quarterly*, 22, 1–21.

Berg, J. M. 2016. Balancing on the Creative Highwire: Forecasting the Success of Novel Ideas in Organizations. *Administrative Science Quarterly*, 61, 433–468.

Berger, P. L. and Luckmann, T. 1966. *The Social Construction of Reality: A Treatise in the Sociology of Knowledge.* London, Penguin.

Berns, G. S., Laibson, D., and Loewenstein, G. 2007. Intertemporal Choice—Toward an Integrative Framework. *Trends in Cognitive Sciences*, 11, 482–488.

Bernstein, E. S. 2012. The Transparency Paradox: A Role for Privacy in Organizational Learning and Operational Control. *Administrative Science Quarterly*, 57, 181–216.

Bilton, C. and Cummings, S. 2014. *Handbook of Management and Creativity.* Cheltenham, Edward Elgar.

Birch, A. H. 1975. Economic Models in Political Science: The Case of 'Exit Voice, and Loyalty'. *British Journal of Political Science*, 5, 69–82.

Blank, S. 2019. Why Companies Do 'Innovation Theater' Instead of Actual Innovation. *Harvard Business Review* [Online]. Available: https://hbr.org/2019/10/why-companies-do-innovation-theater-instead-of-actual-innovation [Accessed 13 July 2022].

Blumer, H. 1954. What is Wrong with Social Theory? *American Sociological Review*, 19, 3–10.

Bobadilla, N. and Gilbert, P. 2017. Managing Scientific and Technical Experts in R&D: Beyond Tensions, Conflicting Logics and Orders of Worth. *R&D Management*, 47, 223–235.

Bolman, L. and Deal, T. 2013. *Reframing Organizations: Artistry, Choice, and Leadership.* Hoboken, NJ, Jossey-Bass.

Boltanski, L. and Thévenot, L. 2006. *On Justification.* Princeton, NJ, Princeton University Press.

Bouty, I. and Gomez, M.-L. 2015. Creativity at Work: Generating Useful Novelty in Haute Cuisine Restaurants. *In*: R. Garud, B. Simpson, A. Langley, and H. Tsoukas (eds) *The Emergence of Novelty in Organizations.* Oxford, Oxford University Press, 216–245.

Brock, T. D. 1995. The Road to Yellowstone—and Beyond. *Annual Review of Microbiology*, 49, 1–29.

Brown, T. 2008. Design Thinking. *Harvard Business Review*, 86, 84–92.

Buchanan, R. 1992. Wicked Problems in Design Thinking. *Design Issues*, 8, 5–21.

Burns, T. and Stalker, G. M. 1961. *The Management of Innovation*. Oxford, Oxford University Press.

Burt, R. S. 2004. Structural Holes and Good Ideas. *American Journal of Sociology*, 110, 349–399.

Bushe, G. R. and Marshak, R. J. 2009. Revisioning Organization Development: Diagnostic and Dialogic Premises and Patterns of Practice. *Journal of Applied Behavioral Science*, 45, 348–368.

Bycroft, M. 2014. Psychology, Psychologists, and the Creativity Movement: The Lives of Method Inside and Outside the Cold War. *In*: M. Solovey and C. Hamilton (eds) *Cold War Social Science: Knowledge Production, Liberal Democracy, and Human Nature*. New York: Palgrave Macmillan, 197–214.

Canato, A., Ravasi, D., and Phillips, N. 2013. Coerced Practice Implementation in Cases of Low Cultural Fit: Cultural Change and Practice Adaptation During the Implementation of Six Sigma at 3M. *Academy of Management Journal*, 56, 1724–1753.

Carlson, S. 1951. *Executive Behaviour*. Stockholm, Strömbergs.

Cederström, C. and Spicer, A. 2015. *The Wellness Syndrome*. New York, Wiley.

Chakrabarti, A. K. 1974. The Role of Champion in Product Innovation. *California Management Review*, 17, 58–62.

Chambers, A. 2009. Africa's Not-So-Magic Roundabout. The Guardian [Online]. Available: https://www.theguardian.com/commentisfree/2009/nov/24/africa-charity-water-pumps-roundabouts [Accessed 13 July 2022].

Cheney, G., Santa Cruz, I., Peredo, A. M., and Nazareno, E. 2014. Worker Cooperatives as an Organizational Alternative: Challenges, Achievements and Promise in Business Governance and Ownership. *Organization*, 21, 591–603.

Cohen, W. M. and Levinthal, D. A. 1990. Absorptive Capacity: A New Perspective on Learning and Innovation. *Administrative Science Quarterly*, 35, 128–152.

Cohen, M. D., March, J. G., and Olsen, J. P. 1972. A Garbage Can Model of Organizational Choice. *Administrative Science Quarterly*, 17, 1–25.

Collinson, D. 2012. Prozac Leadership and the Limits of Positive Thinking. *Leadership*, 8, 87–107.

Cooper, R. G. 1990. Stage-Gate Systems: A New Tool for Managing New Products. *Business Horizons*, 33, 44–54.

Cooper, R. G. 2008. Perspective: The Stage-Gate® Idea-to-Launch Process—Update, What's New, and NexGen Systems. *Journal of Product Innovation Management*, 25, 213–232.

Crawford, M. 2009. *Shop Class as Soulcraft: An Inquiry into the Value of Work*. New York, Penguin.

Cropley, A. 2006. In Praise of Convergent Thinking. *Creativity Research Journal*, 18, 391–404.

Cropley, D. H., Kaufman, J. C., and Cropley, A. J. 2008. Malevolent Creativity: A Functional Model of Creativity in Terrorism and Crime. *Creativity Research Journal*, 20, 105–115.

Csikszentmihalyi, M. 1990. The Domain of Creativity. *In*: M. A. Runco and R. S. Albert (eds) *Theories of Creativity*. Newbury Park, Sage, 190–212.

Csikszentmihalyi, M. 1996. *Creativity: The Psychology of Discovery and Invention*. New York, Harper Collins.

Cyert, R. C. and March, I. G. 1963. *A Behavioural Theory of the Firm*. New York, Prentice Hall.

Czarniawska, B. 2001. Having Hope in Paralogy. *Human Relations*, 54, 13–21.

Daft, R. L., Murphy, J., and Willmott, H. 2020. *Organization Theory & Design: An International Perspective*. Andover, Cengage Learning.

Dalsgaard, P. 2014. Pragmatism and Design Thinking. *International Journal of Design*, 8, 143–155.

Dane, E. 2018. Where is My Mind? Theorizing Mind Wandering and Its Performance-Related Consequences in Organizations. *Academy of Management Review*, 43, 179–197.

Davis, G. F. 2009. The Rise and Fall of Finance and the End of the Society of Organizations. *Academy of Management Perspectives*, 23, 27–44.

Davis, T. 2012. *Explainer: What is Wave–Particle Duality* [Online]. The Conversation. Available: https://theconversation.com/explainer-what-is-wave-particle-duality-7414 [Accessed 13 July 2022].

Dawson, V., D'Andrea, T., Affinito, R., and Westby, E. L. 1999. Predicting Creative Behavior: A Reexamination of the Divergence between Traditional and Teacher-Defined Concepts of Creativity. *Creativity Research Journal*, 12, 57–66.

De Bono, E. 2014. *Lateral Thinking: An Introduction*. London, Vermillion.

De Rond, M. 2014. The Structure of Serendipity. *Culture and Organization*, 20, 342–358.

De Vaan, M., Stark, D., and Vedres, B. 2015. Game Changer: The Topology of Creativity. *American Journal of Sociology*, 120, 1144–1194.

Kets de Vries, M., and Miller, D. 1984. The Neurotic Organization: Diagnosing and Changing Counterproductive Styles of Management. San Francisco, Jossey Bass.

Dean, J. W., Brandes, P., and Dharwadkar, R. 1998. Organizational Cynicism. *Academy of Management Review*, 23, 341–352.

Denis, J.-L., Langley, A., and Rouleau, L. 2007. Strategizing in Pluralistic Contexts: Rethinking Theoretical Frames. *Human Relations*, 60, 179–215.

Dewey, J. 1981. The Need for a Recovery of Philosophy. *In*: J. J. McDermott (ed.) *The Philosophy of John Dewey*. Chicago: University of Chicago Press, 58–97.

Dickinson, M. H. 1999. Bionics: Biological Insight into Mechanical Design. *Proceedings of the National Academy of Sciences*, 96, 14208–14209.

Diehl, M. and Stroebe, W. 1987. Productivity Loss in Brainstorming Groups: Toward the Solution of a Riddle. *Journal of Personality and Social Psychology*, 53, 497–509.

Dillon, J. T. 1982. Problem Finding and Solving. *Journal of Creative Behavior*, 16, 97–111.

Dodgson, M., Gann, D., and Salter, A. 2006. The Role of Technology in the Shift Towards Open Innovation: The Case of Procter & Gamble. *R&D Management*, 36, 333–346.

Dombrowski, C., Kim, J. Y., Desouza, K. C., Braganza, A., Papagari, S., Baloh, P., and Jha, S. 2007. Elements of Innovative Cultures. *Knowledge and Process Management*, 14, 190–202.

Dougherty, D. 1992. Interpretive Barriers to Successful Product Innovation in Large Firms. *Organization Science*, 3, 179–202.

Drazin, R., Glynn, M. A., and Kazanjian, R. K. 1999. Multilevel Theorizing about Creativity in Organizations: A Sensemaking Perspective. *Academy of Management Review*, 24, 286–307.

Dubinskas, F. A. 1993. Modeling Cultures of Project Management. *Journal of Engineering and Technology Management*, 10, 129–160.

Dunne, D. and Martin, R. 2006. Design Thinking and How It Will Change Management Education: An Interview and Discussion. *Academy of Management Learning & Education*, 5, 512–523.

Eagleton, T. 1991. *Ideology: An Introduction*. London, Verso.

Edelman, M. 1964. *The Symbolic Uses of Politics*. Urbana and Chicago, University of Illinois Press.

Edmondson, A. 1999. Psychological Safety and Learning Behavior in Work Teams. *Administrative Science Quarterly*, 44, 350–383.

Edson, G. 2009. *Letter from the CEO*. Available: https://playpumps.wordpress.com/page/2/ [Accessed 13 July 2022].

Egholm, L. 2014. *Philosophy of Science: Perspectives on Organisations and Society*. Copenhagen, Hans Reitzels Forlag.

Ehrenreich, B. 2010. *Smile or Die: How Positive Thinking Fooled America and the World*. London, Granta Books.

Einola, K. and Alvesson, M. 2019. The Making and Unmaking of Teams. *Human Relations*, 72, 1891–1919.

Einstein, B. 2017. Here's Why Juicero's Press is So Expensive. Bolt. Available: https://blog.bolt.io/ juicero/ [Accessed 13 July 2022].

Elsbach, K. D. and Hargadon, A. B. 2006. Enhancing Creativity through 'Mindless' Work: A Framework of Workday Design. *Organization Science*, 17, 470–483.

Elsbach, K. D. and Kramer, R. M. 2003. Assessing Creativity in Hollywood Pitch Meetings: Evidence for a Dual-Process Model of Creativity Judgments. *Academy of Management Journal*, 46, 283–301.

Emirbayer, M. and Mische, A. 1998. What is Agency? *American Journal of Sociology*, 103, 962–1023.

Enders, J., Kehm, B. M., and Schimank, U. 2015. Turning Universities into Actors on Quasi-Markets: How New Public Management Reforms Affect Academic Research. *In*: D. Jansen and I. Pruisken (eds) *The Changing Governance of Higher Education and Research*. Dordrecht, Springer, 89–103.

Endrissat, N., Islam, G., and Noppeney, C. 2015. Enchanting Work: New Spirits of Service Work in an Organic Supermarket. *Organization Studies*, 36, 1555–1576.

Engwall, M., Kling, R., and Werr, A. 2005. Models in Action: How Management Models are Interpreted in New Product Development. *R&D Management*, 35, 427–439.

Ewenstein, B. and Whyte, J. 2009. Knowledge Practices in Design: The Role of Visual Representations as 'Epistemic Objects'. *Organization Studies*, 30, 7–30.

Eysenck, H. J. 2003. Creativity, Personality and the Convergent–Divergent Continuum. *In*: M. A. Runco (ed.) *Critical Creative Processes*. Cresskill, Hampton Press, 95–114.

Feldman, M. S. 2000. Organizational Routines as a Source of Continuous Change. *Organization Science*, 11, 611–629.

Feldman, M. S. and March, J. G. 1981. Information in Organizations as Signal and Symbol. *Administrative Science Quarterly*, 26, 171–186.

Feldman, M. S. and Pentland, B. T. 2003. Reconceptualizing Organizational Routines as a Source of Flexibility and Change. *Administrative Science Quarterly*, 48, 94–118.

Ferraro, F., Pfeffer, J., and Sutton, R. I. 2005. Economics Language and Assumptions: How Theories Can Become Self-Fulfilling. *Academy of Management Review*, 30, 8–24.

Festinger, L., Riecken, H. W., and Schachter, S. 1956. *When Prophecies Fail*. New York, Harper Torchbooks.

Fleming, L., Mingo, S., and Chen, D. 2007. Collaborative Brokerage, Generative Creativity, and Creative Success. *Administrative Science Quarterly*, 52, 443–475.

Fleming, P. 2005. Workers' Playtime?: Boundaries and Cynicism in a 'Culture of Fun' Program. *Journal of Applied Behavioral Science*, 41, 285–303.

Fleming, P. 2009. *Authenticity and the Cultural Politics of Work: New Forms of Informal Control*. Oxford, Oxford University Press.

Fleming, P. and Spicer, A. 2014. Power in Management and Organization Science. *Academy of Management Annals*, 8, 237–298.

Florida, R. 2005. *Cities and the Creative Class*. New York, Routledge.

Florida, R. 2012. *The Rise of the Creative Class*. New York, Basic Books.

Ford, C. M. 1996. A Theory of Individual Creative Action in Multiple Social Domains. *Academy of Management Review*, 21, 1112–1142.

Fortwengel, J., Schüßler, E., and Sydow, J. 2017. Studying Organizational Creativity as Process: Fluidity or Duality? *Creativity and Innovation Management*, 26, 5–16.

Fournier, V. and Grey, C. 2000. At the Critical Moment: Conditions and Prospects for Critical Management Studies. *Human Relations*, 53, 7–32.

Franklin, S. W. 2023. *The Cult of Creativity*. Chicago, University of Chicago Press.

Freeman, R. E., Harrison, J. S., Wicks, A. C., Parmar, B. L., and De Colle, S. 2010. *Stakeholder Theory: The State of the Art*. Cambridge, Cambridge University Press.

Friedman, M. 1970. A Friedman Doctrine—The Social Responsibility Of Business is to Increase its Profits [Online]. *The New York Times*. Available: https://www.nytimes.com/1970/09/13/archives/a-friedman-doctrine-the-social-responsibility-of-business-is-to.html [Accessed 13 July 2022].

Frost, P. J. and Egri, C. P. 1990. Influence of Political Action on Innovation. *Leadership & Organization Development Journal*, 11, 4–12.

Fukuyama, F. 1989. The End of History? *The National Interest*, 16, 3–18.

Gabriel, Y. and Carr, A. 2002. Organizations, Management and Psychoanalysis: An Overview. *Journal of Managerial Psychology*, 17, 348–365.

Gabriel, Y., Muhr, S. L., and Linstead, S. 2014. Luck of the Draw? Serendipity, Accident, Chance and Misfortune in Organization and Design. *Culture and Organization*, 20, 334–341.

Garber, M. 2012. *The Future of Advertising (Will be Squirted into Your Nostrils as You Sit on a Bus)* [Online]. The Atlantic. Available: https://www.theatlantic.com/technology/archive/2012/07/the-future-of-advertising-will-be-squirted-into-your-nostrils-as-you-sit-on-a-bus/260283/ [Accessed 13 July 2022].

Gartner, W. B. 2007. Entrepreneurial Narrative and a Science of the Imagination. *Journal of Business Venturing*, 22, 613–627.

Garud, R., Gehman, J., and Kumaraswamy, A. 2011. Complexity Arrangements for Sustained Innovation: Lessons from 3M Corporation. *Organization Studies*, 32, 737–767.

Geertz, C. 1973. *The Interpretation of Cultures*. New York, Basic Books.

Geller, J. S. 2011. *Open Letter to BlackBerry Bosses: Senior RIM Exec Tells All as Company Crumbles Around him* [Online]. BGR Media. Available: https://bgr.com/general/open-letter-to-blackberry-bosses-senior-rim-exec-tells-all-as-company-crumbles-around-him-95272/ [Accessed 13 July 2022].

Gentner, D. 1983. Structure-Mapping: A Theoretical Framework for Analogy. *Cognitive Science*, 7, 155–170.

George, J. M. 2007. Creativity in Organizations. *Academy of Management Annals*, 1, 439–477.

Getzels, J. W. 1975. Problem-Finding and the Inventiveness of Solutions. *Journal of Creative Behavior*, 9, 12–18.

Giddens, A. 1984. *The Constitution of Society*. Cambridge, Polity Press.

Gillingham, K., Kotchen, M. J., Rapson, D. S., and Wagner, G. 2013. The Rebound Effect is Overplayed. *Nature*, 493, 475–476.

Girschik, V. 2020. Shared Responsibility for Societal Problems: The Role of Internal Activists in Reframing Corporate Responsibility. *Business & Society*, 59, 34–66.

Göpel, M. 2016. *The Great Mindshift: How a New Economic Paradigm and Sustainability Transformations go Hand in Hand*. Dordrecht, Springer.

Graaf, T. and Gruendler, D. 2019. The Visibility Paradox: Escaping the Panopticon of Enterprise Social Networks. Masters thesis, Lund University.

Granovetter, M. 1973. The Strength of Weak Ties. *American Journal of Sociology*, 78, 1360–1380.

Granovetter, M. 1985. Economic Action and Social Structure: The Problem of Embeddedness. *American Journal of Sociology*, 91, 481–510.

Gregg, M. 2011. *Work's Intimacy*. New York, Wiley.

Gros, F. 2014. *A Philosophy of Walking*. London, Verso.

Guattari, F. and Deleuze, G. 1987. *A Thousand Plateaus: Capitalism and Schizophrenia*. Minneapolis, University of Minnesota Press.

Guilford, J. P. 1950. Creativity. *American Psychologist*, 5, 444–454.

Gulick, L. 1937. Notes on the Theory of Organization. *In*: J. M. Shafritz, J. S. Ott, and Y. S. Jang, *Classics of Organization Theory*. Andover, Cengage, 87–95.

Habermas, J. 1968. *Knowledge and Human Interests*. Boston, MA, Beacon.

Hacking, I. 1999. *The Social Construction of What?* Boston, MA, Harvard University Press.

Hahn, T. and Knight, E. 2021. The Ontology of Organizational Paradox: A Quantum Approach. *Academy of Management Review*, 46, 362–384.

Håkonsen Coldevin, G., Carlsen, A., Clegg, S., Pitsis, T. S., and Antonacopoulou, E. P. 2019. Organizational Creativity as Idea Work: Intertextual Placing and Legitimating Imaginings in Media Development and Oil Exploration. *Human Relations*, 72, 1369–1397.

Hall, P. A. and Soskice, D. (eds) 2001. *Varieties of Capitalism: The Institutional Foundations of Competitive Advantage*. Oxford: Oxford University Press.

Hamel, G. and Breen, B. 2007. *The Future of Management*. Cambridge, MA, Harvard Business School Press.

Hannan, M. T. and Freeman, J. 1977. The Population Ecology of Organizations. *American Journal of Sociology*, 82, 929–964.

Hansen, M., Nohria, N., and Tierney, T. 1999. What's Your Strategy for Knowledge Management. *Harvard Business Review*, 77, 106–116.

Hargadon, A. and Bechky, B. A. 2006. When Collections of Creatives become Creative Collectives: A Field Study of Problem Solving at Work. *Organization Science*, 17, 484–500.

Hargadon, A. and Sutton, R. I. 1997. Technology Brokering and Innovation in a Product Development Firm. *Administrative Science Quarterly*, 42, 716–749.

Hartelius, E. J. and Browning, L. D. 2008. The Application of Rhetorical Theory in Managerial Research: A Literature Review. *Management Communication Quarterly*, 22, 13–39.

Hartmann, M. 2014. In the Gray Zone. With Police in Making Space for Creativity. PhD thesis, Copenhagen Business School.

Hartmann, M. R. K. and Hartmann, R. K. 2023. Hiding Practices in Employee-User Innovation. *Research Policy*, 52, 2-12.

Harvey, S. 2014. Creative Synthesis: Exploring the Process of Extraordinary Group Creativity. *Academy of Management Review*, 39, 324–343.

Harvey, S. and Kou, C.-Y. 2013. Collective Engagement in Creative Tasks: The Role of Evaluation in the Creative Process in Groups. *Administrative Science Quarterly*, 58, 346–386.

Hassi, L. and Laakso, M. 2011. Conceptions of Design Thinking in the Design and Management Discourses. *Proceedings of IASDR2011*, Delft, 1–10.

Hatch, M. J. 1999. Exploring the Empty Spaces of Organizing: How Improvisational Jazz Helps Redescribe Organizational Structure. *Organization Studies*, 20, 75–100.

Hatch, M. J. 2011. *Organizations: A Very Short Introduction*. Oxford, Oxford University Press.

Heidegger, M. 1927. *Sein und Zeit*. Tübingen, Niemeyer.

Hernes, T. 2014. *A Process Theory of Organization*. Oxford, Oxford University Press.

Hirschman, A. O. 1970. *Exit, Voice, and Loyalty: Responses to Decline in Firms, Organizations, and States*. Boston, MA, Harvard University Press.

Hislop, D., Bosua, R., and Helms, R. 2018. *Knowledge Management in Organizations: A Critical Introduction*. Oxford: Oxford University Press.

Hochschild, A. 1983. *The Managed Heart: Commercialization of Human Feeling*. Berkeley, University of California Press.

Hua, M.-Y., Harvey, S., and Rietzschel, E. 2022. Unpacking 'Ideas' in Creative Work: A Multidisciplinary Review. Academy of Management Annals. Published online 15 March.

Huet, E. and Zaleski, O. 2017. *Silicon Valley's $400 Juicer May Be Feeling the Squeeze* [Online]. Bloomberg. Available: https://www.bloomberg.com/news/features/2017-04-19/silicon-valley-s-400-juicer-may-be-feeling-the-squeeze [Accessed 13 July 2022].

Hughes, D. J., Lee, A., Tian, A. W., Newman, A., and Legood, A. 2018. Leadership, Creativity, and Innovation: A Critical Review and Practical Recommendations. *The Leadership Quarterly*, 29, 549–569.

Hutter, M. and Stark, D. 2015. Pragmatist Perspectives on Valuation: An Introduction. *In*: A. Berthoin Antal, M. Hutter, and D. Stark (eds) *Moments of Valuation: Exploring Sites of Dissonance*. Oxford: Oxford University Press, 1–15.

Huzzard, T., Hellström, A., Lifvergren, S., and Conradi, N. 2014. A Physician-Led, Learning-Driven Approach to Regional Development of 23 Cancer Pathways in Sweden. *In*: S. A. Mohrman and A. B. Shani (eds) *Reconfiguring the Ecosystem for Sustainable Healthcare*. Bingley, Emerald, 101–133.

IPCC. 2022. *Climate Change 2022: Impacts, Adaptation and Vulnerability* [Online]. Available: https://reliefweb.int/report/world/climate-change-2022-impacts-adaptation-and-vulnerability?gclid=Cj0KCQjwu-KiBhCsARIsAPztUF3FoNmyTLElXzmtHAK_sC5DfnBtxI_4fgVA4i8iUZsq1ZXSm5N6UzsaAnZcEALw_wcB [Accessed 13 July 2022].

Isaacson, W. 2011. *Steve Jobs*. New York, Simon & Schuster.

Jackall, R. 1988. *Moral Mazes: The World of Corporate Managers*. Oxford, Oxford University Press.

Jackson, T. 2009. *Prosperity Without Growth: Economics for a Finite Planet*. London, Routledge.

James, W. 1907. *Pragmatism: A New Name for Some Old Ways of Thinking*. New York, Longmans, Green & Co.

Janis, I. 1982. *Groupthink*. Boston, MA, Houghton Mifflin.

Japp, F. R. 1898. Kekulé Memorial Lecture. *Journal of the Chemical Society, Transactions*, 73, 97–138.

Jevons, W. S. 1865. *The Coal Question: An Inquiry Concerning the Progress of the Nation, and the Probable Exhaustion of our Coal Mines*. London, Macmillan.

Johansson-Sköldberg, U., Woodilla, J., and Çetinkaya, M. 2013. Design Thinking: Past, Present and Possible Futures. *Creativity and Innovation Management*, 22, 121–146.

Johns, G. 2006. The Essential Impact of Context on Organizational Behavior. *Academy of Management Review*, 31, 386–408.

Just, S. N., De Cock, C., and Schaefer, S. M. 2021. From Antagonists to Allies? Exploring the Critical Performativity of Alternative Organization. *Culture and Organization*, 27, 89–97.

Katzenbach, J. R. and Smith, D. K. 1993. The Discipline of Teams, *Harvard Business Review*, 71, 111–120.

Kayes, D. C. 2004. The 1996 Mount Everest Climbing Disaster: The Breakdown of Learning in Teams. *Human Relations*, 57, 1263–1284.

Keinänen, M. 2016. Taking your Mind for a Walk: A Qualitative Investigation of Walking and Thinking Among Nine Norwegian Academics. *Higher Education*, 71, 593–605.

Kieser, A., Nicolai, A., and Seidl, D. 2015. The Practical Relevance of Management Research: Turning the Debate on Relevance into a Rigorous Scientific Research Program. *Academy of Management Annals*, 9, 143–233.

Killingsworth, M. A. and Gilbert, D. T. 2010. A Wandering Mind is an Unhappy Mind. *Science*, 330, 932.

Kimbell, L. 2011. Rethinking Design Thinking: Part I. *Design and Culture*, 3, 285–306.

Kreiner, K. 2012. Organizational Decision Mechanisms in an Architectural Competition. *In*: L. Alessandro and J. R. Harrison (eds) *The Garbage Can Model of Organizational Choice: Looking Forward at Forty*. Bingley, Emerald, 399–429.

Kroezen, J., Ravasi, D., Sasaki, I., Żebrowska, M., and Suddaby, R. 2021. Configurations of Craft: Alternative Models for Organizing Work. *Academy of Management Annals*, 15, 502–536.

Kunda, G. 1992. *Engineering Culture: Control and Commitment in a High-Tech Corporation*. Philadelphia, PA, Temple University Press.

Lamont, M. 2012. Toward a Comparative Sociology of Valuation and Evaluation. *Annual Review of Sociology*, 38, 201–221.

Langley, A., Smallman, C., Tsoukas, H., and Ven, A. H. V. D. 2013. Process Studies of Change in Organization and Management: Unveiling Temporality, Activity, and Flow. *Academy of Management Journal*, 56, 1–13.

Lasch, C. 1991. *The Culture of Narcissism: American Life in an Age of Diminishing Expectations*. New York, Norton.

Lawrence, P. R. and Lorsch, J. W. 1967. Differentiation and Integration in Complex Organizations. *Administrative Science Quarterly*, 12, 1–47.

Lawson, B. 2006. *How Designers Think: The Design Process Demystified*. New York, Elsevier.

Lee, F., Edmondson, A. C., Thomke, S., and Worline, M. 2004. The Mixed Effects of Inconsistency on Experimentation in Organizations. *Organization Science*, 15, 310–326.

Leonardi, P. M. 2014. Social Media, Knowledge Sharing, and Innovation: Toward a Theory of Communication Visibility. *Information Systems Research*, 25, 796–816.

Leonardi, P. M. and Vaast, E. 2017. Social Media and Their Affordances for Organizing: A Review and Agenda for Research. *Academy of Management Annals*, 11, 150–188.

Lepore, J. 2004. The Disruption Machine: What the Gospel of Innovation Gets Wrong. *The New Yorker* [Online]. Available: https://www.newyorker.com/magazine/2014/06/23/the-disruption-machine [Accessed 13 July 2022].

Lepper, M. R. and Greene, D. 2015. *The Hidden Costs of Reward: New Perspectives on the Psychology of Human Motivation*. London, Psychology Press.

Levin, S. 2017. Squeezed Out: Widely Mocked Startup Juicero is Shutting Down. *The Guardian* [Online]. Available: https://www.theguardian.com/technology/2017/sep/01/juicero-silicon-valley-shutting-down [Accessed 13 July 2022].

Levitt, B. and March, J. G. 1988. Organizational Learning. *Annual Review of Sociology*, 14, 319–338.

Lewis, M. W. 2000. Exploring Paradox: Toward a More Comprehensive Guide. *Academy of Management Review*, 25, 760–776.

Lingo, E. L. and O'Mahony, S. 2010. Nexus Work: Brokerage on Creative Projects. *Administrative Science Quarterly*, 55, 47–81.

Loewenstein, J. and Mueller, J. 2016. Implicit Theories of Creative Ideas: How Culture Guides Creativity Assessments. *Academy of Management Discoveries*, 2, 320–348.

Lüscher, L. S. 2018. *Managing Leadership Paradoxes*. London, Routledge.

Lüscher, L. S. and Lewis, M. W. 2008. Organizational Change and Managerial Sensemaking: Working Through Paradox. *Academy of Management Journal*, 51, 221–240.

Luyckx, J., Schneider, A., and Kourula, A. 2022. Learning from Alternatives: Analyzing Alternative Ways of Organizing as Starting Points for Improving the Corporation. *In*: R. E. Meyer, S. Leixnering, and J. Veldman (eds) *The Corporation: Rethinking the Iconic Form of Business Organization*. Bingley, Emerald, 209–231.

Mackinnon, D. W. 1978. *In Search of Human Effectiveness*. Buffalo, NY, The Creative Education Foundation.

Mainemelis, C., Kark, R., and Epitropaki, O. 2015. Creative Leadership: A Multi-Context Conceptualization. *Academy of Management Annals*, 9, 393–482.

March, E. 2009. *When Innovation is Child's Play* [Online]. WIPO. Available: https://www.wipo.int/wipo_magazine/en/2009/02/article_0013.html [Accessed 13 July 2022].

March, J. G. 1991. Exploration and Exploitation in Organizational Learning. *Organization Science*, 2, 71–87.

March, J. G. and Simon, H. 1958. *Organizations*. New York, Wiley.

Marcuse, H. 1964. *One Dimensional Man: Studies in the Ideology of Advanced Industrial Society*. London, Routledge.

Martin, R. 2009. *The Design of Business: Why Design Thinking Is the Next Competitive Advantage*. Cambridge, MA, Harvard Business Press.

Maslow, A. H. 1943. A Theory of Human Motivation. *Psychological Review*, 50, 370–396.

Maslow, A. H. 1950. Self-Actualizing People: A Study of Psychological Health. *Personality*, Symposium 1, 11–34.

Maslow, A. H. 1962. *Towards a Psychology of Being*. Princeton, NJ, Nostrand.

Mathias, B. D., Huyghe, A., Frid, C. J., and Galloway, T. L. 2018. An Identity Perspective on Coopetition in the Craft Beer Industry. *Strategic Management Journal*, 39, 3086–3115.

McDonald, C. 2019. Intolerable Genius: Berkeley's Most Controversial Nobel Laureate. *California* [Online]. Available: https://alumni.berkeley.edu/california-magazine/winter-2019/intolerable-genius-berkeleys-most-controversial-nobel-laureate [Accessed 13 July 2022].

McGee, M. C. 1980. The 'Ideograph': A Link Between Rhetoric and Ideology. *Quarterly Journal of Speech*, 66, 1–16.

McNemar, Q. 1964. Lost: Our Intelligence? Why? *American Psychologist*, 19, 871–882.

Meadows, D., Donella, M., Randers, J., and Behrens, W. W. 1972. *Limits to Growth*. New York, Universe Books.

Mintzberg, H. 1973. *The Nature of Managerial Work*. New York, Harper & Row.

Mintzberg, H. 1980. Structure in 5's: A Synthesis of the Research on Organization Design. *Management Science*, 26, 322–341.

Miron-Spektor, E. and Erez, M. 2017. Looking at Creativity Through a Paradox Lens: Deeper Understanding and New Insights. *In*: M. Lewis, W. K. Smith, P. Jarzabkowski, and A. Langley (eds) *Handbook of Organizational Paradox: Approaches to Plurality, Tensions and Contradictions*. Oxford, Oxford University Press, 434–452.

Mischel, W. 1977. The Interaction of Person and Situation. *In*: D. Magnusson and N. S. Endler (eds) *Personality at the Crossroads: Current Issues in Interactional Psychology*. Hillsdale, Erlbaum, 333–352.

Mohr, L. B. 1982. *Explaining Organizational Behavior*. San Francisco, Jossey-Bass.

Moorman, C. and Miner, A. S. 1998. Organizational Improvisation and Organizational Memory. *Academy of Management Review*, 23, 698–723.

Morgan, G. 1997. *Images of Organization*. London, Sage.

Morrot, G., Brochet, F., and Dubourdieu, D. 2001. The Color of Odors. *Brain and Language*, 79, 309–320.

Mueller, J. S., Melwani, S., and Goncalo, J. A. 2012. The Bias Against Creativity: Why People Desire but Reject Creative Ideas. *Psychological Science*, 23, 13–17.

Mumford, M. D., Scott, G. M., Gaddis, B., and Strange, J. M. 2002. Leading Creative People: Orchestrating Expertise and Relationships. *The Leadership Quarterly*, 13, 705–750.

Myers, D. G. and Diener, E. 2018. The Scientific Pursuit of Happiness. *Perspectives on Psychological Science*, 13, 218–225.

Navis, C. and Glynn, M. A. 2011. Legitimate Distinctiveness and the Entrepreneurial Identity: Influence on Investor Judgments of New Venture Plausibility. *Academy of Management Review*, 36, 479–499.

Nickerson, R. S. 1998. Confirmation Bias: A Ubiquitous Phenomenon in Many Guises. *Review of General Psychology*, 2, 175–220.

Nicolini, D., Mengis, J., and Swan, J. 2012. Understanding the Role of Objects in Cross-Disciplinary Collaboration. *Organization Science*, 23, 612–629.

Nidditch, P. H. (ed.) 1975. *John Locke: An Essay Concerning Human Understanding*. Oxford, Oxford University Press.

Nohria, N. and Gulati, R. 1996. Is Slack Good or Bad for Innovation? *Academy of Management Journal*, 39, 1245–1264.

Obstfeld, D. 2005. Social Networks, the Tertius Iungens Orientation, and Involvement in Innovation. *Administrative Science Quarterly*, 50, 100–130.

Oldham, G. R. and Cummings, A. 1996. Employee Creativity: Personal and Contextual Factors at Work. *Academy of Management Journal*, 39, 607–634.

Oppezzo, M. and Schwartz, D. L. 2014. Give Your Ideas Some Legs: The Positive Effect of Walking on Creative Thinking. *Journal of Experimental Psychology: Learning, Memory, and Cognition*, 40, 1142–1152.

O'Reilly, C. 1989. Corporations, Culture, and Commitment: Motivation and Social Control in Organizations. *California Management Review*, 31, 9–25.

O'Reilly, C. A. and Tushman, M. L. 2013. Organizational Ambidexterity: Past, Present, and Future. *Academy of Management Perspectives*, 27, 324–338.

Ortmann, G. and Sydow, J. 2018. Dancing in Chains: Creative Practices in/of Organizations. *Organization Studies*, 39, 899–921.

Osborn, A. 1942. *How to Think Up*. New York, McGraw-Hill.

Osborn, A. F. 1953. *Applied Imagination: Principles and Procedures of Creative Thinking*. New York: Charles Scribner's Sons.

Park, G., Lim, B.-C., and Oh, H. S. 2019. Why Being Bored Might not be a Bad Thing After All. *Academy of Management Discoveries*, 5, 78–92.

Parker, M., Cheney, G., Fournier, V., and Land, C. (eds) 2014. *The Routledge Companion to Alternative Organization*. London, Routledge.

Patriotta, G., Gond, J. P., and Schultz, F. 2011. Maintaining Legitimacy: Controversies, Orders of Worth, and Public Justifications. *Journal of Management Studies*, 48, 1804–1836.

Paulus, P. 2000. Groups, Teams, and Creativity: The Creative Potential of Idea-Generating Groups. *Applied Psychology*, 49, 237–262.

Peck, J. 2005. Struggling with the Creative Class. *International Journal of Urban and Regional Studies*, 29, 740–770.

Pellegrini, E. K. and Scandura, T. A. 2008. Paternalistic Leadership: A Review and Agenda for Future Research. *Journal of Management*, 34, 566–593.

Peltier, E., Glanz, J., Gröndahl, M., Cai, W., Nossiter, A., and Alderman, L. 2019. Notre-Dame Came far Closer to Collapsing than People Knew. This is How it was Saved. *The New York Times* [Online]. Available: https://www.nytimes.com/interactive/2019/07/16/world/europe/notre-dame.html [Accessed 13 July 2022].

Perry-Smith, J. E. and Shalley, C. E. 2003. The Social Side of Creativity: A Static and Dynamic Social Network Perspective. *Academy of Management Review*, 28, 89–106.

Pfeffer, J. and Salancik, G. 1978. *The External Control of Organizations: A Resource Dependence Perspective*. Stanford, CA, Stanford University Press.

Plucker, J. A. and Renzulli, J. S. 1999. Psychometric Approaches to the Study of Human Creativity. *In*: R. J. Sternberg (ed.) *Handbook of Creativity*. Cambridge, Cambridge University Press, 35–61.

Powell, W. W. 1990. Neither Market nor Hierarchy. *In*: B. Staw and L. L. Cummings (eds) *Research in Organizational Behavior*, Vol. 12. London, JAI Press, 295–336.

Prasad, P. 1993. Symbolic Processes in the Implementation of Technological Change: A Symbolic Interactionist Study of Work Computerization. *Academy of Management Journal*, 36, 1400–1429.

Princen, T. 2005. *The Logic of Sufficiency*. Cambridge, MA, MIT Press.

Putnam, R. 2000. *Bowling Alone: The Collapse and Revival of American Community*. New York, Simon & Schuster.

Ranganathan, A. 2018. The Artisan and His Audience: Identification with Work and Price Setting in a Handicraft Cluster in Southern India. *Administrative Science Quarterly*, 63, 637–667.

Razik, T. A. 1970. Psychometric Measurement of Creativity. *In*: P. E. Vernon (ed.) *Creativity: Selected Readings*. Harmondsworth, Penguin Books, 155–166.

Reckhenrich, J., Kupp, M., and Anderson, J. 2009. Understanding Creativity: The Manager as Artist. *Business Strategy Review*, 20, 68–73.

Reckwitz, A. 2002. Toward a Theory of Social Practices: A Development in Culturalist Theorizing. *European Journal of Social Theory*, 5, 243–263.

Rehn, A. 2019. *Innovation for the Fatigued*. London, Kogan.

Rehn, A. and De Cock, C. 2008. Deconstructing Creativity. *In*: T. Rickards, M. Runco, and S. Moger (eds) *Routledge Companion of Creativity*. London, Routledge, 150–161.

Reid, N. and Gatrell, J. D. 2017. Creativity, Community, & Growth: A Social Geography of Urban Craft Beer. *REGION*, 4, 31–49.

Rennstam, J. and Lundholm, S. 2020. Practice Theory. *In*: U. Eriksson-Zetterquist, M. Hansson, and F. Nilsson (eds) *Theories and Perspectives in Business Administration*. Lund, Studentlitteratur, 377–406.

Rexroth, K. 1957. The Vivisection of a Poet. *The Nation*, 185, 450–453.

Rickards, T. and De Cock, C. 2012. Understanding Organizational Creativity: Toward a Multi-paradigmatic Approach. *In*: M. A. Runco (ed.) *The Creativity Research Handbook*. New York, Hampton Press, 1–32.

Roberts, P. 2014. *The Impulse Society: America in the Age of Instant Gratification*. New York, Bloomsbury.

Robertson, D. 2013. *How LEGO Stopped Thinking Outside the Box and Innovated Inside the Brick* [Online]. Knowledge at Wharton. Available: https://knowledge.wharton.upenn.edu/article/how-lego-stopped-thinking-outside-the-box-and-innovated-inside-the-brick/ [Accessed 13 July 2022].

Robertson, M. and Swan, J. 2003. 'Control—What Control?' Culture and Ambiguity Within a Knowledge Intensive Firm. *Journal of Management Studies*, 40, 831–858.

Roethlisberger, F. J. and Dickson, W. J. 1939. *Management and the Worker*. Cambridge, MA, Harvard University Press.

Rollins, H. E. (ed.) 1958. *The Letters of John Keats, 1814–1821*. Boston, MA, Harvard University Press.

Rosa, H. 2013. *Social Acceleration: A New Theory of Modernity*. New York, Columbia University Press.

Rosa, H., Dörre, K., and Lessenich, S. 2017. Appropriation, Activation and Acceleration: The Escalatory Logics of Capitalist Modernity and the Crises of Dynamic Stabilization. *Theory, Culture & Society*, 34, 53–73.

Ross, A. 2004. *No-Collar: The Humane Workplace and Its Hidden Costs*. Philadelphia, PA, Temple University Press.

Rothermel, R. C. 1993. *Mann Gulch Fire: A Race that Couldn't Be Won*. General Technical Report. Ogden, UT, US Department of Agriculture, Forest Service, Intermountain Research Station.

Rothstein, H. 2015. *Det Fanns Utrymme för Något Annorlunda* [Online]. Affärs Världen. Available: https://www.affarsvarlden.se/artikel/det-fanns-utrymme-for-nagot-annorlunda-6762449 [Accessed 13 July 2022].

Roy, D. 1959. 'Banana Time': Job Satisfaction and Informal Interaction. *Human Organization*, 18, 158–168.

Runco, M. 2014. *Creativity Theories and Themes: Research, Development and Practice*. London, Academic Press.

Ryan, R. M. and Deci, E. L. 2000. Intrinsic and Extrinsic Motivations: Classic Definitions and New Directions. *Contemporary Educational Psychology*, 25, 54–67.

Sarasvathy, S. D. 2009. *Effectuation: Elements of Entrepreneurial Expertise*. Cheltenham, Edward Elgar.

Sasaki, I., Ravasi, D., and Micelotta, E. 2019. Family Firms as Institutions: Cultural Reproduction and Status Maintenance Among Multi-Centenary Shinise in Kyoto. *Organization Studies*, 40, 793–831.

Saunders, H. D. 1992. The Khazzoom-Brookes Postulate and Neoclassical Growth. *The Energy Journal*, 13, 131–148.

Sawyer, R. K. 2011. *Explaining Creativity: The Science of Human Innovation*. Oxford, Oxford University Press.

Scarbrough, H., Panourgias, N. S., and Nandhakumar, J. 2015. Developing a Relational View of the Organizing Role of Objects: A Study of the Innovation Process in Computer Games. *Organization Studies*, 36, 197–220.

Schaefer, S. and Paulsson, A. 2013. The Emotional Rollercoaster: Leadership of Innovation and the Dialectical Relationship Between Negative and Positive Emotions. *In*: J. Lemmergaard and

S. L. Muhr (eds) *Critical Perspectives on Leadership: Emotion, Toxicity, and Dysfunction*. Cheltenham, Edward Elgar, 105–127.

Schaefer, S. M. 2019. Wilful Managerial Ignorance, Symbolic Work and Decoupling: A Socio-Phenomenological Study of 'Managing Creativity'. *Organization Studies*, 40, 1387–1407.

Schmidt, T., Braun, T., and Sydow, J. 2019. Copying Routines for New Venture Creation: How Replication can Support Entrepreneurial Innovation. *In*: M. S. Feldman, L. D'Aderio, K. Dittrich, and P. Jarzabkowski (eds) *Routine Dynamics in Action: Replication and Transformation*. Bingley, Emerald, 55–78.

Schön, D. A. 1979. Generative Metaphor: A Perspective on Problem-Setting in Social Policy. *In*: A. Ortony (ed.) *Metaphor and Thought*. Cambridge, Cambridge University Press, 137–163.

Schön, D. A. 1983. *The Reflective Practitioner*. New York, Basic Books.

Schüßler, E., Svejenova, S., and Cohendet, P. 2021. Organizing Creativity for Innovation: Situated Practices and Process Perspectives. *In*: E. Schüßler, P. Cohendet, and S. Svejenova (eds) *Organizing Creativity in the Innovation Journey*. Bingley, Emerald Publishing Limited, 1–16.

Seaton, R. 2019. *More Seniors are Embracing Technology. But Can They Use It? UCSD Researchers Suggest Asking Them*. [Online]. Forbes. Available: https://www.forbes.com/sites/robinseatonjefferson/2019/06/28/more-seniors-are-embracing-technology-but-can-they-use-it-ucsd-researchers-suggest-asking-them/?sh=2a599db23233 [Accessed 13 July 2022].

Sennett, R. 1998. *The Corrosion of Character*. New York, W. W. Norton.

Sennett, R. 2007. *The Culture of the New Capitalism*. New Haven, CT, Yale University Press.

Sennett, R. 2008. *The Craftsman*. London, Penguin.

Silverman, D. 1970. *The Theory of Organizations: A Sociological Framework*. London, Heineman.

Simon, H. A. 1997. *Models of Bounded Rationality: Empirically Grounded Economic Reason*. Boston, MA, MIT Press.

Simons, D. J. and Chabris, C. F. 1999. Gorillas in our Midst: Sustained Inattentional Blindness for Dynamic Events. *Perception*, 28, 1059–1074.

Simpson, P. F., French, R., and Harvey, C. E. 2002. Leadership and Negative Capability. *Human Relations*, 55, 1209–1226.

Slawinski, N. and Bansal, P. 2015. Short on Time: Intertemporal Tensions in Business Sustainability. *Organization Science*, 26, 531–549.

Smircich, L. 1983. Concepts of Culture and Organizational Analysis. *Administrative Science Quarterly*, 28, 339–358.

Smircich, L. and Morgan, G. 1982. Leadership: The Management of Meaning. *Journal of Applied Behavioral Science*, 18, 257–273.

Smith, W. K. and Lewis, M. W. 2011. Toward a Theory of Paradox: A Dynamic Equilibrium Model of Organizing. *Academy of Management Review*, 36, 381–403.

Snyder, M. and Ickes, W. 1985. Personality and Social behavior. *In*: G. Lindzey and E. Aronson (eds) *Handbook of Social Psychology*. New York, Random House, 883–947.

Sonenshein, S. 2016. Routines and Creativity: From Dualism to Duality. *Organization Science*, 27, 739–758.

Sorrell, S. 2009. Jevons' Paradox Revisited: The Evidence for Backfire from Improved Energy Efficiency. *Energy Policy*, 37, 1456–1469.

Spicer, A. 2017. *Business Bullshit*. London, Routledge.

Spoelstra, S. 2018. *Leadership and Organization: A Philosophical Introduction*. London, Routledge.

Stark, D. 2009. *The Sense of Dissonance*. Princeton, NJ, Princeton University Press.

Stewart, R. 1967. *Managers and Their Job*. Maidenhead, McGraw-Hill.

Storey, J. and Salaman, G. 2005. *Managers of Innovation: Insights into Making Innovation Happen*. Malden, MA, Blackwell.

Styhre, A. and Eriksson, M. 2008. Bring in the Arts and Get the Creativity for Free: A Study of the *Artists in Residence* Project. *Creativity and Innovation Management*, 17, 47–57.

Styhre, A. and Sundgren, M. 2003. Creativity as Connectivity: A Rhizome Model of Creativity. *International Journal of Internet and Enterprise Management*, 1, 421–436.

Styhre, A. and Sundgren, M. 2005. *Managing Creativity in Organizations*. Basingstoke, Palgrave.

Sutton, R. I. and Hargadon, A. 1996. Brainstorming Groups in Context: Effectiveness in a Product Design Firm. *Administrative Science Quarterly*, 41, 685–718.

Suzman, J. 2020. *Work: A History of How We Spend Our Time*. London, Bloomsbury Circus.

Synnott, M. 2015. Legendary Climber Alex Honnold Shares His Closest Call. *National Geographic* [Online]. Available: https://www.nationalgeographic.com/adventure/article/ropeless-climber-alex-honnolds-closest-call [Accessed 13 July 2022].

Taylor, C. and Barron, F. 1963. A Look Ahead: Reflections of the Conference Participants and Editors. *In*: C. Taylor and F. Barron (eds) *Scientific Creativity: Its Recognition and Development*. New York, Wiley, 372–389.

Taylor, F. W. 1911. *The Principles of Scientific Management*. New York, Harper & Brothers.

Taylor, J. R. and Van Every, E. 2000. *The Emergent Organization: Communication as its Site and Surface*. Mahwah, NJ, Lawrence Erlbaum Associates.

Terborg, J. R. 1981. Interactional Psychology and Research on Human Behavior in Organizations. *Academy of Management Review*, 6, 569–576.

Thévenot, L., Moody, M., and Lafaye, C. 2000. Forms of Valuing Nature: Arguments and Modes of Justification in French and American Environmental Disputes. *In*: M. Lamont and L. Thévenot (eds) *Rethinking Comparative Cultural Sociology: Repertoires of Evaluation in France and the United States*. Cambridge, Cambridge University Press, 229–273.

Treem, J. W. and Leonardi, P. M. 2013. Social Media Use in Organizations: Exploring the Affordances of Visibility, Editability, Persistence, and Association. *Annals of the International Communication Association*, 36, 143–189.

Trist, E. L. and Bamforth, K. W. 1951. Some Social and Psychological Consequences of the Longwall Method of Coal-Getting: An Examination of the Psychological Situation and Defences of a Work Group in Relation to the Social Structure and Technological Content of the Work System. *Human Relations*, 4, 3–38.

Tsoukas, H. and Chia, R. 2002. On Organizational Becoming. *Organization Science*, 13, 567–582.

Turco, C. J. 2016. *The Conversational Firm: Rethinking Bureaucracy in the Age of Social Media*. New York, Columbia University Press.

Tushman, M. L. and Scanlan, T. J. 1981. Characteristics and External Orientations of Boundary Spanning Individuals. *Academy of Management Journal*, 24, 83–98.

Ungar, S. 2000. Knowledge, Ignorance and the Popular Culture: Climate Change versus the Ozone Hole. *Public Understanding of Science*, 9, 297–312.

UNICEF. 2007. *An Evaluation of the PlayPump® Water System as an Appropriate Technology for Water, Sanitation and Hygiene Programmes*. New York, UNICEF.

Unsworth, K. 2001. Unpacking Creativity. *Academy of Management Review*, 26, 289–297.

Uzzi, B. 1996. The Sources and Consequences of Embeddedness for the Economic Performance of Organizations: The Network Effect. *American Sociological Review*, 61, 674–698.

Van Werven, R., Bouwmeester, O., and Cornelissen, J. P. 2015. The Power of Arguments: How Entrepreneurs Convince Stakeholders of the Legitimate Distinctiveness of their Ventures. *Journal of Business Venturing*, 30, 616–631.

Van Werven, R., Bouwmeester, O., and Cornelissen, J. P. 2019. Pitching a Business Idea to Investors: How New Venture Founders Use Micro-Level Rhetoric to Achieve Narrative Plausibility and Resonance. *International Small Business Journal*, 37, 193–214.

Vargas, M. 2020. *What Happened to Juicero? The Doug Evans story* [Online]. Slidebean. Available: https://slidebean.com/story/doug-evans-juicero-juicer [Accessed 13 July 2022].

Vaughan, D. 1996. *The Challenger Launch Decision*. Chicago, University of Chicago Press.

Vinsel, L. 2018. Design Thinking Is a Boondoggle: Its Adherents Think It Will Save Higher Ed. They're Delusional. Chronicle of Higher Education [Online]. Available https://www.chronicle.com/article/design-thinking-is-a-boondoggle/ [Accessed 13 July 2022].

Von Hippel, E. 1988. *The Sources of Innovation*. Oxford, Oxford University Press.

Von Weizsäcker, E., Lovins, A., and Lovins, H. 1998. *Factor Four: Doubling Wealth, Halving Resource Use*. London, Earthscan.

Vuori, T. O. and Huy, Q. N. 2016. Distributed Attention and Shared Emotions in the Innovation Process: How Nokia Lost the Smartphone Battle. *Administrative Science Quarterly*, 61, 9–51.

Wajcman, J. 2014. *Pressed for Time*. Chicago, University of Chicago Press.

Wallas, G. 1926. *The Art of Thought*. New York, Harcourt.

Walton, K. 1990. *Mimesis as Make-Believe: On the Foundations of the Representational Arts*. Boston, MA, Harvard University Press.

Ward, T. B. 1994. Structured Imagination: The Role of Category Structure in Exemplar Generation. *Cognitive Psychology*, 27, 1–40.

Ward, T. B. 2004. Cognition, Creativity, and Entrepreneurship. *Journal of Business Venturing*, 19, 173–188.

Watson, T. J. 1994. *In Search of Management: Culture, Chaos and Control in Managerial Work*. London, Routledge.

Weber, M. 1978. *Economy and Society: An Outline of Interpretive Sociology*. Berkeley, University of California Press.

Weick, K. E. 1976. Educational Organizations as Loosely Coupled Systems. *Administrative Science Quarterly*, 21, 1–19.

Weick, K. E. 1979. *The Social Psychology of Organizing*. Reading, MA, Addison-Westley.

Weick, K. E. 1984. Small Wins: Redefining the Scale of Social Problems. *American Psychologist*, 39, 40–49.

Weick, K. E. 1993. The Collapse of Sensemaking in Organizations: The Mann Gulch Disaster. *Administrative Science Quarterly*, 38, 628–652.

Weick, K. E. 1995. *Sensemaking in Organizations*. Thousand Oaks, CA, Sage.

Weick, K. E. 1998. Introductory Essay—Improvisation as a Mindset for Organizational Analysis. *Organization Science*, 9, 543–555.

Weiner, R. P. 2012. *Creativity and Beyond: Cultures, Values, and Change*. Albany, NY, SUNY Press.

Whitehead, A. N. 1925. Science and the Modern World. New York, MacMillan.

Whittington, R. 2006. Completing the Practice Turn in Strategy Research. *Organization Studies*, 27, 613–634.

Whyte, W. H. 1956. *The Organization Man*. New York, Simon & Schuster.

Wickert, C. and De Bakker, F. 2019. How CSR Managers Can Inspire Other Leaders to Act on Sustainability. Harvard Business Review [Online]. Available https://hbr.org/2019/01/how-csr-managers-can-inspire-other-leaders-to-act-on-sustainability [Accessed 13 July 2022].

Wickert, C. and Risi, D. 2019. *Corporate Social Responsibility*. Cambridge, Cambridge University Press.

Wickert, C. and Schaefer, S. M. 2015. Towards a Progressive Understanding of Performativity in Critical Management Studies. *Human Relations*, 68, 107–130.

Williams Scott, D. 2002. Self-Esteem and the Self-Censorship of Creative Ideas. *Personnel Review*, 31, 495–503.

Willmott, H. 1993. Strength is Ignorance; Slavery is Freedom: Managing Culture in Modern Organizations. *Journal of Management Studies*, 30, 515–552.

Wollastan, S. 2019. Alone with No Safety Equipment, Alex Honnold Defies Gravity. *The Irish Times* [Online]. Available: https://www.irishtimes.com/sport/other-sports/alone-with-no-safety-equipment-alex-honnold-defies-gravity-1.3809994 [Accessed 13 July 2022].

Woodman, R. W., Sawyer, J. E., and Griffin, R. W. 1993. Toward a Theory of Organizational Creativity. *Academy of Management Review*, 18, 293–321.

Zerbe, W. J. and Paulhus, D. L. 1987. Socially Desirable Responding in Organizational Behavior: A Reconception. *Academy of Management Review*, 12, 250–264.

Index

For the benefit of digital users, indexed terms that span two pages (e.g., 52–53) may, on occasion, appear on only one of those pages.

Note: Tables and figures are indicated by an italic *t* and *f* following the page/paragraph number.